The Soviet presence and purposes in Latin America are a matter of great controversy, yet no serious study has hitherto combined a regional perspective (concentrating on the nature and regional impact of Soviet activity on the ground) with diplomatic analysis, examining the strategic and ideological factors that influence Soviet foreign policy. Nicola Miller's lucid and accessible survey of Soviet–Latin American relations over the past quarter-century demonstrates clearly that existing, heavily 'geo-political' accounts distort the real nature of Soviet activity in the area, closely constrained by local political, social and geographical factors.

In a broadly chronological series of case-studies Dr Miller argues that, American counter-influence apart, enormous physical and communicational barriers obstruct Soviet–Latin American relations, and that the lack of economic complementarity imposes a natural obstacle to trading growth: even Cuba, often cited as 'proof' of Soviet designs upon the area, is only an apparent exception.

NICOLA MILLER is a Research Fellow of King's College, Cambridge

Soviet relations with Latin America 1959–1987

Cambridge Soviet Paperbacks: 1

Cambridge Soviet Paperbacks is a completely new initiative in publishing on the Soviet Union. The series will focus on the economics, international relations, politics, sociology and history of the Soviet and Revolutionary periods.

The idea behind the series is the identification of gaps for upper-level surveys or studies falling between the traditional university press monograph and most student textbooks. The main readership will be students and specialists, but some 'overview' studies in the series will have broader appeal.

Publication will in every case be simultaneously in hardcover and paperback.

Soviet relations with Latin America 1959–1987

NICOLA MILLER

King's College, Cambridge

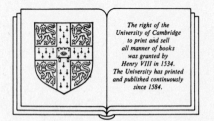

The right of the
University of Cambridge
to print and sell
all manner of books
was granted by
Henry VIII in 1534.
The University has printed
and published continuously
since 1584.

CAMBRIDGE UNIVERSITY PRESS

Cambridge
New York   Port Chester
Melbourne   Sydney

Published by the Press Syndicate of the University of Cambridge
The Pitt Building, Trumpington Street, Cambridge, CB2 1RP
40 West 20th Street, New York, NY 10011, USA
10 Stamford Road, Oakleigh, Melbourne 3166, Australia

© Cambridge University Press 1989

First published 1989

Printed in Great Britain at the University Press, Cambridge

British Library cataloguing in publication data
Miller, Nicola.
Soviet relations with Latin America.
1959–1987. – (Cambridge Soviet paperbacks).
1. Soviet Union. Foreign relations with Latin America, 1959–1987.
2. Latin America. Foreign relations with Soviet Union. 1959–1987.
I. Title.
327.4108

Library of Congress cataloguing in publication data
Miller, Nicola.
Soviet relations with Latin America, 1959–1987 / Nicola Miller.
    p.   cm. – (Cambridge Soviet paperbacks).
Based on the author's thesis (D.Phil. – Oxford University).
Bibliography.
Includes index.
ISBN 0 521 35193 6
1. Latin America – Relations – Soviet Union.
2. Soviet Union – Relations – Latin America.
3. Soviet Union – Foreign relations – 1945–   .
4. Latin America – Foreign relations – 1948–   .
5. Communism – Latin America – History – 20th century.
I. Title. II. Series.
F1416.S65M55   1989.
303.4'8247'08–dc19   88–34135   CIP

ISBN 0 521 35193 6   hard covers
ISBN 0 521 35979 1   paperback

Contents

Acknowledgements

Much of the material in this book was presented as a D.Phil. dissertation, undertaken at St Antony's College, Oxford, and supported by an Economic and Social Research Council post-graduate research award. I would like to thank my two thesis supervisors, Laurence Whitehead and Mary McAuley, for all their advice and encouragement. My two examiners, Alan Angell and Margot Light, also made many helpful comments which stimulated the process of revising the manuscript. I also gratefully acknowledge the support of the Nuffield Foundation in funding further research in Nicaragua and at the London School of Economics.

Introduction

Much of the literature (particularly work published in the United States) concerned with the Soviet Union's relations with the Third World tends to discuss Soviet behaviour solely in geo-political/strategic terms. The authors of such studies generally regard the USSR as an expansionist nation ultimately seeking world domination, which aims to 'fill any vacuum' left by the United States. There are two crucial deficiencies in such an approach to the study of Soviet foreign policy (regardless of whether or not one shares this view of the Soviet Union). Firstly, the analysis tends to proceed as if the USSR were the only 'actor' on the stage, all other parties, that is the Western nations and the Third World countries themselves, being merely passive observers of an aggressive Soviet foreign policy.[1] Thus we are presented with statements such as 'Undoubtedly, the Soviets would like to upgrade and expand their naval presence in the Caribbean. ... Unfettered, the Soviet Union is likely to establish additional naval facilities in the region in order to create a stronger and more permanent presence than it now has' (Valenta: 1983, p. 294). It is safe to assume that any power ideally strives for optimum security and therefore maximum influence: however, an analysis that proceeds from the hypothesis of an 'unfettered' Soviet Union is unlikely to explain the main determinants of Soviet policy in the developing world.

Secondly, such an analysis fails to take sufficient account of changes over time. It will acknowledge the strategic developments which have taken place since the mid-1950s, most notably the attaining by the USSR of nuclear 'parity' with the United States in the early 1970s and the increase in Soviet conventional military strength to the extent that the USSR now has a fully global naval presence. Less attention will be paid to international political factors such as shifts in the relations

---

[1] Examples of this approach applied to Soviet–Latin American relations are Herman: 1973; Theberge: 1974; Leiken: 1982; Gouré and Rothenberg: 1975.

between the superpowers and in their respective links with China, the increasing participation of the developing nations in world politics (exemplified by the existence of the Non-Aligned Movement and the campaign for a New International Economic Order), the internal political development of the Third World nations under discussion, and shifts in regional alliances. Nor is sufficient account taken of changes in the ideology and the perceptions of policy-makers, of possible Soviet modifications of foreign policy in response to the consequences of earlier decisions, or of internal developments within the USSR which may contribute to an overall reassessment of foreign-policy priorities. For example, Soviet knowledge of the Third World and analysis of international relations has developed and expanded considerably since the late 1950s. Thus it is likely that Soviet leaders are taking far more informed decisions now about their response to events in developing countries than could have been the case three decades ago. They have also had far more experience of dealing with Third World countries, much of which has contributed to a markedly less positive assessment of what can be achieved there than was being put forward in the early stages of the decolonisation process. This, together with a sober re-evaluation of the prospects for economic progress in the Soviet Union and an increasing pressure on Soviet leaders to fulfil their promises to the Soviet population, prompted unequivocal statements in the early 1970s to the effect that revolution-ary leaders in the Third World should not operate on the basis that unlimited largesse would be forthcoming from Moscow. The 1970s have seen the increasingly pragmatic allocation of Soviet aid.

Because I believe that all such factors should be taken into account and that analysis of Soviet relations with Third World nations should be set firmly in the context of the foreign policies of the countries themselves with due consideration for the role of the United States and China (powerful rivals for influence in the area), the following chapters explore the hypothesis that Soviet foreign policy towards Latin America is determined primarily by political and economic variables, which act as constraints on the realisation of the maximum ideological/strategic goals so often emphasised in the literature. Chapter 1 indicates what these variables might be, highlighting them within the context of a historical account of Soviet involvement in the region.

Beyond the points made in the first chapter, only a limited amount can be said about Soviet relations with Latin America in aggregate (even with the exception of Cuba). For this reason, the book is based around a series of case studies covering Soviet relations with individual Latin American countries. Chapter 2, however, presents the essential ideological background to Soviet–Latin American relations, covering each side's perceptions of the other, offering reasons for and against the acceptance of Marxist ideas in Latin America, and contrasting the evolutions of Soviet and Latin American Marxist thought. The aim is to assess the extent to which Latin America is likely to be receptive to the oft-mentioned Soviet ideological offensive. Although this chapter contains a brief history of the evolution of the Communist movement in Latin America, a detailed treatment of Soviet relations with individual Communist parties was adjudged to be outside the scope of this work and the topic is introduced only where it is deemed to be relevant to Soviet state-to-state relations with Latin American countries.

An important variable determining the making of foreign policy is the constraining influence of previous decisions. The establishing of an alliance with Cuba is obviously the single most important decision taken by the Soviet Union with respect to Latin America – a decision made, moreover, at a time when Soviet links with Latin America (and to a lesser extent with the Third World generally) were so minimal that they were virtually operating on a *tabula rasa*. The decision to support Castro had extensive ramifications for Soviet foreign policy worldwide, but the effects on its relations with Latin America were particularly marked. It is still commonly asserted, or accepted implicitly, that 'The factors which made possible the development of Soviet–Cuban ties still shape Soviet policy elsewhere in the region' (Rothenberg: 1983, p. 1). To the contrary, chapter 3, which emphasises the events of 1959–62, the initial years of Soviet commitment, argues that the Soviet–Cuban embrace was the product of highly specific historical circumstances (the only factor analogous to the contemporary situation being the role of the United States), and that the Soviet Union played an essentially reactive, rather than instigative role.

The Soviet-Cuban connection obviously overshadows Moscow's relations with any other nation in the subcontinent or the Caribbean, to such an extent that no attempt has been made here to explore the full ideological, political, strategic and economic ramifications of this relationship. Chapter 4, however, attempts to consider how either side might weigh up the costs and benefits of its commitment, in order to throw some light upon what the 'lessons of Cuba' might have been, both in terms of Soviet policy towards Latin America and Latin American attitudes towards the USSR.

Chapter 5 discusses Chile under Allende's Popular Unity government (1970–3) as the first major opportunity the Soviet Union was offered (and, significantly, rejected) to gain substantial influence in any Latin American country since the Cuban revolution. To provide a counterweight to the other examples, chapter 6 examines Moscow's relations with the major Latin American powers – Argentina, Brazil, Mexico and Venezuela – which, in geo-political terms, represent the greatest prizes that Moscow could win in Latin America. It will be argued that these relations, conditioned almost entirely by economic and diplomatic factors, represent the norm of Soviet relations with Latin America. Argentina, as the USSR's foremost trading partner in the region (apart from Cuba) since 1978, is an apparent exception to the overall lack of complementarity between Latin America and the Soviet Union, and Brazil too offers a potentially significant scope for exchange. As a final case study, the penultimate chapter considers the Soviet response to the most recent socialist experiment in Latin America – the 1979 revolution in Nicaragua – and sets Moscow's policy towards the Sandinista government in the context of the crisis throughout Central America. On this basis, the conclusion aims to isolate the variables shaping the Soviet Union's differential treatment of Latin American countries.

1 The Soviet interest in Latin America

Latin America is clearly not an area of vital security interest to the Soviet Union, notwithstanding the importance Moscow attaches to the preservation of a socialist Cuba (see chapter 4). It is the United States, rather than the USSR, which is significantly dependent on Latin America for its raw materials, and Moscow's interest in this respect is largely confined to the as yet unexplored potential of Antarctica. Soviet strategic concerns in Latin America stem from the region's status as a high priority area for the United States and the challenge thereby posed to the USSR as a rival superpower.

Indeed Latin America, as the Third World region furthest from the USSR and nearest to the United States, has traditionally been an area of low priority for Moscow. It was not until the late 1960s that the Soviet Union began to build a relatively stable and extensive network of diplomatic links in the sub-continent. According to CIA estimates, Latin America (excluding Cuba)[1] was allocated only 5.6 per cent of the aid extended by the Soviet Union to all non-Communist developing countries over the period 1954–78, and received less than 2.5 per cent of Soviet military deliveries to the Third World. Conventional trading links have been even weaker: between 1975 and 1978 Latin America supplied barely 1 per cent of Soviet imports and absorbed less than one quarter per cent of Soviet exports.

A number of factors combined to explain why this was the case prior to 1959. Firstly, until the 1950s foreign trade played only a very subsidiary role in the inward-looking Soviet economy, as Stalin pursued a policy of autarky. Within that schema, trade with the geographically remote countries of Latin America naturally occupied a position of low priority. Thus there was little incentive to overcome the second factor, namely that Moscow's early view of Latin America was governed by what became known as the law of 'geographical

---

[1] Unless indicated to the contrary, references to 'Latin America' in this chapter do not include post-1959 Cuba.

fatalism'. Soviet officials saw little hope either of establishing formal political ties or of promoting revolution in countries forced to live within the shadow of the United States and its 1823 Monroe Doctrine. (It is worth noting that the Monroe Doctrine, which aimed to exclude all European influence from the American continent, consisted of two parts, the first of which was designed to deter Russian expansionism down the northwest US Pacific coast. The tsarist threat receded in 1867, when Russia sold Alaska to the United States, and the doctrine subsequently became better known for its challenge to the perceived intention of the European Holy Alliance to help Spain reconquer its former colonies. By extension it has become widely interpreted as the formulation of Washington's view that any intrusion by European powers into the Americas would be regarded as an act of hostility towards the United States.) This assumption seemed to be justified when Argentina and Bolivia, having shown some signs of willingness to recognise the Soviet Union, succumbed to British pressure not to do so. In the pre-war years Moscow had state-to-state relations with only two Latin American nations: Mexico (1924–30) and Uruguay (1926–35). After the USSR joined the Allied cause following the Nazi invasion of the Soviet Union in June 1941, the United States launched a huge propaganda effort directed towards persuading Latin American governments that they should establish relations with Moscow. Most accordingly did so, although several (notably the 1943–6 military regime in Argentina) chose to postpone the decision until the Allied victory was imminent.[2]

As soon as the war was over, however, most Latin American countries broke off or refused to recognise their ties with the USSR. Only Mexico, Uruguay and Argentina retained links throughout the Cold War period. This fact, along with the 1947 Inter-American Treaty of Reciprocal Assistance (in effect a restatement of the principles behind the Monroe Doctrine), confirmed that, in the context of Moscow's then rigid categorisation of the world into 'capitalist' or 'Communist', the Latin American nations were firmly entrenched in the capitalist camp. In 1951 Stalin, denouncing the exclusion from the United Nations of the People's Republic of China, berated the twenty Latin American republics for being the 'most solid and obedient army of the United States' (*Pravda* interview with Stalin, 17 February 1951, p. 1).

[2] Relations were established as follows: Cuba – Oct. 1942; Mexico – Nov. 1942; Uruguay – Jan. 1943; Colombia – Feb. 1943; Costa Rica – May 1944; Chile and Nicaragua – Dec. 1944; Venezuela and the Dominican Republic – March 1945; Brazil, Bolivia, Guatemala, El Salvador and Ecuador – April 1945; Argentina – June 1945.

Even after Khrushchev announced, at the Twentieth Congress of the Communist Party of the Soviet Union (CPSU) in 1956, that the Soviet Union had abandoned its strictly bipolar view of the world and was ready to open up relations with the developing nations, there was little change in Moscow's attitude towards Latin America, which had recently been 'vindicated' by US covert involvement in the 1954 overthrow of the Arbenz government in Guatemala. In his 1956 speeches Khrushchev placed new emphasis on the 'peaceful road' to socialism which, it was asserted, might be taken by those of the newly independent and underdeveloped states which, albeit not ready to take the fully socialist road, were nevertheless 'anti-imperialist' in orientation. In retrospect it seems clear that this ideological shift was made, as were a whole series of later ones, because the Soviet Union in its role as emerging superpower (rather than as leading socialist nation) wished to respond to a perceived change in the world situation in a more positive way than was permitted by the orthodox formulations. The new pre-eminence of the 'peaceful road' was clearly aligned with Khrushchev's drive for 'peaceful coexistence' with the United States. It also enabled the Soviet Union to pursue a more active policy towards developing countries in order to take advantage of the rapid decolonisation which followed in the wake of the Second World War, none of which, with the exception of North Vietnam, was a result of action by local Communist forces. This was a time of great Soviet optimism about the potential of the Third World: the fact that Latin America was not included in Khrushchev's 'zone of peace' of African and Asian nations is a telling indication of the region's ill-defined status and low priority in Soviet eyes.

The third factor which is relevant to an explanation of the limited development of early Soviet–Latin American ties is that significant sectors of the Latin American elites were (indeed, in some cases still are) deeply imbued with a strong anti-Communism. This derived largely from fears amongst Latin American ruling groups of a threat to their own positions, concerns which have been played upon and reinforced by Great Britain in the 1920s because of its considerable stake in the Argentine economy, and subsequently by the United States. Anti-Communism lay behind several setbacks to early Soviet initiatives in the area, notably the closure of the first trading office in Latin America, Iuzhamtorg (set up in Buenos Aires in 1927), by the military regime of General José Uriburu who came to power in a 1930 *coup*. Furthermore, tensions ensuing from the USSR's need to support its claim to be the vanguard of world revolutionary movements and its interests as a nation state (and subsequently as a world superpower) were felt particularly acutely in these early years. In the 1930s Moscow's attempts to pursue a two-track policy, combining increased Comintern militancy with endeavours to cultivate state-to-state relations, strained the Soviet Union's weak diplomatic links to breaking point. Mexico severed its relations with the USSR in January 1930 after the Comintern had made a clumsy and ill-judged bid to exploit the uncertainty caused by a right-wing rebellion against the Portes Gil government (see pages 39–40). In 1935 Uruguay acceded to Brazilian pressure to break links with Moscow because of allegations, apparently not unfounded, that the Soviet trading office in Montevideo had been used as a conduit for funds to the Brazilian insurgents. The closure of this last remaining branch of Iuzhamtorg '[brought] Soviet trade with Latin America virtually to a standstill' (Zinoviev: 1981, p. 100). The pro-Washington stance of most post-war regimes in Latin America, along with the onslaught of anti-Communist propaganda generated by the Cold War, were the main reasons for the refusal of all but three nations to have diplomatic relations with the USSR during that period, and of all but one (Perón's Argentina, which was undergoing a near-total trade embargo imposed by Washington) to engage in commercial activity.

Since the late 1950s, however, the importance of all of the above factors has diminished to the extent that, even taken together, they no longer offer more than a partial explanation for the restricted nature of Soviet–Latin American relations. As far as the first factor is concerned, foreign trade has clearly assumed greater importance to the Soviet economy in recent years. To what extent this is the case is a matter for debate; however, the fact that trade with the developing nations is intended to play some part is indicated by the *Guidelines for the Economic and Social Development of the USSR for 1981–5 and for the Period Ending in 1990* adopted at the 26th CPSU Congress in 1981, which envisage '[the development], on a longterm and equitable basis, [of a] mutually beneficial exchange of goods . . . with developing countries' (in Koshelev: 1982, pp. 8–9). Specifically with respect to Latin America, Soviet commentators have written, 'The socialist countries . . . are interested in widening their trade and economic ties with Latin America, particularly in the form of regular purchases of individual foodstuffs which either do not grow in the temperate climate of the socialist countries (coffee, cocoa-beans, bananas, and so on) or whose production at home is not yet sufficient to meet the population's needs completely' (a discreet reference to grain and meat, which the Soviet

Union has purchased in substantial quantities in Latin America)
(Zhuravleva: 1983, p. 44).

Some observers have attributed the Soviet Union's apparent willingness to carry a high trade deficit with almost all of its trading partners
in Latin America to the fact that it is using trade primarily as a political
instrument in order to increase its influence within the region.[3] While
there may have been isolated instances which appear to confirm this
interpretation (for example, in 1970 the Soviet Union bought up Costa
Rica's excess of coffee, which may well have been a factor contributing
to the establishment of diplomatic relations the following year), other
such instances have been similarly small-scale and the evidence
overall is against it. The Soviet Union has shown itself anxious to
expand trade with, for example, Mexico, with which Moscow already
has good and well-established political relations.[4] Moreover it 'has
been confirmed independently from various Soviet sources' that
'Moscow finds Latin American offerings attractive' (Blasier: 1983,
p. 50). Most Soviet imports from the area consist of essential foodstuffs and the Soviet Union would in any case have to buy many of
them, notably grain, meat and wool, in hard currency markets. In
addition there are constraints imposed by the Soviet economy itself: it
is likely that, as Cole Blasier suggests, 'Soviet resources are still so
limited as to discourage purely political use. Domestic needs for
resources are so great that the USSR cannot afford to take many losses
in Latin America for purely political purposes. Moreover, other
geographic areas closer to home take priority (Blasier: 1983, p. 54).
Persistent Soviet attempts to penetrate the Latin American market
with its machinery and equipment indicate a distinct reluctance to
acquiesce in the continuance of the existing trading imbalance. In the
light of the above considerations, I would argue that the Soviet Union
has a genuinely economic interest in expanding its trading links with
Latin American countries, and that it wishes to apply purely commercial principles to such dealings.

---

[3] This section has made no mention of Soviet 'aid' to Latin America. The reason for this
is that outright grants are very few (normally limited to emergency funds after natural
disasters) and Soviet aid usually takes the form of lines of credit for the purchase of
Soviet equipment. While the terms are concessionary compared to Western commercial loans, it appears that these credits are 'primarily . . . an inducement to Latin
American governments to buy Soviet goods' and 'similar to US Export-Import Bank
credits' (Blasier: 1983, p. 66).
[4] In 1977 the first inter-parliamentary meeting between representatives of the Mexican
Congress and the Supreme Soviet was held in Mexico City. Such meetings are
intended to balance similar sessions established eighteen years previously with the US
Congress. *Latin America Weekly Report*, 25 March 1977, p. 96.

As for the second factor, the January 1959 revolution in Cuba irreversibly changed the perceptions of Soviet policy-makers concerning the opportunities available to them in Latin America. This event was acclaimed as having 'destroyed the myth of geographical fatalism with respect to the United States and Latin America' (A. F. Shul'govskii, 'Rasstanovka klassovikh sil v borbe za osvobozhdenie', in Avarina and Danilevich: 1963, pp. 482–4). The triumph of Fidel Castro's 26 July Movement took the Soviet Union completely by surprise. As late as October 1958 Khrushchev referred in the same breath to 'the tragic fate of Guatemala' and 'the heroic but unequal struggle of the Cuban people'.[5] This reflects the fact that Soviet assessments of events in Latin America were then made almost wholly on the basis of information received from local Communist parties. The Cuban Communist Party, in a message to the Eleventh Congress of the Communist Party of Chile signed by Juan Marinello and Blas Roca and dated November 1958, had deplored the 'disunity of the opposition forces' and called for 'national unity' in order to overthrow Batista and form a 'democratic coalition government'.[6] It is unlikely that the Cuban Communists were sending the CPSU a different evaluation of the situation in their country. However, after the Cuban revolution Soviet analysts began to include Latin America in their discussions of the underdeveloped world, and a series of initiatives were taken by Moscow both to overcome its ignorance of the area and to increase its presence there.

In 1961 an Institute of Latin America was established at the Academy of Sciences in Moscow, on the recommendation of Anastas Mikoian, who had recently returned from Cuba. Previously, a very limited number of Latin America specialists had worked within the Institute of World Economy and International Relations or the Institute of Universal History. The Latin America Institute has since expanded to become 'the largest, and probably the most prolific, research centre devoted exclusively to Latin America in the world, with over one hundred full-time researchers' (Blasier: 1983, p. 171). In 1969, when the initiation of diplomatic relations with recently established nationalist regimes in Peru, Bolivia, Ecuador and Colombia had considerably broadened the Soviet diplomatic presence, the Institute launched a regular publication, *Latinskaia Amerika*. This journal, which

[5] Interview with a Brazilian journalist on 3 October 1958, *Mezhdunarodnaia zhizn*, no. 11, 1958, pp. 3–6.
[6] Communist Party of Chile, *Documentos del XI Congreso Nacional realizado en noviembre de 1958* (Talleres Gráficos Lautaro, Santiago de Chile, 1959), p. 43, in Halperin: 1965, p. 64.

covers most aspects of Latin American affairs with the emphasis on contemporary socio-political developments, was originally published bi-monthly in Russian and three or four times a year in Spanish. Since 1980, in the light of events in Central America, both editions have been produced monthly and the presentation of the Spanish version has become far more lively and colourful. The journal has 10,000 subscribers, most of them in Latin America and the United States. Under the editorship of Sergei Mikoian (son of the late Politburo member) it has sponsored and published regular 'round-table' discussions on salient issues in Latin American studies such as the nature and degree of Latin America's dependence and the social and political role of the military. One American political scientist argues that the debate on Latin America is the most sophisticated and open of all published Soviet debates on the outside world (Hough: 1981). (Debate about Cuba, however, was not permitted to surface in print until very recently.)

It is clear that the Soviet Union, which now has far more information and greater understanding of Latin America than in the early 1960s, no longer regards the area as a monolithic whole. There appear to be four main Soviet categories for Latin American regimes: (i) 'revolutionary democratic' states or (a label rarely applied) states of 'socialist orientation', such as post-1979 Nicaragua and 1979–83 Grenada; (ii) capitalist, yet 'progressive' and 'anti-imperialist' regimes which are willing to be friendly to the Soviet Union and stand up to the United States, such as Mexico and Panama (particularly under General Omar Torrijos (1969–81), who negotiated a treaty with the Carter administration providing for complete Panamanian sovereignty over the Canal by 1999, a campaign that was strongly supported by Moscow). The Alfonsín government elected in Argentina in late 1983 would probably also be included in this category, as would the recently elected (1984) administration in Uruguay (President Julio María Sanguinetti called for expanded economic relations with the USSR shortly before his inauguration) and the APRA government led by Alán García in Peru which, since its election victory in May 1985, has taken an active role in the Non-Aligned Movement, vying for the leadership and backing its challenge with moves to extend diplomatic recognition to the Palestine Liberation Organisation; (iii) capitalist, 'liberal-bourgeois' governments that are oriented towards Washington, for example, Venezuela, Peru under Belaúnde, Colombia (before1982), Costa Rica and Jamaica; (iv) 'right-wing', 'reactionary' military dictatorships generally not liked, but supported by the United States. The latter category, (which did not include the 1976–83 military regime in Argentina) is usually divided into two groups: those which have relations with the USSR, i.e., pre-democratisation Brazil and Uruguay, and those which do not, i.e., Chile, Paraguay, pre-1985 Guatemala, and Duvalier's Haiti (Valenta: 1983, pp. 291–2 and Blasier: 1983, pp. 87–91). Soviet specialists identify the main political force within the region as nationalism and, just as in the 1960s countries were judged by their policy position regarding Cuba, the touchstone now is their degree of independence from the United States. Moscow's current policy in Latin America is aimed at undermining US influence while seeking to develop its own ties with the more 'progressive' and independent governments, and events have demonstrated that anti-Communism can no longer be regarded as a significant impediment to the success of such a policy.

In the 1960s, the Soviet Union rapidly discovered that its connection with Cuba led to the complication and distortion of its relations with other Latin American nations at the same time as it presented them with new opportunities in the region. The 1962 Cuban missile crisis severely damaged the USSR's image in Latin America, and Moscow's claims to be seeking peaceful coexistence were further undermined by Castro's outspoken advocacy of guerrilla warfare and his stated policy of support for such endeavours in Latin America (see chapter 4). During the 1970s, however, the basic conflict between Soviet interests as superpower and as revolutionary vanguard was contained, albeit not completely resolved. Castro's material aid to groups embracing guerrilla warfare was effectively halted after the death of Che Guevara in 1967, polemic with the Soviet Union died down, and in the early 1970s Havana launched a successful diplomatic initiative to establish its own ties with Latin American governments. Towards the end of the decade Communist party strategy in Latin America, with its renewed emphasis on broad political alliances and electoral participation, was brought more firmly into line with Moscow's overall foreign-policy stance. In most Latin American countries the Communist parties are now an accepted part of the political scene, largely because of their willingness to engage in the horse-trading of Latin American politics. Individual parties have offered their backing to a wide variety of regimes, ranging from the Peruvians' support for Velasco, the Panamanians' generally favourable stand towards Torrijos and the Argentine Communists' (critical) support for the 1976 military coup led by General Videla. By the late 1960s all of the orthodox parties, with the partial exception of Colombia, had clearly distanced themselves from the armed struggle. Guerrilla groups such as Carlos Marighela's

National Liberation Action in Brazil, Uruguay's Tupamaros and the Montoneros in Argentina operated without Communist support and indeed were founded in the belief that the Moscow faithful lacked either the will or the capacity to engage in armed struggle. Moreover, the unexpectedly progressive nature of the military government which came to power in Peru in 1968 provided an effective counter-weight to Castroite arguments. These factors, together with an overall reduction in East-West tension (symbolised by detente, the SALT accords and the Helsinki conference) and the emergence of nationalist governments in Latin America, facilitated an increasing Soviet diplomatic presence. Whereas in the early years of the 1960s only two Latin American nations resumed relations with Moscow – Brazil in 1961 and Chile in 1964 – by the end of the decade a host of countries were willing to renew links: Colombia in 1968, Peru, Bolivia and Ecuador in 1969, Venezuela and Guyana in 1970 and Costa Rica in 1971. Moscow has taken various measures aimed at overcoming Latin American mistrust of the Soviet Union, including academic and cultural exchanges, which are facilitated by the Soviet friendship societies now existing in most Latin American countries. Soviet cultural initiatives have traditionally been focused on Mexico, but in recent years Soviet musicians and dancers have toured in other parts of Latin America, often with spectacular success. More importantly, Soviet diplomats have by and large restrained from trying to cultivate political ties with groups considered unacceptable to the government in question and, when accused of doing so, have apologised and made every effort to smooth over the situation, in dramatic contrast to the vehement denials and abusive tirades which any such allegation elicited in the 1930s. As the 1970s progressed, Moscow succeeded in establishing and maintaining diplomatic links with the majority of Latin American and Caribbean states. By the early 1980s, only pariah regimes such as Pinochet in Chile, Stroessner in Paraguay, Duvalier in Haiti and the Guatemalan military still refused to recognise the Soviet Union – which would probably not want relations with them in any case. Indeed, over the past decade Moscow has enjoyed far more trouble-free relations in Latin America than has Castro.

A similar pattern has occurred in the development of economic relations. Since the 1950s the USSR has tried to persuade Latin American governments that trade with the eastern bloc should be 'a major element in the Latin American countries' drive for economic independence', since it would enable them 'to gain more favourable terms with the industrially developed capitalist states, to consolidate their forces in the struggle against foreign monopolies [and] to expand their export (*sic*) and develop their industry and agriculture' (Gladkov: 1975, p. 11). In the cold war climate of the early 1950s only Perón's Argentina showed any sign of having seen the merits of this argument (see chapter 6), and during the following decade the political costs of Moscow's connections with a militant Castro further obstructed commercial relations with the Latin American mainland. However, in the early 1980s, anti-Communism *per se* is probably more of a nagging difficulty than a significant obstacle to trade, at least at governmental level. Trading links have survived right-wing military coups in Argentina (1976), Brazil (1964), Uruguay (1973) and Bolivia (1971, 1978, 1979, 1980), countries which have accounted for the bulk of Soviet trade with Latin America over the past two decades. The only partial exception is Peru: after Morales Bermúdez took over from Velasco in 1975 the military regime drifted rightwards and trade with the Soviet Union sharply diminished. This is largely due, however, to the fact that a significant proportion of Peru's imports from the Soviet Union consists of arms – clearly a highly sensitive commodity. Thus, neither Latin American political developments nor Latin American suspicions of the USSR – although either or both may lie behind isolated set-backs to Soviet policy – can any longer be considered a significant factor in the overall development of commercial relations.

What, then, are the main constraints on Soviet attempts to project its power into the sub-continent and to consolidate a strong economic presence there? Perhaps the most obvious and important factor to take into account is still the long-established and deeply entrenched socio-political and economic ascendancy of the United States of America. As indicated above, the Cuban revolution induced Soviet leaders to modify the view (hitherto almost as firmly believed in the Kremlin as in the White House) that the Latin American nations were destined to remain trapped in a position of subservience to the United States. However, the Soviet Union still has to contend with the need, perhaps more pressing than in most areas of the world, to keep a wary eye on Washington when considering its options in South and, since 1979 particularly, Central America. The majority of Latin American governments have to operate under much the same constraints and, although nationalist tendencies have intermittently rendered this factor advantageous to the USSR, it has more consistently worked against Moscow. Economic and political realities in Latin America determine that any government, whatever its orientation, will ultimately have to find a *modus vivendi* with Washington.

The second factor, which constitutes an additional hypothesis which will be explored in the following chapters, is that there are highly significant and fundamental economic and geographical determinants which have acted in the past to constrain Soviet activities in the region and which will remain a crucial obstacle to an increased Soviet presence, even in the context of a more favourable political climate. It will be argued that such factors may have had considerable influence on what are widely believed to have been exclusively 'political' decisions. Foremost among these economic constraints is the markedly low level of complementarity in the structure of production of the two regions. Furthermore, although 'planned' convergence arising out of favourable political conditions in individual countries cannot be excluded as a possibility, the economic costs inherent in any such operation are likely to be increased considerably in Latin America because of the formidable physical barriers to communications and trade with the Soviet Union.

Prior to the 1960s, Soviet economic relations with Latin America were highly sporadic, unstable and confined to only a few countries, principally Argentina and Uruguay. Soviet trade with Latin America at the time of the Cuban revolution compared distinctly unfavourably with its trade with Asia and Africa. In 1955 Soviet trade amounted to 122 million rubles with Asia, 40 million rubles with Africa and 58 million rubles with Latin America. In 1958 the figures were 459 million rubles, 189 million rubles and 58 million rubles respectively. By 1962, while trade with Asia reached 636 million rubles, and with Africa 265 million rubles, it was still only 96 million rubles with Latin America (excluding Cuba) (*Mirovaia ekonomika i mezhdunarodnye otnosheniia*, no. 3, 1964, p. 87). This is still the case today. In 1987 the Soviet Union exchanged 3,583.7 million rubles' worth of goods with Asia (excluding Vietnam, China, North Korea, Mongolia, Afghanistan and Japan), 1,399.8 million rubles' worth with Africa and only 969.4 million rubles' worth with Latin America (*Foreign Trade* (Moscow), no. 1, 1988). Although Moscow undertook a trade push in Latin America in the late 1960s (offering credits of $100 million to Brazil in 1966, $57 million to Chile in 1967, $2 million to Colombia and $20 million to Uruguay in 1968) and saw its efforts pay off to some extent with a steady increase in turnover between the two regions during the 1970s, the true extent of the Soviet economic presence in Latin America is by no means as great as many observers claim (see appendix for detailed figures on Soviet trade with Latin America). Moscow has increased the number of countries with which it has commercial dealings from four in 1960 to over twenty by the end of the 1970s, but the volume of trade has not exceeded $30 million with more than eight (Argentina, Brazil, Uruguay, Peru, Bolivia, Mexico, Colombia and Nicaragua) and it is only with Argentina, Brazil and Nicaragua that it has risen above the $100 million level. Before Soviet purchases of Argentine grain boosted overall trade figures in the early 1980s, the USSR's trade with Havana exceeded its dealings with the rest of Latin America by a ratio of approximately four to one. With the exception of the freak year 1981 the ratio since has been about two to one.

Four phases can be identified in the development of economic relations between the two regions: (1) In the 1920s tentative links were initiated by the new Soviet government, which was anxious to secure diplomatic recognition and to explore the potential for trade with Latin America as part of its attempt to break out of what was perceived as an economic blockade by the Western nations. These approaches (directed primarily at the River Plate nations and Mexico) were thwarted by the difficulties of sustaining commerce over such long distances and by the political complications discussed above. (2) In the 1950s nationalist leaders in a few Latin American countries (Argentina, Brazil and Uruguay), at critical junctures when their economies were undergoing varying degrees of pressure, sought to explore the potential political and/or economic benefits of relations with the Soviet Union. (3) With the onset of detente and the new multipolarity of the post-1970 world, the majority of Latin American countries followed the lead of the regional powers in establishing economic links with the Soviet Union. The 1970s saw what one Soviet commentator described as 'a real change for more active trade with the USSR' (Zinoviev: 1981, p. 100), with some consolidation of earlier initiatives. Perhaps one of the more important developments of the 1970s was that Moscow secured mutual most-favoured-nation status trading agreements with a majority of Latin American countries.[7] Such accords are all-important to Soviet officials in that they offer a clear indication of Latin American interest in trading with the USSR, act as the official sanction which enables the Soviet trade bureaucracy to move into action, and facilitate the organisation involved in the completion of transactions. Moscow also has trade missions in most Latin American capitals, and where trade has become at all significant joint inter-governmental

[7] Agreements were signed as follows: Argentina (1971), Bolivia (1970), Brazil (1969), Colombia (1968), Costa Rica (1970), Ecuador (1969), El Salvador (1974), Grenada (1980), Guyana (1973), Jamaica (1978), Mexico (1973), Nicaragua (1980), Panama (1979), Peru (1969) and Uruguay (1969).

commissions have been set up with the aim of promoting fulfilment of the trading agreements. In addition, from the Soviet point of view, 'Within the whole spectrum of measures taken to promote trade between the USSR and Latin America, of greatest importance have been the agreements reached between the USSR Chamber of Commerce and Industry and the Chambers of Commerce in some Latin American countries including Argentina, Brazil, Peru, Colombia and Mexico' (Zinoviev: 1981, pp. 101–2). Personal contacts have also improved: one Soviet commentator reports that 'In the past, visits of Soviet and Latin American businessmen to each other for commercial talks or for an appraisal of export and import requirements were incidental; nowadays hundreds of businessmen and experts from Latin America come to the Soviet Union each year and as many Soviet specialists visit the Latin American countries' (Gladkov: 1975, pp. 11–12). In the early 1970s, four shipping lines (Baltamerica, Baltpacific, Baltcaribbean and Baltgulf) were established by the Soviet Union to facilitate transportation which, in view of the distances involved, can be a costly and problematic operation even today.

The most notable consequences of the new Soviet initiative were that in 1975 Mexico signed an agreement with Comecon, and trade with both Argentina and Brazil reached a peak in 1981 when both countries refused to take part in the grain embargo introduced by President Carter as one of his sanctions against the Soviet invasion of Afghanistan. (4) Since 1981, however, there has been a distinct slackening of impetus in relations, largely because of the disillusionment experienced by both the USSR and the Latin American countries about what could be expected from each other. Trade with Argentina and Brazil has failed to realise its potential. Neither have Soviet–Mexican economic links developed to the extent anticipated in the 1975 agreement. Trade turnover with other countries, such as Colombia, Bolivia, Peru and Uruguay, still tends to fluctuate from year to year, lacking a coherent pattern of expansion. The reasons for this are outlined below and discussed in detail in chapter 6.

Despite the more stable pattern of Soviet–Latin American trade since the 1970s and its firmer organisational base, its most prominent characteristic is still a sharp imbalance in favour of the Latin American nations. The Soviet Union has a trade deficit with virtually all of its Latin American partners. (The exception is Venezuela, but to date Moscow's trade with Caracas has been almost negligible.) In 1978 Moscow's imports from the area outweighed exports by a ratio of four to one, obliging the USSR to pay in hard currency for most of its Latin

American purchases. There is scarcely an article published in Moscow concerning the development of Soviet–Latin American trade which does not cite this factor as the principal and most enduring obstacle to the further expansion of commercial relations.

Part of the explanation for the slow and uneven progress of Soviet–Latin American economic links can be found in the nature of the Soviet economy. As indicated above, trade now has an acknowledged role to play in Soviet development. However, it clearly performs a much less crucial or well-defined function than is the case in the Western capitalist economies. To this extent, Soviet foreign traders, who came late to the Latin American markets, may be disadvantaged in their competition with capitalist suppliers either because their own authorities prevent them from participating in the bidding for a project or because they cannot mobilise the Soviet bureaucracy in time to meet deadlines. Moreover, in 1973 one deputy minister of foreign trade described the deficiencies in Soviet marketing as follows: 'While we were only beginning to understand that before entering the marketplace we had to study it, determining which machinery could or could not be supplied where, as well as how to organise the work involved, capitalist firms had already created a whole science to deal with the question, coordinating production, advertising and commercial activity into a single discipline' (N. Smeliakov, *Novy mir*, 12 (Dec.) 1973, 216–17). An additional problem is that Soviet organisations are automatically barred from competing for infra-structural projects sponsored by the World Bank or the Inter-American Development Bank, which require bidders to be members of these institutions.

However, a more basic explanation for the persistent trade imbalance is that the economies of the two regions have developed in such a way that the scope for exchange always has been (and remains) severely limited. At first sight it may appear that the general pattern of Soviet trade with the Third World, consisting of the export of capital goods and equipment in return for raw materials, could be applied successfully in Latin America. On closer examination, however, it emerges that the Soviet Union is self-sufficient in many of the traditional Latin American primary exports and indeed is exporting some of them in competition with Latin American supplies. This applies to, for example, gold, petroleum, copper, iron ore, lead, silver, nickel and zinc. The most obvious exception is tin, the main export of Bolivia, which may help to explain the Soviet Union's especial enthusiasm for its relations with Bolivia, which have survived that country's numerous changes of government. (In 1984, Bolivia was the only country in Latin America with Communists in the government: one of its two Communist ministers had responsibility for the mining industry.) The bulk of the USSR's purchases in Latin America consists of primary agricultural produce, for example, tropical crops such as coffee and cocoa, and, most notably, grain and meat.

As far as Soviet exports are concerned, Latin American economies, which have generally attempted import-substitution industrialisation in the consumer goods sector rather than in capital-intensive heavy industry, might be considered a potentially receptive market for Soviet machinery and equipment. Soviet officials have themselves consistently indicated that they have hopes in this respect. With very few exceptions, however, this has not proved to be the case, largely because Latin American states have retained a high degree of integration with, and dependence on, the developed capitalist economies.

One of the main reasons for the Soviet failure to undermine Latin American reliance on Western imports is that Soviet industrial machinery and equipment is widely considered to be inferior in quality to its capitalist produced counterparts. It is possible that some Latin American judgements that Soviet goods are uncompetitive are founded in the belief that Soviet producers take less trouble over 'aesthetic' qualities, such as finish, than do their Western rivals. However, as late as 1979 a Soviet researcher wrote that no system existed for checking and analysing technical and economic information relating to product quality, and that 'present methods of assessing the quality of goods manufactured for export or already delivered to the foreign consumer cannot provide an adequate view of how well they are produced' (Gruzinov: 1979, p. 191). Thus, although trade with the Soviet Union would enable Latin Americans to benefit from lower prices and improved credit terms, to conserve scarce foreign exchange and, according to opinions recently expressed in Latin America, to receive better guarantees and local servicing, it is still generally the case that both public and private sector companies prefer to deal with the West.

There is one main exception to the above generalisation, namely, energy supplies. From an early stage the Soviet Union has tried to exploit Latin American dependence on imported oil. The first attempt to penetrate the Latin American market was made in the early 1930s, when Moscow found itself with a surplus of oil in a world marketing network tightly controlled by the major multi-nationals. Chile and Argentina were both offered barter deals, involving the exchange of

Chilean nitrates (demand for which had recently collapsed because of German development of synthetic substitutes) and Argentine agricultural products for Soviet crude oil, along with assistance in the setting up of their own national refineries. The refusal of foreign-owned oil companies operating in Chile to handle Soviet crude lent weight to the arguments of nationalists who wanted to accept the Soviet offer, which was heatedly debated in the Chilean Congress for two years before the incoming elected conservative government of Alessandri felt strong enough to reject it. In Argentina, serious negotiations with the state oil firm YPF were broken off after the 1930 *coup*. Only with Uruguay did the Soviet Union achieve a limited agreement involving the supply of petroleum products; this led to the creation of a state distribution company to handle the Soviet supplies which, in 1932, took 39 per cent of the Uruguayan market. The intention was that the Uruguayans would construct a state refinery to process Soviet crude, so that they would no longer need to buy the more expensive refined products. Two years before the refinery became operational, however, Montevideo severed all links with Moscow.

Again, in the late 1950s, the Soviet Union found itself with a surplus of oil, and this time succeeded in negotiating agreements with Uruguay and Argentina in 1958, and with Brazil in 1959. Mexico was offered credits tied to the purchase of petroleum equipment, but rejected the initiative (Philip: 1982, p. 342). Bolivia used a similar offer of Soviet technical assistance to the nationalised oil company YPFB to pressurise President Eisenhower into reversing his policy of refusing to supply credits to state-owned enterprises (a major factor behind Argentina's acceptance of the deal). The Uruguayan agreement consisted of a barter arrangement (Soviet oil for Uruguayan wool), which suited Montevideo since it had a large surplus of wool and a shortage of foreign exchange. In 1958 and 1959 Uruguay sold 16 per cent of its wool exports to Communist countries, the bulk of which went to the Soviet Union. However, resistance on the part of the Uruguayan government to Soviet overtures in 1959 for a larger share of the market indicated that the agreement had been little more than a contingency measure on the part of Montevideo. In retaliation, the Soviet Union threatened to curtail its purchases altogether, and in the midst of this dissension better prospects for the wool trade together with modifications in US tariff regulations concerning wool made it unnecessary to reverse the decline in Uruguay's short-lived burst of trade with the Soviet Union. The Argentine agreement was thwarted largely by the

March 1962 *coup* which brought to power a right-wing military government which promptly suspended the 1953 trade agreement with the USSR. The most successful of the three accords was with Brazil, whose President Kubitschek needed both to find new export outlets and to conserve foreign exchange in the aftermath of a rapid industrial expansion policy which had placed severe strains on his country's economy.

In recent years several Latin American countries have sought to reduce their reliance on imported oil by harnessing potential hydro-electric resources. Thus the Soviet Union has retained its interest in meeting Latin America's energy needs, for the USSR's world-class technology and expertise in the field of hydro-electric engineering enable it to compete easily and indeed advantageously with the West in this respect. The Soviet Union has supplied equipment for two hydro-electric stations in Brazil (at Capivari and Sobradinho). In 1973 the Soviet company Elektromashexport was granted the contract for fourteen turbines and generators for the Salto Grande project (sponsored jointly by Argentina and Uruguay), which went into operation in 1981. The USSR is also supplying equipment for thermal electric stations at San Nicolás, Luján de Cuyo and Costanera, and has prepared the design for the huge $4 billion Paraná Medio scheme. A contract has been signed with Colombia for the design and supply of generators for the Urrá 1 and Urrá 2 complex, a deal worth approximately $500 million. In Peru, the Soviet Union is part of a consortium involved in the Olmos project to bring water across the Andes to irrigate the drought-ridden northern coast.

A second potential means of reducing the Soviet trade deficit with Latin America would be through the sale of arms. As yet, however, such initiatives have proved largely unfruitful. With the exceptions of revolutionary Cuba, Nicaragua and Grenada (all denied ready access to Western arms supplies), Peru is the only country willing to receive Soviet materiel. From 1973–5 the Soviet Union sold Peru aircraft, tanks, surface-to-air missiles and artillery on very generous terms and when, in 1978, the Peruvians found themselves unable to maintain payments for their weapons, the Soviet Union rolled over the debt until 1981–8, indicating their reluctance to relinquish this sole market. Arms were offered to Allende's Chile, but were refused, and various rumours in 1982-3 to the effect that the Argentine generals had ordered Soviet weapons have so far proved unsubstantiated. It is possible that Mexico has also been approached, but again there is no indication that the latter has proved responsive to such an offer. Apart from the political objections many Latin American governments would have to the purchase of Soviet armaments, the traditional predominance of the United States as supplier of military hardware to the region, along with the increasing strength of Brazil as an arms exporter ($1 billion worth in 1981), are highly significant obstacles to the expansion of Soviet arms sales to Latin America. Moreover, there are no major unresolved conflicts between states (such as persist in, for example, the Middle East) to be exploited by a potential arms supplier.

2 'Communist subversion' in Latin America? – The impact of Marxist thought

Exponents of the ideological-strategic approach outlined in the introduction frequently draw attention to the Soviet propaganda offensive in Latin America. As they correctly point out, this has broadened and diversified over the past twenty-five years. Thus we are told, for example, that in the late 1980s there are 10,000 Latin American students enrolled in Soviet universities compared with the 144 who were attending Patrice Lumumba in 1960; that in 1982 Latin Americans could tune in to Soviet radio broadcasting for 105 hours per week compared with only 63 in 1962 and that at least seventeen Soviet journals are now translated and distributed in Latin America, six of which also appear in Portuguese (Blasier: 1983, pp. 12–13 and pp. 191–2; Goldhamer: 1972, p. 147).

Whilst the relevance of such information should not be denied, to present it divorced from the Latin American context leads to a seriously distorted picture of Soviet–Latin American relations. Too often evidence which merely indicates the existence of a greater Soviet propaganda effort in Latin America is upheld as confirmation of a corresponding degree of success in instigating 'subversion'. The first point to be made in response to this is that current Soviet initiatives are clearly designed to foster a positive attitude towards the USSR as a country which has a viable socio-economic system and offers valuable commercial opportunities, rather than trying to incite the masses to Soviet-style revolution. The propaganda effort is very low-key compared to the diplomatic and trading activities discussed in chapter 6 and in general appears to be intended to complement them. However, even if, for the sake of argument, it is assumed that this is not the case and that the USSR is directing substantial resources to the winning of Latin America for Communism, it is still necessary to extend the analysis further. Issues which must be incorporated are the extent to which Latin Americans – either the educated elites or the mostly under-educated masses – are receptive or responsive to Marxist propaganda. In what ways, if any, do they perceive Marxism to be relevant to Latin American conditions? How much latitude does the political structure of Latin American countries allow for the development of Marxist-based organisations? It is the purpose of this chapter to suggest answers to these questions.

The most fundamental barrier to the penetration of Marxism into Latin America throughout the period under discussion has been the Catholic Church. This remained a crucial obstacle until well into the 1960s, when attempts began to synthesise the two ideologies, in what has become known as Liberation Theology. Contemporary Nicaragua, however, offers a revealing example of the problems which still confront Marxist leaders of a predominantly peasant-based economy. The contradiction was less dramatic for the revolutionaries in Cuba, where the Church's influence was not great, partly because of the presence of vestiges of African religion from the slave culture and partly because of the comparatively developed state of Cuba's economy and educational system. Argentina, Chile and Uruguay are also relatively urbanised and secularised societies where the role of the Church was less significant than in, say, Mexico, Brazil or Colombia.

In its assertion of a total world-view, the Church was also important in terms of creating a receptivity to a certain kind of all-embracing ideology. Mexican novelist Carlos Fuentes has lamented that 'We are the sons of rigid ecclesiastical societies. This is the burden of Latin America – to go from one Church to another, from Catholicism to Marxism, with all its dogma and ritual' (in Riding: 1986, p. 429). For dissident Catholics, Marxism was the only ideology which could provide a sufficiently all-encompassing vision to replace what they had rejected, replicating the Church's concepts of dogma, orthodoxy and heresy. This was a particularly important factor in the conversion of intellectuals, particularly writers and artists, who have played a key role in the dissemination of Marxism in Latin America.

The examples are numerous. José Mariátegui and César Vallejo, who travelled to the Soviet Union three times in 1928–31, both played important roles in the foundation of the Peruvian Socialist Party. Jorge Amado and the Mexican muralists (José Orozco, David Siqueiros – who was involved in a plot to kill Trotsky – and Diego Rivera, who was Trotsky's main protector in Mexico) were all active. In Chile, Pablo Neruda was an established poet with a continent-wide reputation before his conversion to Communism under the impact of the Spanish Civil War – particularly the murder of García Lorca, whom he saw as the bearer of the spirit of Republican Spain. In 1969, when the Chilean

Communist Party opted to announce their own presidential candidate in order to force a decision from the other parties in the Popular Unity coalition about whom to support, their nominee was Pablo Neruda. After he became a Communist, Neruda consciously tried to write a different kind of poetry incorporating a political message and which would be comprehensible to working people, the most famous and successful example of which is his *Canto General*. This was apparently one of only two books which Che Guevara carried with him to Bolivia (the other being an arithmetic textbook), and Che told Neruda that he used to read it to the guerrillas in the Sierra Maestra, and presumably in Bolivia as well (Neruda: 1974, p. 439). The importance of such figures in terms of their ability to carry the message of Marxism to working people is suggested by Neruda's account of how, travelling the nitrate region of Chile as a senator in 1945, 'at hundreds of meetings, all very far away from each other, I heard a constant plea: that I should read my poems. Many times they asked me for them by title. Of course I never knew whether anybody understood very much of my verses. It was difficult to tell, in that atmosphere of absolute silence, of sacred respect in which they listened to me' (Neruda: 1974, p. 240). In Cuba, the avant-garde poet Rubén Martínez Villena played a leading role in events of the 1920s and 1930s, and Nicolás Guillén joined the Communist Party in 1937. Other leading writers, whilst not fully committing themselves to the Communist movement, have been fellow-travellers, the most notable recent example of which is Nobel prize-winning novelist Gabriel García Márquez. The importance of these cultural bearers of Marxism, whose glamour, charisma and intellectual weight have done much to enhance the acceptance of Marxist ideas in Latin America, is hard to over-estimate. (Officials in the Soviet Union have also understood the significance of cultural ambassadors: for example, they sent their leading film director, Eisenstein, to make a film in Mexico.) A strong and enduring link has been established between Marxism and culture. Many of the leading Sandinistas in revolutionary Nicaragua are poets and writers. Minister of Culture Ernesto Cardenal (who is also an ordained priest), in particular, has used poetry workshops as a prominent means of raising consciousness amongst working people.

What attracted Latin American artists and writers to Marxism? The influence of intellectual life in Europe was important for many leading figures, particularly those who travelled and lived there, for example, Mariátegui, Vallejo, Siquieros and Neruda. Of particular importance was the *Clarté* movement founded by French intellectual Henri Barbusse in 1919, which called on intellectuals to engage in the struggle against ignorance and its perpetrators. In his 1927 *Manifesto to intellectuals*, Barbusse argued that they should do everything possible to help the birth of a new society. *Claridad* movements arose in Peru (where both Mariátegui and Haya de la Torre were involved), Argentina, Chile (where the magazine published some of Neruda's early poems) and Brazil. As indicated above, the Spanish Civil War was a deeply felt experience for Neruda, also for Octavio Paz, César Vallejo, David Siquieros and others.

At a more general level, however, artists embraced Marxism because of its ability to offer a total world-view, an intellectually palatable explanation for underdevelopment and social injustice, a Utopian (and historically determined) solution and a programme for immediate political action in which intellectuals were called upon to play a role. Marxism was appropriate for those who, like Vallejo and Neruda, were intellectuals who were not particularly comfortable with their consequently privileged status. Neruda explains what he got out of being a member of the Communist party in personal terms: 'I found in my party, the Communist Party of Chile, a large group of simple people, who had left personal vanity, *caudillismo* and material interests far behind. I felt happy to know honourable people who were fighting for the common good, that is to say, for justice' (Neruda: 1974, p. 435).

Perhaps the clearest example of Marxism being embraced as a substitute for a rejected Catholicism is offered by César Vallejo, whose poetry is constructed around biblical images both before and after his conversion to Communism and whose proletarian heroes 'appear as new Christs' urging redemption through collective love (Vallejo: 1970, p. 69). Vallejo expressed his concept of revolution as follows: 'Revolution does not mean the fall of the Tsar or the seizure of power by the workers. What it means is what is happening today in the hearts of families and of the peoples' (Vallejo: 1970, p. 66). For him, as for Neruda and others, Communism was less a political philosophy than a metaphysical need.

A final introductory point concerns the importance of differentiating between Marxism and Marxism-Leninism in Latin America. This distinction is frequently blurred by those who choose to see all who assume radical leftist positions as 'tools of international Communism'. The resulting confusion entails a highly inaccurate assessment of the extent of Soviet control over the diverse groups in Latin America which claim a 'Marxist' orientation. As will be made clear in the following brief history of Marxist thought in Latin America, there has been very little interplay between the evolutions of Marxism-Leninist prescriptions for revolutionary development in Latin America, as shaped by Soviet ideologues, and the way that

Latin Americans themselves have applied Marxism to their situation. Trotskyism and Maoism have both had an impact in Latin America, which has also produced its own distinct versions of Marxist theory in Castroism and Guevarism. In order to make the comparison, this history is divided into five main periods: (1) before 1917; (2) 1917–35; (3) 1936–58; (4) 1959–75; and (5) 1975 to date.

Pre-1917

Despite the evidence put forward by Soviet historians to assert a Marxist tradition in Latin America antedating the Russian revolution, it is difficult to draw any conclusion other than that Marxism as a basis for worker organisation became a significant force in the region, with few exceptions, in the wake of the Bolshevik triumph. Nevertheless, the events of the nineteenth and early twentieth centuries established a crucial background for the diffusion of Marxist ideas.

In the relatively prosperous years of the late nineteenth century Latin American intellectuals were primarily concerned not with the economic progress of their nations, but with their development away from a state of 'barbarism' to one of 'civilisation' along European lines. Great faith was placed in the efficacy of (secular) education as a means of inculcating democratic and national values. Positivism, with its emphasis on orderly, scientific advancement, was in vogue amongst the intelligentsia. Thus the ideology of the Church, in addition to its power as an institution, was beginning to be challenged. However, the prevailing hegemony of Catholic ideals is revealed by the way in which Marxism was initially received in Latin America. For intellectuals, encouraged by Rodó's *Ariel* (1900) to seek a 'disinterested ideal' for Latin American development in contrast to the utilitarianism of the United States, socialism was 'romantic and individualistic . . . the expression of a desire more moralistic than social' (Zea: 1963, pp. 23–4). Latin American philosophers who were interested in its potential for eliminating poverty made no attempt to formulate a 'scientific' programme for political action on the part of the working classes. For workers, Marxism was a 'doctrine much like the doctrine of emancipation preached by Jesus Christ. For them it was an intuitive idealisation of justice and well-being. It meant more bread for the hungry, higher wages, and fewer hours of work. It meant civil, social, human liberation and, thus, a greater spirit of democracy' (Santiago Iglesias, in Aguilar: 1968, p. 76).

It was in the Southern Cone countries where industrialisation, the pre-requisite of a proletariat, came earliest to Latin America, in the middle to late nineteenth century. It was introduced by confident elites who were strong enough to pay minimal wages and subject workers to appalling and often highly dangerous conditions (particularly in the mining industry), extremely arduous hours of work and quick – if necessary, brutal – repression of worker demands. It also brought European immigrants, who were to play a crucial role in the introduction of Marxist ideas to Latin America, flooding into these countries, where newly built ports and railways were facilitating the spread of new political theories. Thus, the intellectual climate was transformed by refugees from the failed Paris Commune, and from Spain, Italy and Germany, who had 'brought with them their socialistic education, which led to the general practice of mutual aid among the immigrants – a practice little known to the people of Argentina' (Juan Justo, in Aguilar: 1968, p. 79). The importance of the Europeans is indicated by a revealing description by Juan Justo of a German Vorwärts Club formed in 1882 in Buenos Aires, which 'was truly an international movement. The public meetings were conducted, in turn, in Spanish, Italian, French and German' (in Aguilar: 1968, p. 79). Many of the immigrants were supporters of the First and Second Internationals and had considerable experience in the labour movements of their native countries. Excluded from the political process in their newly adopted lands, where they were not allowed to vote, and anxious to ensure a higher standard of living in the New World than they had enjoyed at home, they were instrumental in the creation of early workers' organisations and political parties in Latin America.

The ideas of Marx and Engels were introduced by the First International (1864–76), which had sections in several Latin American countries. The Second International, launched in 1889, prompted the formation of the Argentine Socialist Party in 1896. Socialism had only a limited impact, however, confined (at least in terms of parties) to the countries where immigration was highest – Argentina, Chile and Uruguay. The most significant of these parties was undoubtedly Luis Recabarren's United Socialist Workers' Party, founded in Chile in 1912, which later formed the basis of the Chilean Communist Party. The Socialist parties suffered from the consequences of the Second International's theory of revolution in stages (which led the Argentine Socialist Party to support US interventions in the Caribbean) and its under-estimation of the power of nationalism. The collapse of the Second International under the impact of the First World War, which dealt a severe blow to socialist illusions, demonstrated the need for an alternative solution to the workers' plight.

More appealing than socialism to the still largely artisanal work-force of most Latin American countries was anarchism and its collectivist variant, anarcho-syndicalism, which was a highly potent force amongst nascent labour movements, above all in Argentina, but also in Brazil, Peru and Mexico, and to a lesser extent in Uruguay, Chile, Bolivia, Ecuador, Colombia and Cuba. The anarchist movement and its radicalism provided a crucial background for the introduction of Marxist ideas. As with socialism, its inherent limitations were as important in this respect as its positive aspects: Luis Recabarren founded his Socialist Workers' Party partly out of a conviction that anarchist prohibitions on party and parliamentary activity were short-sighted and had to be rejected. Changes in the structure of the work-force (greater concentration into single industries and decline of artisanal activity, especially after the First World War) also tended to reduce the relevance of anarchism and to leave a vacuum for Marxist ideas. At a purely practical level, the anarchist and socialist press provided a forum for the dissemination of information about the October revolution, where it was given an enthusiastic reception. However, anarchism remained an influential competitor to the Communist movement until well into the late 1920s.

Chilean Communist Elías Lafertte offers the following revealing explanation of the fluidity of the political situation at the time, of how Marxism was introduced into the Chilean Socialist Workers' Party, and of how the evolution of the party was influenced by a blend of Marxist and anarchist ideas and attitudes:

People came from all camps. There were Democratic party militants, anarchists, people with no party, workers, small businessmen, intellectuals, professional people. But the working class was predominant, from the nitrate *pampa*, from Iquique, from the bakers' unions. Many anarchist ideas and customs flourished in our ranks: for instance, resistance to the law, free love, anti-clericalism. We were not really Marxists. Marxism came in good time to the Socialist Workers' Party after study, after reading the books from Europe, from international contacts, from the travels of our comrades, from the contact with the Communist International. But we had in our midst ... the capacity to fight, to resist injustice, to organise, the sentiment of unity, the pride of the proletariat and above all class consciousness. (Laferrte: 1961, p. 101)

1917–1935

Impact of the Russian revolution

There is no doubt that the October 1917 victory of the Russian revolution captured the imagination of the reform-minded Latin American intelligentsia. It came at a time when dislocation of the Latin American economies as a result of the First World War caused widespread unemployment and increasingly militant labour unrest. This had also triggered an assertive economic nationalism amongst a small but significant sector of the Latin American elites. In this context of the search for a model which would resolve Latin America's economic and social contradictions, events in Russia had all the impact of an apparently successful solution. Argentina's José Ingenieros, for example, saw the Bolshevik triumph as the harbinger of a new era. Moreover, anarchists and socialists who offered alternative ways forward had few tangible achievements with which to support their arguments. The immediate response from intellectuals and students was a euphoric sense that if it could happen in backward Russia then why not in Latin America? Eudocio Ravines, the former Peruvian Communist, describes how in 1917 'all the events in Russia went straight to my heart. Every morning I read the news avidly, and in it I saw gradually a possibility of believing in something again . . . I could find genuine analogies between the [Peruvian] Indian and what I imagined the Russian *muzhik* to be' (Ravines: 1951, p. 13). It is difficult to overestimate the prestige of the Soviet leaders amongst the university communities in Latin America during these years.

It was on their own initiative that Recabarren's Socialist Workers' Party (in 1922) and weaker versions in Argentina (1921) and Uruguay (1920) gained admission to the Communist International. In Brazil (1921) and Mexico (1919) existing anarcho-syndicalist groups were converted to Bolshevism. In Mexico, where revolution had antedated the Russian uprising by seven years, the establishment of a 'bourgeois' republic in the 1917 Constitution of Querétaro had highlighted the lack of an effective organisation of the working-class. According to former Mexican Communist Valentín Campa, the attitudes to the Russian revolution of intellectuals such as Ricardo Flores Magón, who was not a Marxist but initially saw the Bolsheviks as 'the true internationalists', and leaders such as Emiliano Zapata, were influential in the decision to form a Communist party. Campa describes how the conversion from anarcho-syndicalism to Bolshevism took place: 'Somewhat gen-eralised opinions [arose] amongst unionists and also amongst numerous intellectuals as to the need to create a party of the working class. The process [took place] on a confused basis in which there were some theoretical elements, but in which intuition and discontent [played] a considerable part' (Campa: 1978, pp. 59–60). At this stage it would have been surprising if the theoretical basis for action had been anything other than weak: there was scant Marxist literature in Mexico available in Spanish. Material from the Bolshevik Party and later the Third International was received only sporadically by individuals, although what did arrive was circulated with significant impact. Mexico was also the object of early Comintern interest: Moscow was keen to promote Communist activity in Mexico in order to distract the United States from intervening against the Soviet Union, and dispatched Mikhail Borodin in 1919 partly to achieve this end. Agents from the Mexican party were later instrumental in founding Communist parties in Cuba (1925) and Central America.

Thus Communist parties were functioning in the major Latin American countries by 1923, and had been set up in most others by the end of the decade. However, the number of people willing to make the commitment to Communist Party membership remained disproportionately small. For example, at the Fifth Comintern Congress in 1924 delegates from their respective countries reported 1,000 members in Mexico, 3,500 in Argentina, 2,000 in Chile, 600 in Uruguay and in Brazil, where the party was illegal, 350 members (Cerdas Cruz: 1986a, p. 98). The Communist movement failed to extend its influence much beyond this restricted minority.

One of the most important reasons for this is that the Latin American elites reacted quickly and in most cases effectively to the social and economic changes brought about by the industrialisation, urbanisation and immigration of the late nineteenth and early twentieth centuries. At the socio-economic level, the traditionally powerful agricultural interests established themselves in positions of control in industry and commerce, and were remarkably successful in transferring landowner-peasant patronage relationships from the countryside to the cities. At the political level, labour organisations or parties based on working-class interests suffered persecution throughout Latin America. The rapid response of the elites is typified by events in Peru in 1919. A three-day strike declared by the workers of Lima-Callao in January of that year in support of lower food prices and the demand for an eight-hour day brought the army out to disperse them. Labour organisation and activism was clearly still in its early stages: notwithstanding this, dictator General Leguía, who took power in July

1919, announced that he had done so 'not only to liquidate the old state of affairs, but also to detain the advance of Communism which, because it is premature among us, would produce dreadful consequences' (Skidmore and Smith: 1984, p. 206).

The pattern of repression was repeated across Latin America. In Venezuela, the dictatorship of Juán Vicente Gómez attacked all workers' movements and the Communist Party was outlawed from the 1920s until 1945. In Brazil, the Communist Party was illegal from 1922 to 1945, and the abortive Communist-led uprising in 1935 (see page 41) provided a pretext for a comprehensive crackdown on the entire left. The Chilean Communist Party was proscribed by dictator Ibáñez from 1927 to 1931, and in Argentina the 1930 *coup* by the armed forces presaged a fifteen-year period of illegality for the PCA. Suppression of the Communist-inspired 1932 insurgency in El Salvador (see page 41) was truly ferocious and resulted in the complete destruction of the party apparatus and the execution of its leaders (including the man whose name has been adopted by the current guerrilla movement in El Salvador, Farabundo Martí). Similar difficulties were experienced by almost all of the Latin American Communist parties during these years. In most countries persecution was preemptively instigated by an elite which had identified the threat to its position from worker or peasant organisation, rather than constituting a defensive reaction to Communist activity itself. (One possible exception to this was Mexico, where the Communists were more or less tolerated until they made a misjudged and Comintern-inspired attempt to exploit an abortive right-wing *coup* against the Portes Gil government in 1929 – see pages 39–40. Legality was restored to them in 1935.) Thus the willingness of the Latin American elites to use repression to safeguard their interests severely hampered the Communists in their attempts to recruit cadres. However, the restricted influence of the Communists must be attributed in part to the subordination of their parties to the Communist International, which manifested a distinct lack of interest, knowledge or understanding of the local conditions within which they had to operate.

The Comintern's attitude towards Latin America must be seen in the context of its view of how the national liberation movement in 'colonial' countries should be evaluated in relation to the world socialist revolution. This raised the question of what policy the Comintern ought to adopt towards such movements, which in its turn was intimately related to the security concerns of the fledgling Soviet state. The first Comintern Congress in 1919 devoted almost exclusive attention to events in Germany, where revolution was believed to be imminent. Trotsky's *Manifesto to the proletariat of the world* failed to mention Latin America. At this stage, liberation of the colonies was regarded as being crucially dependent upon the overthrow of existing state structures in the metropoli. This extreme Euro-centric viewpoint was called into question following the fading of prospects for pro-letarian revolution in Europe, an upsurge in the activities of national liberation movements and the emergence of the national and colonial question within Soviet Russia itself. At the Second Congress in 1920 Indian delegate M. N. Roy's counter-thesis that the fate of the revo-lution in Europe depended upon the success or otherwise of the revolution in colonial countries was adopted in a weaker form. However, although theoretically this assigned a primary role to the struggles of colonial peoples (a position which seemed to be at least partially vindicated by events in Turkey, Persia, India and China), Soviet foreign-policy considerations determined that discussion of colonial problems be suppressed at the 1921 Third Congress. Great Britain had recently signed a commercial treaty with the Soviet Union, in which the latter promised to abstain from propaganda that would incite the peoples of Asia to act contrary to British interests, and for security reasons an aid pact was signed with Kemal Ataturk, in spite of his massacres of Turkish Communists.

Soviet security concerns with respect to Latin America were obvi-ously minimal and were confined to Mexico and the River Plate nations. In addition to Mexico (see above), Soviet attention was also directed towards Argentina and Uruguay because of their role as food suppliers to Great Britain, whom the Soviet government regarded as another potential aggressor. It is hardly surprising that, at this stage, Moscow assigned little theoretical importance and a low priority in practice to the fate of the revolution in far-flung Latin America, obliged to live within the shadow of the United States and its 1823 Monroe Doctrine. This relegation of Latin American affairs reflected Lenin's conviction that 'there were more urgent revolutionary tasks which must have priority. It would be a long time before revolution could succeed in the New World. Conditions might mature in the near future. But American imperialism was on the alert to intervene as it had done in the past' (Roy: 1964, p. 346). The USSR devoted more energy and resources to the development of diplomatic and trading ties with these nations than it did to establishing effective operational links with the Communist parties. Mexico, which had relations with the Soviet Union from 1924 to 1930, was courted by Alexandra

Kollontai (ambassador 1926–9), and trade was carried out with Argentina and Uruguay despite the acknowledged difficulties of transporting goods across the Equator. As a result of British pressure on Argentina, the only country apart from Mexico to maintain relations with the USSR was Uruguay (1925–35). Thus political links were largely confined to the Comintern network which, notwithstanding this fact, was initially extremely weak.

The failure of the revolution in Europe, together with events in China and elsewhere, forced the colonial issue back on to the agenda at the Fourth (1922), Fifth (1924) and Sixth (1928) Comintern Congresses. At the Fifth Congress the colonial question began to be perceived as an essential factor for the triumph of socialism on a world scale. A delegate from Mexico argued that the United States had become the centre of gravity of imperialism, and it was this growing awareness of the importance of the United States which prompted the Comintern's rising interest in Latin America, as the 'colonial' economic base of the new imperialism. It was after this Congress, in 1925, that the Argentine Communist Party was instructed to establish a South American Bureau, through which most of Comintern's operations in the area were directed. A Caribbean branch was opened in New York in 1928. However, it was only in 1929 that a separate Secretariat for Latin America was formed within the Comintern's Moscow administration; hitherto relations with Latin American Communist parties had been handled through a 'Latin Secretariat' which also covered Southern Europe.

The potential role of Latin America in any conflict between the United States and Great Britain had become a main concern of Comintern policy by 1928, when its Sixth Congress was held. For the first time, Latin America was significantly represented and its revolutionary potential discussed, a development also partly attributable to events in Nicaragua where Augusto Sandino was raising a nationalist banner to challenge US imperialism. Within the Comintern schema (outlined at the 1928 Congress) Latin America's fundamentally agrarian economic structure required that it attain the capitalist stage of development before a transition to socialism was possible. Its century of political independence forestalled the possibility of 'skipping' this stage, as was proposed for the colonial countries of the East. This analysis appeared to be substantiated by the small size of the proletariat in most Latin American countries, and by the agrarian and peasant character of the Mexican revolution. Latin American Communists were directed to work for a 'democratic-bourgeois' revolution. The main tenets of this were nationalisation of foreign concessions, expropriation of large landed estates (although it was not specified to whom they should be transferred, an omission reflecting the ambivalent attitudes regarding the role of the peasantry, which proved one of the most controversial issues in the debates between Latin American and Soviet Marxisms), repudiation of the national debt, rejection of imperialist control over the economy, the fight for an eight-hour day and the 'stamping out of semi-slave-like conditions of labour'.[1]

However, although the resolutions of Congress specified that the revolution in Latin America could only be democratic-bourgeois at this stage, they also said that, because of the weakness of the national bourgeoisie and their links to imperialism, Latin American Communist parties should work at the same time for the eventual dictatorship of the proletariat. This echoed the ambivalence of the original 1920 Lenin and Roy theses on the colonial question in general, formulated as an interim measure in what Lenin saw as an inconclusive debate at the Second Congress. The theses advocated both support for national liberation movements and agitation to ensure that workers and peasants were prepared for the Soviet revolution which was to follow, a policy contradiction which was never resolved. The basic problem with Comintern attempts to formulate a strategy for revolution in the colonies was that issues such as the nature of the revolution and the role of classes were examined by means of a formal analogy with the Russian revolution, rather than a structural analysis of the specific conditions in individual countries (Cerdas Cruz: 1986a, p. 41). This led to fundamental inadequacies in the Comintern approach, which were graphically demonstrated by its relationship with the nationalist leader Sandino of Nicaragua, who fought against a US occupation force from 1927 to 1934. Comintern officials first tried to convert Sandino to Communism (battling for influence with APRA) and then, having failed, denounced him as a traitor. The Comintern's aim was to convert a nationalist struggle into a broader social struggle (in accordance with part of its remit), but Comintern officials made no serious attempt to fulfil the second part of the resolutions adopted at the Sixth Congress by setting up a Communist party in Nicaragua, which could have given the Sandinista movment an organisational base and therefore the possibility of continuity (Cerdas Cruz: 1986a, pp. 363–97).

[1] 'Revolutionary prospects and tasks in Latin America: Sixth Comintern Congress theses on the revolutionary element in colonial and semi-colonial countries', *Inprecorr*, viii/88, 12 December 1928, pp. 1,660–1 and 1,675, in Clissold: 1970, p. 78.

Clearly one of the major difficulties of applying the standard Comintern model of a vanguard Communist party with a proletarian base to the Latin American situation was that the proletariat in the majority of these countries was small in size, rural in origin and lacking in organisation and political consciousness. It is noteworthy that the two figures who made the most substantial contribution during this period to the formulation of a Marxist-based model which was more directly relevant to Latin American reality both came from Peru, where the above features were particularly accentuated and where, therefore, the Comintern prescription seemed least appropriate. The first of these men was Victor Raúl Haya de la Torre, founder of the *Alianza Popular Revolucionaria Americana* (APRA), who initially established contact with the Comintern and whose model was in fact not dissimilar to that proposed by the Soviet theorists, although he differed greatly on questions of strategy and tactics. The second was José Mariátegui, a socialist whose position was almost directly opposed to Moscow's on all the major points at issue. These were: (1) the nature of Latin America's existing economic structure and its relation to world capitalism; (2) the role and characteristics of the 'national bourgeoisie'; (3) attitudes towards the peasantry; and (4) the indigenous question.

Haya de la Torre rejected the Comintern premise that Latin America was set on the same course of development as the European industrial nations. He disputed Lenin's contention that imperialism constitutes the last stage of capitalism, arguing that in Latin America it represented only the first stage. While accepting the Comintern classification of Latin American agrarian structures as 'feudal' or semi-feudal, he maintained that what was happening in Latin America was not that capitalism was superseding feudalism, but rather that the two systems tended to coexist. He stressed the deformed nature of Latin American capitalism, with its bourgeoisie of foreigners, the enduring alliance between imperialist bourgeoisie and native landowners, a weak, impoverished *petite bourgeoisie* threatened by foreign competition, and a very small proletariat.

In terms of tactics the implications of this analysis were a repudiation of the Leninist thesis that capitalism could be overthrown in backward countries before the revolution took place in industrial Europe. Early Comintern documents on Latin America – authorship unknown – had explicitly denied the applicability of the national-democratic stage and called for an agrarian, anti-imperialist and anti-capitalist revolution.[2] In contrast, Haya de la Torre insisted that the orthodox Marxist theory concerning stages of production had to be applied to Latin America, and he urged completion of the democratic 'bourgeois' stage of political development through a combined anti-imperialist and anti-feudalist revolution. The revised 1928 Comintern theses on Latin America, as indicated above, came closer to this position, although differences remained over the nature of Latin American development and the issue of the possible coexistence of feudalism and capitalism. Tactical positions were completely at variance: Haya de la Torre rejected the concept of the vanguard party and sought to build an alliance of workers, peasants, the *petite bourgeoisie* and the 'national' bourgeoisie – similar in concept to the Chinese Kuomintang.

Mariátegui also challenged the Comintern theory of an 'autonomous' stage of capitalist development in Latin America. He maintained that Latin America had already been drawn into the capitalist system in a dependent role, and that the activities of imperialism would ensure that it would retain this colonial status. He disputed the idea that Latin American agrarian structures were 'feudalist', arguing that they too existed in dependent relation to a capitalism which was ultimately supported by their very primitivism. The conclusion he drew, in stark contrast to Haya de la Torre, was that the revolution in Latin America could only be socialist, and that the united front, gradualist tactics advanced by the Comintern (and by APRA) were invalid in a continent overshadowed by the United States and deeply penetrated by monopoly capital. He wrote, 'Only a socialist Latin or Spanish America can pit itself effectively against plutocratic, imperialist North America. The era of free competition in the capitalist economy is over in all areas and in all respects. We are in the age of the monopolies, one might say of the empires. The Latin American countries came late to capitalist competition. The destiny of these countries, within the capitalist order, is that of mere colonies.'[3]

Mariátegui's assertion of the need for a socialist revolution excluded the possibility of coopting the bourgeoisie, whom he believed had an intrinsic interest in collaborating with imperialism. He advocated revolution based on a worker-peasant alliance, and drew substantially

---

[2] 'Sobre la revolución en América Latina. Llamamiento a la clase obrera de los dos Américas', *L'Internationale Communiste*, no. 15, January 1921, pp. 3,311–14 and 3,321–4, in Löwy: 1982, pp. 73–9; 'A los obreros y campesinos de América del Sur', *La Correspondance Internationale*, no. 2, 20 January 1923, pp. 26–7, in Löwy: 1982, pp. 80–1.

[3] Mariátegui, *La revolución socialista latinoamericana* ('Carta colectiva del grupo de Lima', June 1929), in Löwy: 1982, p. 106.

on evidence of a communitarian life-style amongst the Incas to present a somewhat mystical vision of a racially integrated, socialist Peru. Whereas Marxism-Leninism does not always take a wholly positive attitude towards the peasantry, identifying *petit bourgeois* tendencies – particularly amongst the less impoverished – which can make them a sometimes unreliable ally, Mariátegui and subsequent Latin American Marxists have pointed to a dual oppression – both economic and racial. The role of the peasantry in the revolution or its relationship with the industrial proletariat was never satisfactorily defined by the Comintern. This neglect of the indigenous peasantry helps to explain the appeal of Maoism in Latin America and the over-estimation of the revolutionary potential of the rural areas by Castroism and Guevarism.

The differences in approach of Soviet officials and Latin Americans had, by the time of the Sixth Congress, already led to tensions between Latin American Communists and their Soviet mentors. One Comintern categorisation that the nationalistically minded Latin Americans found particularly unpalatable was the description of their countries as 'semi-colonies'. Jules Humbert-Droz, a Swiss friend of Lenin's, as head first of the Latin Secretariat and then of the Latin American Secretariat, was the Comintern official most concerned with Latin America until 1931. He then resigned his post after incurring Stalin's mistrust because of his association with Bukharin. He reported after the Sixth Comintern Congress that 'As a rule, when we tell our Latin American comrades, on meeting them for the first time, that the situation of their country is that of a semi-colony and consequently we must consider the problems concerning it from the viewpoint of our colonial or semi-colonial tactics, they are indignant at this notion and assert that their country is independent, that it is represented in the League of Nations, has its own diplomats, consulates, etc.'[4]

Latin Americans also resented the lack of interest shown in their region. Peru's Victor Raúl Haya de la Torre, after meeting Trotsky, Chicherin, Lunacharskii and Frunze, testified that they knew 'little or nothing about conditions in our America' (Haya de la Torre: 1961 pp. 158–9). When Bukharin, in his speech to the Sixth Congress, emphasised that the Latin American Communist parties 'had an important role to play in the development of national and agrarian

[4] 'Questions of the Latin American countries. Co-report on questions of the revolutionary movement in the colonial countries. Sixth World Congress of the Comintern International (Full Report)', *Inprecorr*, 17 October 1928, p. 1,300, in Caballero: 1986, p. 71.

revolutions', Brazilian delegate Fernando Lacerna somewhat tartly pointed out that a Communist movement had existed in Latin America since 1920 but it was only in 1928 that 'the Communist International [had] shown its interest in Latin America for the first time' (*La Correspondance Internationale* (organ of the Communist International), 1928, in Alba: 1964, p. 188). The following year a Latin American delegate at the Tenth Plenum of the Committee of the Communist International stated bluntly that Latin American Communist parties needed 'stronger organisational and more effective political support' from the Comintern (Alba: 1959, p. 136).

If the Latin Americans had their nationalist sensibilities ruffled by the refusal of the Comintern to recognise that they were in the best position to analyse the situation in their own countries, and were disappointed by the level of support received from Moscow, Comintern officials in their turn were unenthusiastic about the evolution of the Latin American Communist parties and their approach to revolutionary politics. In 1926 the South American Bureau complained that the process of 'Bolshevisation' had been insufficiently implemented in the Chilean party, which had returned representatives and senators to Congress and had been involved in the drafting of the new Constitution of 1925 (Angell: 1972, p. 32). This lack of Bolshevik militancy (and the reluctance to comply with Moscow's directives) was particularly galling for the Comintern since, as one of its own documents acknowledged, 'the Chilean Communist Party is the one with the most influence amongst the masses out of all the South American Communist Parties'.[5] Mexico was also regarded as a promising base for the expansion of Comintern influence, but Moscow's distrust of the Mexican Communists was such that in March 1926 the Comintern took a decision to entrust the Communist Party of the United States with special responsibility in the same area: the Mexican Communist Party was therefore effectively under a dual tutelage (Clissold: 1970, p. 10).

In 1929 a serious dispute over tactics arose between the Communist International and the Mexican Communists. When a right-wing revolt broke out against the newly-elected president Portes Gil, the Communists, who were highly influential with the Peasant Leagues, instructed them to fight on behalf of the government to help quell the uprising. The Comintern, however, disapproving strongly of these

---

[5] *Directive from the South American Secretariat of the Comintern for the Bolshevisation of the Chilean CP*, Nov. 1926, in Clissold: 1970, pp. 129–30.

tactics, obliged the Mexican Communists 'to send directives to the peasant leaders instructing them to turn their arms against the government and fight an action on two fronts with a view to precipitating social revolution' (Clissold: 1970, p. 6). The attempt of one of the leaders concerned to implement these extreme tactics resulted in his being caught and summarily executed by the local military commander. Notwithstanding this, at the First Latin American Communist Congress in Buenos Aires in June 1929, the Comintern delegate castigated the Mexicans for their failure to take effective advantage of the situation.[6]

Other disputes arose and, in general, Comintern officials were inclined to be disparaging of their Latin American comrades. Alexander Lozovskii, head of the Profintern, who was closely involved with the Latin American Communist parties, wrote:

Today, in Latin America we have a young movement, a movement which incorporates hundreds of thousands of workers, but which is, from the ideological point of view, very confused and, from the organisational point of view, very weak. Revolution is not made by proclamations, strikes cannot be declared every twenty-four hours, and in order to struggle against the bourgeoisie it is not enough to have a weekly publication or a hundred militants. What is needed is an organisation which is strong enough to combat and overthrow the capitalist state.

In Latin America there is too much talk about social revolution. All Latin American manifestoes conclude with 'Long live the social revolution'. This is all very well, and I am not against it. But there are a number of comrades who have too primitive an idea of social revolution. They believe that if socialist revolution has not arrived today, it will come tomorrow.[7]

The Third Period (1929–1935)

As Stalin asserted his dominance over the Comintern during what is known as the 'Third Period' (1929–35), Soviet doctrine (related to the perceived need to defeat social democracy in Europe) became correspondingly extreme, insisting that the only authentic revolution was one led by an orthodox Marxist-Leninist party. Communist parties were exhorted to eschew all alliances and push forward with armed insurgence whenever the opportunity arose. This led the Chilean Communist Party to lose substantial support by its opposition to the short-lived Socialist Republic declared by Colonel Marmaduke

---

[6] *Statement by the Comintern delegate at the First Latin American Communist Congress*, Buenos Aires, 3 June 1929: excerpts, in Clissold: 1970, pp. 89–90.

[7] A. Lozovskii, *El movimiento sindical Latinoamericano: Sus virtudes y sus defectos* (Montevideo, 1929), in Alba: 1964, p. 199.

Grove in June 1932. The Communists, following their isolationist policy, were the only working-class group to oppose this experiment. In Cuba, the Communists played a less than glorious role in the 1933 overthrow of dictator Gerardo Machado. Both parties were further weakened by splits as the Stalin–Trotsky conflict was played out in Latin America. The one major attempt to apply the Third Period model in Latin America, in El Salvador in 1932 (where the Comintern operated through International Red Aid), was quickly and brutally suppressed by a massacre of over 30,000 people.

By contrast, the 1935 insurgency in Brazil was instigated by the Comintern through one of its most trusted Latin American lieutenants, Luis Carlos Prestes (who was not formally a member of the Brazilian Communist Party). According to Peruvian Communist Eudocio Ravines, the decision was a consequence of rivalry within the Comintern hierarchy between Dmitrov, chief proponent of the new Popular Front line adopted at the Seventh Comintern Congress in 1935, and Manuilskii, who still favoured violent tactics. In Brazil, the Popular Front approach was to be used to achieve the seizure of power by armed force, rather than by the non-violent means more usually associated with the Popular-Front era (Ravines: 1957, pp. 255–7).

The Communist International failed to turn any political situation to its advantage during the years 1917 to 1935, largely because of the rigidity of its model and its lack of interest in the actual conditions of Latin America. Attempts by Latin American Communists to implement the ultra-leftism and isolationism of the 'Third Period' (tactics which had been formulated to respond to the very different political conditions prevailing in Europe) resulted in considerable loss of support and influence for many of these parties. Nevertheless, by 1935, the definitively Stalinised Comintern and its network of party faithful comprised the main organisational basis of Marxism in Latin America, and therefore provided a vital touchstone for all other sectors of the Left, which were forced to define themselves in relation to its characterisation of the Latin American revolution.

One major consequence of Communist International neglect of Latin America during the 1920s was that inadequate literature was made available in Spanish for the dissemination of Communist ideas (this was pointed out by a Mexican delegate at the Sixth Congress). In 1927 the South American Secretariat started publishing *La Correspondencia Sudamericana*, which appeared fortnightly at first. In 1930, however, its name was changed to *Revista Comunista*, and the editors explicitly stated their intention to produce a theoretical journal rather than an information bulletin as hitherto. The organ rapidly degenerated, however, into a vehicle for Stalinism. It was really only in this intellectually impoverished form that Marxism-Leninism arrived in Latin America. By this stage, Mariátegui, unconstrained by the rigidities of Stalinist orthodoxy, had already undertaken his original application of Marxism to the Latin American situation. His death in 1930 halted the immediate ascendancy of his version of socialism, but facilitated his canonisation as the prophet of a distinctly Latin American Marxism. His *Seven essays on the interpretation of Peruvian reality* became a standard text (more readily available than most of Marx and Lenin's works) for Latin Americans interested in Marxism. Thus his ideas remained as a potent legacy for the new generation of Marxists which emerged in the 1950s and 1960s.

1936–1958

This period saw the development of two significant trends: the perceived relevance of Marxism to Latin America increased, whilst the stature of the Communist parties markedly declined after reaching a peak in the immediate aftermath of the Second World War. The 1930s witnessed the emerging confrontation with Fascism in Europe, a struggle which was played out on the battlefields of Spain from 1936 to 1939. Franco's hostility to intellectuals of any persuasion meant that intellectuals the world over were driven into the defence of the Spanish Republic. Moreover, the shock of the 1929 Wall Street crash and the ensuing economic depression (which hit the primary-producing nations of Latin America particularly badly as the industrialised countries slashed imports) had two correlated effects. Firstly, the United States economic system was shown to be far from invincible: the myth of the Great American Dream was, if not exploded, at least undermined. Within intellectual circles, this new uncertainty compounded an emerging assertion of Latin America's need to seek its own identity rather than continually strive to emulate the United States. There was a growing awareness that to be Latin rather than Anglo-Saxon should not necessarily imply inferiority. Thus an assertion of cultural identity became closely bound up with the quest for a political model to supersede the North American system.

Secondly, it prompted a recognition of Latin America's economic vulnerability, a search for alternative models of development and a sense that radical solutions had to be found. Latin America's weak position in relation to world capitalism was further confirmed in the aftermath of the Second World War, when drastic reductions in import-demand from the war-torn European economies plunged Latin America back into recession. The increasingly urgent political situation at home and abroad gave Marxism an appropriate context. Thus Latin American nationalism was coupled, albeit loosely at this stage, to the Marxist bandwagon. The 1930s saw the beginning of the development of a primarily student/intellectual sub-culture in which Marxism gradually became the prevalent ideology. With the massive expansion of state education in the aftermath of the Second World War, teachers, freed from the constraints of imparting the Catholic texts, tended to propagate the Church's rival ideology.

The 1935 Seventh Comintern Congress and its emphasis on united-front tactics (stemming from the Soviet leadership's need to build alliances to counter threats from Germany and Japan) gave the Communist parties some chance to regain the ground they had lost by their isolationist, class-against-class policies of the early 1930s. The Chilean party, in alliance with Radicals and Socialists (who had sprung up to challenge the Communists in 1932) won a Popular Front victory in 1938, and in 1946 they collaborated with the Radical Party to win an election (this time without the Socialists) and participated briefly in the government. In Cuba, where the Communists were also relatively strong, class collaborationist tactics gave the party a minis-terial position under Batista (1943–4) and control of the officially recognised *Confederación de Trabajadores de Cuba* (Confederation of Cuban Workers).

The Communist parties inevitably lost credibility as a result of staunchly adhering to the Comintern line throughout the series of volte-face involved in the Nazi–Soviet pact of 1939 and the subsequent German invasion of Soviet Russia in June 1941. They profited, however, from the general admiration for the USSR's contribution to the defeat of Fascism, and attained the peak of their popularity in the immediate aftermath of the war. Once again, however, Communist inability to consolidate this position can be attributed to a combination of swift and effective repression of Communism in Latin America (partly a response to their increased support, partly due to the onset of the Cold War and the pro-US orientation of most Latin American regimes in the late 1940s and 1950s) and failures in tactics by the parties. Post-war instructions from Moscow (the Comintern had been dissolved in 1943) were to maintain the policy of cooperation with democratic forces which had been implemented during the latter stages of the war. Under this banner, Communist parties in several Latin American countries supported not only 'democratic' forces, but openly repressive ones, including Vargas, Manuel Odría in Peru and Medina Angarita (an ally of former dictator Gómez) in Venezuela. In Cuba the Communists' early association with Batista did them great disservice when his second regime (1952–8) became increasingly corrupt and unpopular. Perhaps the greatest blunder of all was the Argentine party's support for Unión Democrática (an alliance of the right-wing oligarchy, the conservative military and the US ambassador) in the fight to prevent the 1946 election of Colonel Perón. This resulted in a perceived split between nationalism and socialism which, as Regis Debray points out, helped to keep 'socialism apart from the mass of the people, and ... gave a certain fascist tinge to all the nationalist and anti-imperialist movements ... the two effects are inseparable' (Debray: 1978, p. 225).

These years also saw the rise of Trotskyism. Leon Trotsky himself arrived in Mexico in early January 1937, having been granted asylum by President Cárdenas. The Comintern's attempts to involve the Mexican Communist Party in Moscow's decision to liquidate Trotsky resulted in violent convulsions within the party, with Valentín Campa and Hernán Laborde expelled. Trotsky was murdered by Stalinists in Mexico City in August 1940. Although many Latin American Communist parties were split by Trotskyism, the only significant Trotskyist party in the region was the Bolivian Workers' Revolutionary party (POR), which became one of the two leading Fourth International affiliates in the world (the other being in Sri Lanka). The POR was set up in 1935 not as a breakaway from an orthodox Communist party (none existed in Bolivia until the formation of the PIR in 1940) but as the party of a group of intellectuals attracted by Trotsky's ideas and personality. The POR had considerable influence in the powerful Bolivian mine-workers' union, the FSTMB, and was responsible for drafting its main charter, the Thesis of Pulacayo, in 1946. By the mid-1950s, however, the POR's importance had diminished, having lost members both to the populist-oriented National Revolutionary Movement (MNR) and to other factions of the Fourth International.

During the late 1940s and early 1950s the Communist movement was further weakened by splits in the parties of Mexico, Venezuela, Colombia, Argentina, Bolivia, Peru and Brazil – mostly over the questions of local tactics discussed above or because of rivalry for the party leadership. Those parties that were not forced into clandestinity demonstrated scant ability to formulate new strategies or even to adapt existing ones to contemporary situations. The ideological bank-ruptcy of the Communists is perhaps most graphically conveyed by quotation of a comment by Soviet Latin Americanist Anatoli Shul'govskii to the effect that in 1945 the Mexican Communist Party had a 'Marxist' ideology comparable to the 'legal Marxism' of tsarist Russia (Löwy: 1982, p. 37). Well over two decades of failure to mount any effective challenge to the established order led to their being seen for what they fundamentally were: bureaucratic 'enclaves' of the international workers' movement with little substantial contribution to make to the debate on Latin American development. Michael Löwy argues that

[As a] professional leadership group, organically structured and hierarchical, the behaviour and thought of the Communist Party of Brazil leadership corresponds with their situation as a social category and their political nature as leadership apparatus of a party belonging to a particular current of the international workers' movement. In the framework of this hypothesis, the organisational, political and ideological relations between the leadership of the PCB and the Third International (and/or the CPSU) are a far more decisive variable for an understanding of their vision of the process and of their strategy than the military petty bourgeois origin of Prestes and other leaders of the party. This same explanatory principle is valid for the other Communist parties of Latin America . . . (Löwy: 1982, p. 29)

However, it was not only on the Left that the search for radical solutions was being pursued. Most significantly in Argentina, Brazil and Mexico, where the organised working classes were large and strong, longer-term strategies to forestall the problems posed by labour militancy were already being implemented. Basic tenets of Catholic social philosophy have contributed to the formation of a Latin American political tradition, the underlying assumptions of which are antipathetic to fundamental Marxist class analysis. In this tradition the state is perceived as the vehicle by which the unity of the nation should be achieved in order to work for the common good. Looking at the major political movements in Latin America in the twentieth century, it is striking how all of the most successful have championed the ideals of integration, national unity and incorporation. At one level, of course, this simply reflects Latin American political realities: these societies are highly fragmented and any governing group will find itself with a diverse power base and the need to sustain its position by means of either coercion or consensus building. However, the ideological position is not an empty one. Perón, Vargas and Cárdenas – who, judged by their mass following, have led the most popular governments of their respective countries – all worked on the basis of an active, aspiring state. Perón expressed the concept thus: 'To the Peronist doctrine, all economic goods were created and are created and exist for man. Therefore we condemn the principles of individualism and collectivism which put man at the service of the economy or the state and we maintain that the economy and the state must secure human happiness by promoting social well-being' (in Stepan: 1978, p. 49).

Indeed one of the main reasons for the failure of Marxists to make headway amongst the Latin American working classes is that labour organisations in many of these countries were originally the creation of the state. Perón (who built up his power from the Ministry of Labour after 1943, was elected president of Argentina in 1946 and governed until 1955) created his movement precisely on the basis of an alliance between nationalist military officers, industrialists and the non-Marxist (largely unrepresented) sections of the working classes. Perón's capacity to deliver the tangible benefits that established unions working against the state apparatus could not hope to obtain for their members (labour's share of the national income increased by twenty-five per cent between 1946 and 1950) ensured that the loyalties of massive sectors of the post-1955 labour movement were to Peronism rather than to Communism or socialism.

A similar process of incorporation took place in Brazil under Vargas (1930–45) and the *Estado Novo* (1937–45). This latter period saw the creation of a labour code (1943) limiting the functioning of unions to a local and plant level and bringing them tightly under the control of the Ministry of Labour. In Mexico, President Cárdenas (1934–40) achieved the incorporation of unions into the state under the aegis of four sub-divisions of the Mexican Revolutionary Party (PRM) (forerunner of today's ruling PRI): agrarian, labour, military and 'popular' (a residual group largely covering the middle classes). The principles behind his approach are embodied in Mexico's 1917 Constitution, as analysed by Frank Tannenbaum:

By implication, the Constitution recognises that contemporary Mexican society is divided into classes, and that it is the function of the State to protect one class against another. The Constitution is therefore not merely a body of rules equally applicable to all citizens, but also a body of rules specially designed to benefit and protect given groups . . . What has in fact happened is that the old idea of the 'estates' has been re-created in Mexican law. The pattern of the older Spanish State, divided into clergy, nobility and commons, has been re-created in modern dress, with peasants, workers and capitalists replacing the ancient model. This is not done formally, but it is . . . evident that a very different kind of social structure is envisioned in the law . . . than that in a liberal democracy. (Morse: 1967, p. 233)

One reason for the weakness of the Communist movement in Mexico is that intellectuals were effectively incorporated into the system until at least the late 1960s, the Mexican government 'preferring the price of appeasing or coopting intellectuals to the perils of ignoring or alienating them'. Thus, 'academics, writers, painters and musicians of minimal renown inherit the right – even the duty – to participate in politics, to give opinions on subjects far removed from their areas of talent, to sit in judgement on the regime, even to denounce the system' (Riding: 1986, p. 427). The price intellectuals pay is that they are dependent on the government for both professional and financial recognition, since 'the most important definition of an intellectual is that he should be recognised by the government as such' (Riding: 1986, p. 428). Thus, for example, Diego Rivera's membership of the Communist party did not stop him from painting radical murals on the walls of government buildings.

There are strong elements of a liberal tradition in Argentina, Chile and (to a lesser extent) Brazil. One of the basic contradictions in the politics of these and other Latin American countries derives from the difficulties of trying to superimpose the liberal concept of a state as a mechanism for ensuring free interplay between competing interest groups onto societies with a built-in tendency to corporatism. Classical democracy's belief in the self-regulation of the individual is recognised as theoretically valid, but the legacy of aristocratic colonial politics means that it is highly restricted in practice. The tensions induced by the conflicts between Marxism versus Liberalism and Liberalism versus corporatism are incarnated in the figure of Salvador Allende, who tried to introduce socialism on the basis of populist support and subsequently refused to sacrifice his belief in 'constitutionalism' until it was too late to save his revolution.

Whereas a strategy of incorporation can be relatively successful when applied by a regime of right-wing orientation which is prepared to support it with repression, it has proved to be ineffective for leftist groups which claim to be advancing the interests of the working class. To date, such experiments have failed under dual pressure – from the Marxist-based Left, which has been unwilling to concede the fight for its class interests, and from the Right, which has continually threatened to halt the reform process. In Peru the Aprista movement founded by Haya de la Torre – an alternative to both Comintern-style Marxism-Leninism and the radical tradition established by Mariátegui

– became discredited owing to its regression into counter-revolutionary responses precisely when its success was greatest. The Apristas – for all their original Marxist inspiration – pursued similar 'incorporating' tactics, trying to maintain a populist coalition in order to build state capitalism. From 1945 to 1948 APRA in government embraced the United States' 'Good Neighbour Policy' and on the agrarian issue defended private property rights, betraying their earlier demands for nationalisation of land. Similar policy reversals were made by *Acción Democrática* in Venezuela and – probably the most important example – by the Bolivian *Movimiento Nacional Revolucionario* (MNR). As early as 1956, economic crisis forced the 1952 Bolivian revolution to confront the contradictions inherent in its class concili-ation model. Faced with the option of further radicalisation or retreat, the MNR chose the latter course, proceeding to expel its left wing in 1964. It is worth noting that the Cuban revolution avoided a similar fate by incorporation of the Communists; the Bolivian experience may well have been in Castro's mind when he was assessing the means by which he could sustain his own revolution.

The success of the Peronist movement and, to a lesser extent, of Vargas and Cárdenas, in gaining widespread acceptance for their visions of national unity cannot be explained without reference to a second major element of the Latin American political tradition which is related to corporatism and which also cuts across class-based Marxist politics: *caudillismo*, and its modern corollary, populism.

At the level of mass impact, the myth of the strong individual, the all-conquering hero, the leader – a myth deriving from the historically dominant role of military actions and actors in the shaping of Latin American nations – is firmly entrenched. It was strengthened by the historical development of Latin American social structures. Large landed estates were run on the basis of patronage relationships between landowners and peasants, which were reinforced by the Catholic institution of *compadrazgo* (god-parenthood). This broad network of clientelism (which has now been transferred to the cities) has combined with the fact that many of these societies are highly fragmented, to create a tendency to unite around a leader rather than around an ideology. (This is especially true when the ideology in question has the doctrinaire, dogmatic and collectively oriented features of Marxism.) Groups such as APRA, which were aiming to create a broad alliance across class boundaries, were obliged to resort to very general slogans, typified by their rallying cry of 'Against Yankee imperialism, for the unity of the peoples of Latin America, for the realisation of social justice', in order to avoid alienating any of their potential supporters. The classic example of the populist leader is Argentina's Perón, whom commentators have found impossible to classify in terms of received ideologies such as Fascism and socialism (although there were elements of both in his style and his policies).

To some extent the *caudillo* phenomenon has worked in favour of Marxism. Moscow established a special relationship with fellow-travelling Mexican labour leader Vicente Lombardo Toledano (similar to their connections with Brazil's Luís Prestes), in recognition of his following not only in the labour movement but also amongst the university communities. Lombardo travelled throughout Latin America drumming up support for the Communist Confederation of the Workers of Latin America (CTAL) formed in 1938, before forming his own Popular Party in Mexico a decade later. His role was effectively one of a papal nuncio, a part which is now played by Fidel Castro, who is the epitome of the charismatic *caudillo*. It was largely by the force of his own personality that Castro took the Cuban people with him along the road of Marxism-Leninism (although he was also tactically astute – for a long time implementing only the minimum conditions of Marxism, allowing rhetoric to fill the vacuum, and emphasising the glorious and dramatic aspects of Marxism, notably the armed struggle and proletarian internationalism). Cubans are *Fidelistas* first and Marxists second, and this pattern of allegiance to a leader rather than to an ideology occurs repeatedly throughout Latin America wherever Marxism has established a working-class base. The Sandinistas in government are somewhat at a loss for their own charismatic figure,[8] but continue to draw amply on the (revised) ideology and mythology of Sandino himself and of the martyred heroes of the revolution.

By extension, this tendency to rally around a leader operates not only at national, but also at local and party political levels, and here its drawbacks are more apparent. Reduced to its minimum, the Latin American idea of a 'party' comes down to a group of friends, which makes the Leninist concept of a totally committed, exclusive vanguard very difficult to accept or implement. This is seen nowhere more clearly than in the Latin American Communist parties which 'prefer systematically an alliance with a strong personality (not to speak of a strongman) rather than with an organised political party which could propose or, worse, impose independent tactics and a different and

---

[8] The two most likely candidates were Carlos Fonseca, who was killed before the revolution came to power, and Edén Pastora, who has since defected.

permanent leadership upon the whole alliance' (Caballero: 1986, p. 109). The most noteworthy consequences of such an attitude was that at the same time as growing numbers of Latin Americans, particularly young people, were looking to Marxism for some kind of solution, the orthodox Communist parties were widely perceived to be inert and impotent.

Thus by the late 1950s both the Comintern version of Marxism-Leninism and a native Marxist-based gradualist model were perceived to be sterile. This period was impoverished in Latin American Marxist thought compared to the 1920s: no figure emerged with the stature of Mariátegui or Haya de la Torre. In the 1950s, however, a new generation of Marxist economists – notably André Gunder Frank, Sergio Bagú and Caio Prado Junior – began experimenting with and developing ideas derived from Mariátegui's work. The theses that Latin American socio-economic structures could not be regarded as simply a local variant of European feudalism, and that the agrarian economy was already incorporated into the capitalist system were restated and developed, and the argument that the revolution in Latin America could only be socialist reasserted. This theoretical position seemed to be vindicated in 1954 by the prompt CIA-organised counter-revolutionary response to the radicalisation of the Communist-supported Arbenz government in Guatemala. This defeat of the most successful application of Communist party popular front tactics appeared to demonstrate that opposition forces within Latin America (backed up by the United States) were too powerful for such a strategy to be ultimately successful.

In this context, I would argue that while the unleashing of widespread revolutionary activity in Latin America in the 1960s must obviously be attributed to the impact of the 1959 Cuban revolution, this event was essentially a catalyst, which supplied a model and a source of inspiration to a radicalised generation who were already looking for an alternative to the Soviet theory of 'revolution in stages'.

1959–1975

The years 1959 to 1975 witnessed a consolidation of radical trends. Perhaps the single most important effect of the Cuban revolution was that it proved beyond all doubt that Marxism was not an exclusively European doctrine and that it could be applied successfully in Latin America. The 1962 *Second Declaration of Havana*, with its call to turn the

Andes into the Sierra Maestra of Latin America, counteracted the Euro-centrism of orthodox Communism. Many became convinced that the region could now find its own way to socialism, without the help of a Communist party or Stalinism. Moreover, Cuba's insistence on 'uninterrupted' revolution made a subsidiary issue of the whole debate about which 'stage' was appropriate. In re-uniting Marxism and nationalism under the anti-imperialist banner, Castro succeeded at one fell stroke where the Communist parties had failed for years.

Thus, in the 1960s, the initiative passed to what became known as the 'New Left' – which in practice referred to all those who sought radical social change in Latin America. Most of those under this broad umbrella adopted a Marxist idiom, and have relied on three 'minimum conditions' of Marxism to act as their rallying point. These are (1) anti-imperialism (in effect, an anti-US stance): increasingly, as Washington insists on defining indigenous anti-US sentiment within the region in terms of 'Communist subversion', Marxism comes to be regarded as the natural channel for such feelings; (2) an acceptance of the Marxist premise of 'the exploitation of man by man'; and (3) a refusal to accept the existing economic order, or to be bound by conventional economic remedies for Latin America's development problems (either of the orthodox 'monetarist' variety which the International Monetary Fund (IMF) is trying to introduce into most major Latin American countries, or of the moderate reform-and-investment strategies pursued by Christian Democratic groups, for example in Chile from 1964 to 1970). For all its fragmentation and factionalism, most of the 'New Left' was also united around the central tenets of Che Guevara's Marxism, which included (1) the necessarily socialist nature of the Latin American revolution (that is, a rejection of the concept of a 'progressive national bourgeoisie' and the 'national democratic' stage, which was perceived as yet another indefinite postponement of the eradication of poverty); (2) the role of the armed struggle as an essential pre-condition for it; (3) the emphasis on the self-disciplined and altruistic 'new man'; and (4) the importance of the countryside and the potential of the peasantry as the new revolutionary class. The theory of *foquismo* (as presented in the works of Regis Debray) took the above positions to their logical conclusion, arguing that a small dedicated band of guerrilla fighters would be sufficient to spark mass peasant revolution in defiance of prevailing political conditions. The guerrilla *foco* would replace the Leninist party as the revolutionary vanguard, and the experience of combat would 'proletarianise' both the guerrilla fighters and the peasantry.

The attraction of *foquismo* to many young, radicalised, middle-class Latin Americans is hard to overestimate, offering as it did the immediacy of a rapid solution and a legitimisation of their participation in the revolutionary process despite their non-proletarian origins. In Nicaragua, for example, the *Frente Sandinista de Liberación Nacional* (FSLN) was formed, in 1962, by cadres disillusioned with the peaceful efforts at reform by the Nicaraguan Communist Party (known as the Partido Socialista Nicaragüense) and, in October 1975, Jaime Wheelock and his Tendencia Proletaria were expelled from an FSLN directorate dominated by Tomás Borge, for the 'sterile dogmatism' of their economic materialism. Similarly, in El Salvador, the formation of the *Fuerzas Populares de Liberación-Farabundo Martí* (forerunner of the current FMLN) in 1970 was a result of a bitter factional fight within the Salvadoran Communist Party over revolutionary tactics, the final split being provoked by the party's backing for the 1969 four-day war against Honduras (Dunkerley: 1982, pp. 87–102).

This new attempt to apply Marxism to the Latin American situation has sought little outside inspiration and, when it has done so, has turned to other Third World countries rather than to Moscow. Maoism, with its emphasis on the countryside surrounding the cities, has been influential, particularly in Peru, where it is strong in the teachers' unions and is the ideology of the Shining Path guerrilla movement. More typically, however, the 'New Left' has drawn on Latin America's own political tradition, resurrecting the work of Mariátegui and embracing earlier, non-Marxist, liberation struggles. Current revolutionary activity in the sub-continent is referred to as the 'Second War of Independence': the nineteenth-century fight to gain political emancipation by ousting the Spanish has been succeeded by the struggle to achieve economic liberation by discarding the yoke of imperialism. This is a crusading, flamboyant Marxism, emphasising the role of the supposedly heroic and glamorous armed struggle. It has attempted to weave the mythology of historical liberation struggles with the martyrdom of its own guerrilla fighters of the 1960s and 1970s to create an unbroken thread of radical revolutionary tradition in Latin America. In Cuba, for example, 'figures of the Wars of Independence, like Martí and Maceo, or of the 1933 revolution [against the dictator Machado] ... give the revolution legitimacy by linking it with the historic past and, at least in the case of the heroes of 1933, they have been in a very real sense the inspiration of the present revolutionary leaders, to a far greater degree than Marx and Lenin' (Lambert: 1977, p. 237). With its assertion of militarism, voluntarism and adventurism, it stands for everything that orthodox Marxists in Latin America had been arguing against for years.

The established Communist parties, however, although over-shadowed at first by the new radicalism, were by no means totally eclipsed by it. In the aftermath of the Cuban revolution, the Communists, forced to contend with Castroite, Maoist and Trotskyist dissenters, all of whom advocated armed struggle, were at times uncertain how to respond to the rise of guerrilla activity in their own countries. In Guatemala and Venezuela support was initially given, and then later with-drawn. However, the majority of established Latin American Communist parties were unwilling to fall into line either with Castro's strategy or his leadership, an attitude most dramatically expressed by the 1966 refusal of Bolivian Communist leader Mario Monje Molina to support Che Guevara in his campaign. As the Venezuelan Communists said, in the midst of polemics with Castro over their withdrawal of support for the guerrilla movement, 'We reject the role of revolutionary "pope" which Fidel Castro arrogates to himself.'

The new movement's influence was undermined by its manifold divisions: Guevarists, Castroites and Maoists proliferated into further factions as differing positions were adopted in response to the rapid succession of events in the 1960s. In particular, Castro's abandonment of the guerrilla strategy, and his favourable attitude to governments such as the reformist military regime in Peru, caused splits between Castroism and Guevarism. The ability of the Communist parties to survive the onslaught from the 'New Left' also bore witness to the fact that the debates over strategy and tactics were real, and had a deeper basis than is suggested by the oft-manifested rivalry for the role of 'true' revolutionary. Communist party critics of the Cuban line stressed its neglect of the role of the masses, its under-estimation of the grip of reformism (*Aprismo*), especially amongst the peasantry, and the need for a party. The pertinence of these arguments to Latin American reality was borne out most clearly by the failure of both rural guerrilla warfare (powerfully symbolised by the death of Che Guevara in Bolivia in 1967) and of attempts to apply the same tactics in an urban situation.[9]

---

[9] Carlos Marighela's ADN in Brazil in the late 1960s proved to be little more than a suicide squad. Argentina's Montoneros (*c.* 1971–6) were far more organised and militarily effective, but sowed the seeds of their own destruction by their political naivety with respect to the potential radicalism of the arch pragmatist Juan Perón. By far the most successful of these groups was Uruguay's Tupamaros, but they were crushed by the full might of extreme military repression after 1973.

Moreover, with the advent to power of the Peruvian military radicals in 1968, the brief rule of left-wing General Torres in Bolivia in 1970 and the election of Chile's Popular Unity in September 1970, the arguments for a 'peaceful road' acquired far greater force. Thus the 1975 Havana Conference of (for the first time since the Cuban revolution) *all* Latin American Communist parties and its rehabilitation of orthodox ideas such as the primacy of the party and the importance of mass organisation, reflected a widespread recognition that the central premise of *foquismo* was false. The staging of this conference must be seen in the context of certain foreign-policy imperatives for Castro (to accommodate himself with the Soviet Union and to re-establish the link between Cuba and the revolutionary process in Latin America). However, subsequent developments in revolutionary tactics in Latin America (both the Nicaraguan FSLN and the Salvadoran FMLN have attempted to combine the use of the armed struggle with the building of a mass movement) indicate that the conference was at least symbolic of real shifts in theoretical position and of a maturing of Latin American Marxist thought.

1975 to date

The necessity for a re-evaluation of tactics was further confirmed by the wave of counter-revolutionary repression which swept Latin America in the mid-1970s, the most dramatic example of which was the abrupt and extraordinarily violent termination of the Allende experiment by a Chilean military which for several decades had prided itself on respecting the nation's democratic traditions. (Also significant was the 1975-onwards descent into repression by the Peruvian military as they desperately sought to regain control of an explosive situation unleashed by their own policies.) If the 1960s had shown that the armed struggle was not in itself sufficient, the most frequently drawn 'lesson of Chile' was that the Left could not afford to dispense with it entirely, since the bourgeoisie ultimately would not hesitate to use force in defence of their interests. Since the mid-1970s there has been an attempt to fuse the voluntaristic, militaristic, flamboyant aspects of Guevarism and Castroism with the tactical positions of more orthodox thought. The 1979 Nicaraguan revolution provoked a fresh round of debate on Communist strategy for Latin America. Roundtable discussions held at the Institute of Latin America early in 1981 revealed that several Soviet ideologists were now prepared to lend credence to the long-discredited theories of guerrilla warfare upheld by Che Guevara. Sergei Mikoian, summarising the arguments, wrote, 'As yet only the armed path has led to the victory of revolutions in Latin America. And the Nicaraguan experience affirms what had been considered refuted by some after the death of Che Guevara and the defeat of a number of other guerrilla movements' (Mikoian: 1980, p. 103).

In 1980 the Communist parties of El Salvador, Chile, Uruguay and Honduras revised their position on armed struggle, although the peaceful road is still the preferred strategy in the majority of Latin American countries. Nevertheless, there is no doubt that Guevarism and other currents of thought have been influential in forcing established Communist parties to rethink their role and recognise the need to be far more responsive than hitherto to the specific circumstances of their own country. In Mexico and Venezuela this has resulted in the development of a new openness towards the broad left, reflected in the formation of the Left Coalition in Mexico in 1977 and the Movement Towards Socialism in Venezuela. In 1978 Mexican Communist theorists and activists 'polemicised with Soviet Latin American specialists over a series of issues relating to the character of Mexican capitalism in the late 1970s . . . The Mexican participants emphasised the mature development of capitalism in their country and the impossibility of distinguishing between local and foreign monopolies . . . The Soviet specialists doubted the existence of local Mexican monopolies and defended an interpretation which ascribed a more progressive character to the Mexican state and which noted the primacy of anti-imperialist struggle' (Carr: 1985, p. 216, footnote 38). The Mexican party has also become increasingly independent of Moscow, condemning the Soviet invasion of Czechoslovakia in 1968 and the 1979 intervention in Afghanistan.

In summary, then, at present advocates of an orthodox Marxist-Leninist (Soviet-inspired) solution to Latin American problems do not enjoy much support, and it seems clear that Communist parties need to develop more flexible strategies and to ally themselves with the broader left if they are to sustain an effective role in political life. The ideologies of indigenous Marxist groups need to be studied in their own right. Within a broadly Marxian framework, these groups encompass a wide range of positions, many of which have only a very tenuous connection with Soviet doctrine. The Soviet Union has little or no influence, let alone control, over the vast majority of them. The vehement anti-US feeling in Nicaragua (so often cited as the latest Communist 'gain' in Latin America) has as much to do with the history of US involvement in the country (not to mention its current support for counter-revolutionary activity) as it does with any Marxist 'indoctrination'. The Sandinista leaders themselves identify four elements which have contributed to the evolution of their ideology, one of which is the Marxism of the student sub-culture in the 1950s, another of which is the example of Cuba. Equally important, however, are Nicaragua's historical tradition of political violence and, above all, the heroic image of General Sandino's struggle against imperialist occupation of his country (Nolan: 1984, p. 13 *passim*). This is not to deny that there are those amongst the Sandinistas who are urging a more orthodox Marxist-Leninist approach to the problems of Nicaraguan development and the need to counter threats from Washington, but to date the Nicaraguan Communist Party (*Partido Socialista Nicaragüense*) has been almost completely excluded from the process of implementing the revolution. It would be an oversimplification to reduce the complex ideology of the movement to the positions of a minority within it, or to assume that such a viewpoint will necessarily prevail.

Moreover, all Marxist groups operating in Latin America confront a formidable array of obstacles, apart from the problems caused by their own factionalism. Firstly, counter-revolutionary forces on the continent, armed and trained (particularly since the Cuban revolution) by the Pentagon, remain impressively strong, and in Central America are backed up by the threat of military action by the United States itself, as recent events in Nicaragua and El Salvador have reaffirmed. Secondly, the strength of the Catholic Church is still a major factor in the failure of Marxism to make any significant inroads into the Latin American masses, particularly the peasantry. Initiatives in the 1970s, by adherents of Liberation Theology, to redefine the relationship between the Church and politics in Third World areas, and the charisma of activists such as the 1960s Colombian guerrilla-priest Camilo Torres, have helped the Sandinistas, three of whose leading figures are ordained priests. However, the potential political pitfalls involved in any attempt to confront the contradictions of a socialist and a Catholic Nicaragua were clearly demonstrated by the events of the Pope's 1982 visit. Although worker-priests have been active in promoting the possibilities for convergence between Christianity and Sandinismo, the head of the Nicaraguan Church Cardinal Obando y Bravo has emerged as a focus for the non-armed Nicaraguan opposition.

Thirdly, the debates over how far to forge a strategy either for winning power or for promoting economic development in a post-revolutionary society have not been satisfactorily resolved, and indeed perhaps cannot be, given that counter-revolutionary response to any successful formula will ensure that it will be that much more difficult to apply the same tactics in another situation. Such is the relation which Nicaragua bears to El Salvador, for example. That Cuba's style of development is still influential in the search for a Marxist-based model for Latin America is confirmed by many of the Sandinista government's policies, for example literacy and health campaigns and the building of mass organisations. Equally, however, Nicaragua's attempts (on Castro's advice) to preserve a mixed economy reveal an awareness of the limitations of the Cuban model. Its diminished stature is mainly due to its continuing economic difficulties and its inability so far to break out of an increasingly stultifying dependence on Soviet aid and trade subsidies. Cuba provides a graphic confirmation of the received wisdom that it is very hard for an under-developed country to proceed to the construction of socialism without first achieving economic independence. There is no doubt that for very many Latin Americans it is a successful capitalist (North American) lifestyle that embodies their hopes and their aspirations, rather than a socialist society which, for all its economic and social advantages, entails restrictions and shortages. A more sober evaluation by the Latin American Left of the prospects for achieving revolution is reinforced by the recognition that the Soviet Union is not going to do what it did for Cuba for any other Latin American country.

3 Castro's Cuba – 'A gift to the Russians'? The Soviet–Cuban embrace, 1959–1962

In the immediate aftermath of Castro's January 1959 victory neither the Soviet Union nor Cuba evinced any great interest in the forging of a closer relationship. There was no Soviet declaration of support for the new government, and Soviet press articles underplayed the revolutionary potential of the Cuban situation. Khrushchev, who was preoccupied with trying to promote a policy of peaceful coexistence with the United States (Khrushchev and Eisenhower met at Camp David in September 1959) whilst at the same time seeking to contain the emerging Sino–Soviet rift, had little thought to spare for the bearded revolutionaries in far-off Cuba. In his memoirs he records:

At the time that Fidel Castro led his revolution to victory and entered Havana with his troops, we had no idea what political course his regime would follow. We knew that there were individual Communists participating in the movement which Castro led, but the Communist Party of Cuba had no contact with him ... When Castro's men captured Havana we had to rely completely on newspaper and radio reports, from Cuba itself and from other countries, about what was happening ... We had no official contacts with any of the new Cuban leaders and therefore nothing to go on but rumours. (Khrushchev: 1970, pp. 488–9)

Neither did the Soviet leaders appear to feel any great need to rectify this situation. It was not until November 1959 that Moscow deemed it necessary even to send a TASS correspondent to Havana.

The main priority on the Soviet foreign-policy agenda at this time was to secure its objectives with regard to Berlin. The failure of Khrushchev's confrontation tactics (on 11 November 1959 he threatened to negotiate a separate peace treaty with the German Democratic Republic if the Western powers did not withdraw their troops within six months) had forced him to moderate his stance, and it was apparent that the Soviet Union would minimise the chances of an agreement on Berlin if it simultaneously pressed hard everywhere else, thereby exacerbating Washington's fears that any concession would be interpreted by Khrushchev as a sign of weakness. Clearly mindful of the likelihood of a US military intervention against Castro (on 10 April 1959 *Izvestiia* published an article entitled 'Those who dream of a repetition of Guatemala'), the Soviet Union took care throughout 1959 not to take any step which might jeopardise its negotiations with the United States. The Kremlin was also anxious to avoid involvement because of the potential loss of face if the USSR's inability to send conventional military support to a friendly country undergoing a successful US action were to be made manifest.

The indications are, however, that Moscow wanted to establish relations with the new Cuban regime as part of its overall campaign for promoting global diplomatic acceptance of the USSR. Soviet recognition was extended to the Castro government a few days after it had taken power, but this was not reciprocated, and it appears to have been the Cubans, concerned not to give Washington any pretext for claiming that Communism had arrived in the Caribbean, who were responsible for the fact that for well over a year after the revolution the two countries did not have diplomatic ties. What is often overlooked because of Cuba's active (although never particularly substantial) support for armed struggle in Latin America later in the 1960s is that, initially, the Castro regime made consistent attempts to build diplomatic relations with its hemispheric neighbours. Cuban leaders visited all the major Latin American capitals and indeed were regular participants in meetings of the Organisation of American States (OAS). The partial success of Cuba's policy is confirmed by the fact that as late as January 1961 Washington was aware that its scope for attacking the Castro regime through the OAS was still limited, and a majority for sanctions not yet assured. (Current Intelligence Weekly Summary, 12 January 1961, *United States Government Declassified Documents* (henceforth *US Declassified*), 1977, 10C.)

Whilst there is no denying that from its early days the Castro government provided safe haven and some aid to the revolutionary groups which flocked to Havana from all over Latin America and the Caribbean – in 1959 Cuba was the launching base for unsuccessful attacks on Haiti, Panama and the Dominican Republic – these activities must be set in context. Apart from the fact that Havana's support for these adventures added up to little more than 'a limited amount of old weapons' in the chaotic early months of revolutionary power (Bourne: 1987, p. 188), 'it must . . . be recognised that giving aid to revolutionaries seeking to overthrow dictatorships is a long-standing tradition for Latin America's democratic Left. Costa Rica's Figueres, Guatemala's Arévalo, even Venezuela's Betancourt – Washington's number one ally in the Alliance for Progress – all played similar roles during the late 1940s . . .' (Robbins: 1984, p. 218). Castro was said to be 'embarrassed' by all but the 14 June expedition against Dominican Republic dictator Trujillo, which was the only one in 1959 launched on Cuban government initiative with, it should be noted, the support of President Rómulo Betancourt (Szulc: 1986, p. 393; Martz and Myers: 1977, p. 337). It was not until 1962, when the Organisation of American States resolved that Cuba had voluntarily placed itself outside the inter-American system, that Castro – finding a temperamental and ideological disposition backed up by pressing security considerations – switched his energies to the export of revolution on a more substantial level. The prime target was Venezuela, whose President Betancourt, convinced that the Cuban revolution posed a threat to his own model of promoting economic and social change within the framework of institutionalised democracy, had personally overruled the objections of his Foreign Minister to signing the OAS August 1960 *Declaration of San José* (a condemnation of all interference in the Americas by non-American states, that is, a watered-down attack on Cuba's ties with the Soviet Union) (Martz and Myers, p. 339).

In April 1959 Castro, despite the misgivings of some of his close associates, visited the United States. Whilst there, he stated publicly that Cuba wanted to maintain good relations and to remain in the OAS. He accepted the direction of a United States public-relations expert to help him present a favourable impression of the revolution, and was described by a Department of State official as 'a man on his best behaviour' throughout the visit (Memo for the President from Christian A. Herter, 23 April 1959, *US Declassified*, 1976, 58F). He also claimed that his government would adhere to the Guantánamo Bay treaty, recognise US property rights and respect concessions granted in 1945 to foreign capital. This broadly non-provocative approach undermined the argument – at least in the eyes of US and Latin American public opinion – that the Cuban revolutionary government threatened US national security. In fact, the US-owned Cuban Electric Company, which was widely accused of inefficient operations and monopoly profits, had already been seized (in January 1959) by the new government. Furthermore, concessions granted to the Cuban Telephone Company by Batista had been cancelled and consumer charges drastically reduced shortly before Castro left Havana for the United States. Both personal conviction and political pressure within Cuba required that any post-revolutionary relationship with the

'Yankees' had to be drastically redefined from the previous 'imperialist' one. The Cuban leader instructed his negotiators not to accept loans from Washington, despite the apparent willingness – even eagerness – of the State Department to extend them. (Felipe Pazos, the former President of the National Bank of Cuba, who accompanied Castro to the United States, wrote in March 1963 that 'In the conversations with the State Department . . . I had the feeling that they were almost forcing me to accept loans . . . ' González: 1968, p. 40, note 3.) Nevertheless, Edward González (1968, p. 44) shows that the Cuban Communists 'worked to preclude the possibility of a rapprochement between Castro and Washington', a fact which indirectly supports the contention that such an accommodation was at least feasible at that time.

Shortly after the US trip, at a meeting of OAS ministers at Punte del Este in Uruguay, Castro made an appeal for US$30 billion for Latin American development over the next ten years. An early bid for Latin American leadership, this, too, could be discounted as a propaganda gesture (and, indeed, such was the response of the US administration). Nevertheless, the indications are that, although Castro was not prepared to sacrifice Cuba's new and hard-won independence by entering into bilateral loan agreements with the 'colossus of the North', he might have been willing to accept US dollars through an intermediary regional organisation. Apparently the Cuban leader was 'very enthusiastic about his private Alliance for Progress scheme' and 'was seriously considering "staying on the American side of the fence as the sponsor of this plan and as the leader of a Nasser-type revolution"' (Javier Pazos, 'Cuba – Was a deal possible in '59?', *The New Republic*, 12 Jan. 1963, in Carla Robbins: 1984, p. 218).

At this stage Castro, at least in public, was holding himself aloof from two disputing tendencies which had emerged from the various parties to the revolution. These may be classified as the 'moderate' left – advocating a democratically based restructuring of Cuban society and a neutralist foreign-policy stance – and the 'radical' left. The latter urged far-reaching reforms that could only be implemented by a revolutionary dictatorship, which would need to realign itself internationally in order to secure protection against the United States. Having distributed his favours fairly equally between these two groups in the first half of 1959 Castro then abruptly and decisively abandoned his on-the-fence posture in favour of the 'radical' position. An indication of what was to follow was given on 12 June when Roberto Agramonte, a moderate who was in favour of conciliation with the United States, was replaced as Secretary of State for Foreign Affairs by radical nationalist Raúl Roa. (Roa, however, was hardly a figure calculated to please Soviet officials. In 1956 he had delivered a scathing attack on Moscow for its invasion of Hungary and was not invited to the Soviet Union until 1971. [Bourne: 1987, p. 199.]) However, the event which clearly signalled the shift in policy was the forced resignation on 17 July of moderate President Urrutia and Castro's installation of Osvaldo Dorticós, a former member of the university committee of the Unión Revolucionaria Comunista (the 1939–45 name of the official Communist Party, later known as the Popular Socialist Party – PSP), in his place. This episode – involving his own stage-managed 'resignation' as Prime Minister – definitively established Castro as the Maximum Leader and arbiter of power in Cuba. A whole series of measures followed promoting the position of radicals – and the Communists – at the expense of the moderates. The culmination of this process was the initiative which paved the way for a Soviet commitment to Cuba: the issuing, in late November 1959, of an invitation to Anastas Mikoian – then in Mexico – to visit the island.

The measures, as detailed by Edward González (1968, pp. 49–53), were as follows: In early August 1959, anti-Communist leaders were removed from the National Directorate of the 26th July Movement and, later in the month, anti-Communist officers were transferred from the Rebel Army to less sensitive civilian posts. In mid-September Castro indicated that the 26th July Movement newspaper *Revolución*'s polemical attacks on the Communists would no longer be tolerated. More significantly, on 17 September Castro announced a new economic course, signifying the phasing out of the mixed economy and the agrarian and redistributive stage of the revolution, and their replacement with a new socialist order, emphasising statism-collectivism and industrialisation. It has been argued that these policies were adopted at Moscow's instigation. However, there is little or no evidence for this. Che Guevara, on an extensive tour in search of new markets for Cuban goods, had met two Soviet representatives in Egypt in August, with whom he concluded an agreement by which the Soviet Union bought 170,000 tons of sugar at the world market price. A further purchase of 333,000 tons of sugar was negotiated at the International Sugar Conference in London on 30 September 1959. Both of these deals appear to have been routine commercial transactions, with scant political significance. Despite the fact that Moscow had severed relations with the dictator Batista in 1952, the USSR had made somewhat erratic purchases of Cuban sugar throughout the 1950s,

which amounted to half a million tons in the peak year, 1955.[1] The fact
that the announcement of Castro's new economic course was ignored
by *Izvestiia, Pravda, New Times* and *International Affairs* is additional
evidence for the argument that at this stage Moscow was interested in
restraining, rather than fostering, radicalisation of the Cuban revolution.

González continues:

By the end of September or early October, the Castro–Communist alliance
appears to have been concluded or tacitly agreed upon, as the PSP pledged
labour's full support for the new economic course. On 16 October, a new
Minister of Labour was appointed to promote trade union 'unity' with the
Communists, a policy that was fully implemented a month later [when] the
labour movement was opened to Communist penetration by Castro's personal
intervention in the National Congress of the Confederation of Cuban Workers
(CTC) on 18 and 21 November . . . In late November, the respected economist
Felipe Pazos was replaced by Guevara as president of the National Bank with
authority to recast the Cuban economy. Finally, toward the end of the year,
the National Institute of Agrarian Reform (INRA) expanded its industrial
activities and accelerated the collectivisation of agriculture.

   In the meantime, Castro had begun to jettison the middle class and to
cultivate support among the peasantry, workers and students through the use
of nationalistic and class appeals. As a result, he gave up any further pretense
of restoring constitutional democracy and relied instead upon the enactment
of a 'direct democracy' between himself and 'the people'. In order to ensure a
personally loyal military apparatus, he also launched the full-scale organisation of the 'popular militias' to be recruited principally from among the
peasantry and the urban lower class. (González: 1968, p. 50 and p. 52)

That Castro had come to regard the Centre-Left as an obstacle to the
course he wanted the revolution to pursue was made clear on 19
October, when he warned, 'It would be better if those who prefer to
remain on the borderline in these hours . . . become enemies; that is,
they would do more damage as companions than enemies' (*Hoy*
(newspaper of the PSP), 21 October 1959, p. 3, in González: 1968,
p. 51). A forcible demonstration of Castro's changed attitude was
given on 21 October when he ordered the arrest of his former
companion-in-arms, the charismatic Major Huber Matos, Commander
of Camaguey Province (an area where there was significant resistance
to the new regime), who had resigned his commission in the Rebel
Army in protest at the increasing Communist influence in the revo-

---

[1] Soviet imports of Cuban sugar 1953–8 (in US dollars) were as follows: 1953 – 763,025;
   1954 – 808,463; 1955 – 36,409,907; 1956 – 14,981,000; 1957 – 41,981,000; 1958 –
   14,072,388. Dirección General de Estadísticas, *10 años de balances comerciales, 1949–58*
   (1960), in Clissold: 1970, p. 37.

lution. Thus it is clear that Castro had deliberately moved to implement socialist and pro-Communist policies before there was any question of Soviet involvement in Cuba and, indeed, before any decisive deterioration had taken place in US–Cuban relations (see pages 66–9). The shift in policy occurred between late May (on 21 May Castro had publicly accused the Communists of 'anti-revolutionary' activities) and mid-July 1959, when the Urrutia affair blew up. What prompted this change?

There is little or no hard evidence to support the theory that Fidel Castro was a 'closet Communist' even during the 26 July 1953 assault on the Moncada barracks, as has been claimed. The core of Fidel's men at this stage consisted of supporters of the *Ortodoxo* party, so-called because of its avowed adherence to the principles of José Martí, a radical thinker in many respects but one who was unequivocally in favour of democratic government for Cuba. Communists from the PSP, with the exception of Fidel's younger brother Raúl, were excluded from the venture, which was anathema to the party line and was subsequently dismissed as 'adventurist'. Raúl Castro, having worked closely with PSP members at the university during 1952, attended the Communist-sponsored Fourth World Youth Congress in Vienna in February 1953 and went on to visit Bucharest, Budapest and Prague. On his return to Havana the following June he enrolled in the Communist Youth. However, Raúl 'was excluded from all secret policy planning and decision-making' (Szulc: 1986, p. 154), and when he joined Fidel's movement in July 1953 (primarily, it seems out of loyalty to his brother rather than conviction as to the political correctness of the enterprise) he did not tell the Communists what he was doing (Lockwood: 1969, p. 163; Szulc: 1986, p. 181).

Khrushchev's statement that the Cuban Communists had no contacts with Castro at the time of his victory is not strictly accurate. The PSP reconsidered their policy of total opposition to the guerrilla strategy late in July 1958, when Carlos Rafael Rodríguez was sent up into the Sierra, where he encountered 'understanding' in Raúl's encampment and 'suspicion' in Fidel's (Thomas: 1977, pp. 220–1). He stayed until 10 August, and returned again in mid-September to remain (although not at Fidel's headquarters) until the end of the war. Rafael Rodríguez claimed that during the course of the first visit Castro gave a verbal acceptance of the idea of an alliance between *Fidelistas* and Communists (Thomas: 1977, p. 224). The indications are that, in Castro's eyes, the failure of the April 1958 general strike had exposed the political and organisational unreliability of many moderate 26th July

Movement leaders (Szulc: 1986, p. 352). In retrospect it is quite clear that, despite the various (and for the most part ill-defined) policy proclamations issued by the 26th July Movement both before and immediately after the revolution, Castro wanted his revolution to instigate radical social change in Cuba. The PSP, as the only party in Cuba with an organisational apparatus throughout the island, potentially offered the discipline and political expertise which would be needed to form a revolutionary government and which seemed to be lacking in Castro's own movement. Thus the possibility of coopting the Communists into the revolution presented itself.

The precise timing of this decision remains a mystery. Tad Szulc presents testimonial evidence for a clandestine agreement between Castro and the PSP 'within days of his arrival in Havana' (Szulc: 1986, p. 376). This possibility cannot be discounted, but it must be borne in mind that Szulc's sources for this are confined to interviews with Blas Roca, Fabio Grobart and Alfredo Guevara, all of whom are 'old' Communists who might well be anxious to give an enhanced impression of their role in the early stages of the revolution.

A second hypothesis (which corresponds closely to the timing of events) is that the decision was taken in the wake of the first major attempt to restructure Cuban society: an Agrarian Reform Law, introduced on 17 May 1959. The limited scope of the moderate provisions of this first law should be emphasised: up to 402 hectares of ordinary farming land were allowed; for cattle farming the maximum was 1,340 hectares. In comparison the agrarian reform introduced by the Chilean Christian Democrats under Eduardo Frei (1964–70) provided for a maximum basic unit of only 80 hectares. The Cuban law made provision for compensation with government bonds, redeemable within twenty years with an annual interest rate of 4.5 per cent. However, the agrarian reform followed a March 1959 Rent Law which greatly dismayed property owners by introducing statutory reductions of 50 per cent for the very poorest tenants (those paying less than 100 pesos per month) and 40–30 per cent decreases for those in higher income brackets. In this context, the agrarian reform was perceived by the middle classes as decisive confirmation of how Castro intended to resolve the contradiction between his promises of social reform and his assurances that the wealthy had nothing to fear, and therefore provoked a swift backlash of opposition within Cuba. Indeed several members of Castro's own cabinet found it unpalatable. Foreign Minister Agramonte was not the only person to be dismissed on 12 June. Elena Mederos, Minister of Social Welfare, Luis Orlando Rodríguez, Minister of the Interior, Ángel Fernández at the Ministry of Justice and Sori Marín at the Ministry of Agriculture, all of whom had at least partially opposed the Agrarian Reform, were also replaced (Thomas: 1977, p. 447).

I would argue that it was this domestic response – signalling that even moderate and gradual reform was unacceptable to the Cuban elite – which was the most immediate cause of the shift in Castro's strategy. The Agrarian Reform also, inevitably, provided the already hostile sectors of the US press and Congress with specific ammunition, and it was at this stage that the cries of 'Communist' first began to be heard. More significantly, the State Department evinced the first sign of active hostility to Cuba by pressurising the British government into rejecting a Cuban order for military helicopters.

Two other factors which have been adduced to explain Castro's shift in position are the failure, in mid-June, of the Cuban-based expedition to liberate the Dominican Republic (Suárez: 1967, pp. 65–9), and the defection of Major Díaz Lanz, Commander of the Rebel Air Force, to the United States shortly afterwards. Díaz Lanz proceeded to testify before the Senate Internal Security Subcommittee on the Communist infiltration of the Cuban armed forces. Neither of these events in themselves (or even together) seems significant enough to account for such a drastic change in policy direction. However, in the context of the volatile reaction, both internal and external, to a relatively mild Agrarian Reform initiative, they may well have served to endorse Castro's conclusion that the social change which he wanted the revolution to effect in Cuba was incompatible with extremely powerful domestic and foreign economic interests. As González remarks, 'Given the Guatemalan precedent [in 1954 the CIA organised the overthrow of left-wing President Arbenz] [Castro] may therefore have calculated that if his regime was inevitably to be labelled as "Communist", he had everything to gain by moving closer to the Cuban Communists who could serve as brokers in obtaining indispensable Soviet assistance' (González: 1968, p. 48).

It would be an oversimplification to ascribe the deterioration of US–Cuban relations during 1959 and 1960 solely to cynical manoeuvrings on the part of Castro (although these certainly took place) or to the imperialist aggression of the United States (although this was undoubtedly evident). In fact both sides (at different times) gave out conciliatory signals, but in the highly charged atmosphere between the two countries each chose to concentrate on the hostile signs and ignore any others.

On the Cuban side, this attitude was brought about by a combination of two factors. Firstly, there is the history of US direct intervention in Central America and the Caribbean, and indeed in Cuba itself. Events in Guatemala in 1954 set a vivid precedent and were a potent reminder that even a glance in the direction of Communism was more than the United States was prepared to countenance. Secondly, from very early days, several leading members of the revolutionary government were arguing that US intervention in Cuba was inevitable. Che Guevara, whose analysis stemmed from his own experiences in Guatemala in 1954 (Hodges: 1977, pp. 15–16), said, in an interview given on 18 April 1959:

The present indications are very clear that they are now preparing to intervene in Cuba and destroy the Cuban revolution. The evil foreign enemies have an old method. First they begin a political offensive, propagandising widely and saying that the Cuban people oppose Communism . . . At the same time they intensify their economic attack and cause Cuba to fall into economic difficulties. Later they will look for a pretext to create some kind of dispute and then utilise certain international organizations they control to carry out intervention against the Cuban people.[2]

Moreover, a Marxist-Leninist analysis of foreign-policy formulation in the United States (which would have been accepted by Guevara and also by Raúl Castro, both extremely powerful figures) implicitly makes two assumptions which have been shown to be inaccurate: firstly, that the 'bourgeoisie' always act in concert, and secondly, that the ruling group has control over the statements of major interest groups within society. Thus the implication is that if the State Department issues a mild statement in response to an issue which is provoking inflammatory articles and speeches in the press and Congress (for example, over the Agrarian Reform Law), then it is simply that the government is hiding its 'real' intentions in order to deceive. Whilst US administrations certainly have instigated 'two-track' policies (for example, in Allende's Chile) these have not proved particularly successful, and it would seem that American foreign-policy-making is rarely as well co-ordinated as this analysis suggests. In fact it can be extremely difficult to isolate the pressures and influences which have gone into the making of any one decision.

Thus, a deterministic view of US actions combines with historical evidence to form the basis of a fear of inevitable US intervention which, while clearly not without a rational foundation, encourages a

[2] Interview given on 18 April 1959 and published in the Chinese journal *World Knowledge*, 5 June 1959, in Guevara: 1967, pp. 9–14, p. 14.

hyper-sensitivity to potential threats which can lead to over-reaction and over-compensation in policy-making. I believe that this Cuban fear of US military action must be taken seriously as a component of Castro's decision-making. It should not be discounted as merely a cynical manipulation on his part in order to restore flagging revolutionary morale by invoking the imperialist threat, even though it has in practice served that purpose. Herbert Matthews, who was close to the Cuban revolutionaries from the late Sierra Maestra days, wrote that 'I made up my mind early in the revolution on the basis of many talks with all the top Cuban leaders that their greatest preoccupation was the conviction that the United States was determined to overthrow the Castro regime' (Matthews: 1969, p. 171).

In fact, throughout this first period, Eisenhower's official policy was to remain aloof, fearful that any direct intervention would make Castro a martyr. In January 1960, shortly before Mikoian's visit, Eisenhower issued another in a series of conciliatory statements, and throughout 1959 Ambassador Philip Bonsal in Havana had worked untiringly to establish grounds for accommodation. The basic attitude of the United States was undeniably one of active hostility. The agenda of a National Security Council meeting as early as 10 March 1959 included as a main item the possibility of bringing 'another government to power in Cuba' (Szulc: 1986, p. 384). Nevertheless, it appears that 'the Intelligence community was split on Cuba. Late in March [1959] ... a special panel on Cuba in the CIA's Board of Estimates concluded in a secret review that Castro was not "a Moscow-oriented Communist" ... The full board rejected that conclusion under pressure from CIA director Allen W. Dulles, architect of the Guatemala approach ...' (Szulc: 1986, p. 385). Almost inevitably, however, day-to-day irritants and culturally blinkered judgements by both sides aggravated the tensions between the two countries even before policy decisions became the source of more substantive disputes. Tad Szulc discusses the problem of the Cuban government's trials of Batista 'war criminals' by revolutionary justice: '... the issue – in the eyes of Fidel Castro and masses of Cubans – was that while the United States government had never protested against the killing and torture of thousands of the old regime's opponents by the Batista police and soldiers (and public opinion took hardly any notice), now that the victorious revolutionaries were punishing their opponents with executions and lengthy prison sentences Americans were indignant [about the lack of Anglo-Saxon judicial guarantees]' (1986, pp. 385–6). Thus the climate for negotiations on a major issue such as

what constituted acceptable compensation for expropriated US properties (the Cubans, desperately short of foreign exchange, were
prepared to offer only 4.5 per cent bonds) was soured.

The United States also argued that Cuban assertions of independence and declarations of neutrality in the Cold War, most notably by
Raúl Roa at the United Nations General Assembly on 24 September
1959, had potential security implications. In fact the Cuban position at
this session was not stridently anti-US. Cuba voted against Washington on several African motions, for example on Algerian independence, but abstained on crucial issues such as the admission of the
People's Republic of China to the United Nations. Both of these points
of contention were symptomatic of the fundamental issue at stake for
Washington, which was that it had lost control of events in Cuba and a
client state which had been regarded virtually as a part of the
American mainland had moved out of the US orbit. However, the only
manifestations of hostility up until October 1959 had been pressure on
its European allies not to supply Cuba with weapons (in mid-October
Washington had blocked the sale of British jet fighters to Cuba).

Thus, when on 21 October a Florida-based plane piloted by Díaz
Lanz bombed Havana, Castro's violent denunciation of the United
States before a mass rally (on 26 October) lacked an 'objective correla-
tive'. It was a product of Castro's evolving strategy for dealing with the
concrete hostility that he anticipated from the United States, rather
than a response to the bombing itself. Peter Bourne reveals that on 16
October 1959 Camilo Cienfuegos (who disappeared in a still unex-
plained air accident only ten days later) was interviewed at the Havana
Riviera Hotel by Alexander Alekseev, a KGB official who quickly
developed an excellent rapport with Castro and played an extremely
important role in the development of relations between Cuba and the
Soviet Union. (After Cuba's incorporation into the Soviet bloc Castro
succeeded in persuading the Kremlin to appoint Alekseev ambassador
to Havana in place of Sergei Kudriatsev who, complained Fidel, was
even more boring than the American Philip Bonsal [Thomas: 1977,
p. 603].) Alekseev asked Cienfuegos to arrange an interview with
Fidel, which took place 'a few days later' at the offices of the agrarian
reform institute. Alekseev – reflecting the Soviet Union's interests at
the time – asked about diplomatic relations, but Castro would say only
that 'what is fundamental now is not diplomatic relations. What is
most important is that the Cuban and Russian people be friends.'
Castro did, however, mention Cuba's desire for trade relations and
Alekseev, presumably perceiving this to be the best way forward,

suggested that the Soviet trade exhibition then in New York should be brought to Havana, and that Anastas Mikoian might come for the opening (Bourne: 1987, p. 189).

The invitation to Mikoian was issued shortly after the Díaz Lanz bombing. Although, unfortunately, we do not know the exact date of the meeting between Alekseev and Castro, it seems highly probable that, as Edward González contends, 'Castro seized upon the [bombing] incident' as a pretext for 'the turn against the Centre-Left and the United States' (González: 1968, p. 51, note 39). As far as we can judge, in the early days at least, anti-Americanism went against the grain of popular feeling within Cuba. Carlos Rafael Rodríguez wrote that in the fifties 'Anti-imperialism was . . . a proscribed word . . . Young people whom we knew to be honest, stung as we were by the sufferings of our Fatherland, lived convinced that Cuba's independence was a Yankee gift and that our denunciations of national oppression were simply ways of serving an idea that they considered to be "anti-Cuban"' ('Reflexiones ante un aniversario', *Hoy*, 29 July 1959, p. 1, cited in Farber: 1983, p. 61). Thus Castro's harangues against Washington were attempts to introduce an anti-American feeling rather than to rally support around one that already existed (which is the case in many Latin American countries). This is suggested by the very vehemence of the speeches and the fact that they always contained prolonged and strident calls on Cuban nationalism (which certainly was a strong popular sentiment). The two factors combined to foster the belief that to be a patriot a Cuban had by definition to be anti-United States.

Further evidence that Castro was pursuing his own course rather than responding to US actions is given by the testimony of US Ambassador Philip Bonsal, who found his efforts to meet with Castro and to pursue negotiations thwarted. In November 1959 the first expropriation of US property took place, an event signalling that the Cubans were no longer willing to accept the need for negotiations on Washington's terms.

What, then, lay behind Castro's invitation to Mikoian? An overriding concern was to find a source of arms supplies to equip the Rebel Army and the people's militia to fight the anticipated US invasion. Herbert Matthews reported that, according to Raúl Castro, the Soviet Union agreed to supply arms during Mikoian's visit (Matthews: 1969, p. 148). In this respect, those who argue that US policy was responsible for Castro's turn towards the Soviet Union are justified: by using its influence to deny access to Western arms supplies, Washington left

Cuba with little option (as it subsequently left Nicaragua) but to purchase weapons from the Eastern bloc.

However, the overture also appears to have been motivated by economic considerations. As early as January 1959 Guevara emphasised the importance of agrarian reform and pointed out that if the constitutional requirements for compensation were met, the reform would be so slow as to be imperceptible. Moreover, to accomplish a programme of rapid industrialisation (the favoured economic strategy of Che, Raúl Castro and Carlos Rafael Rodríguez) the state would have to be in control of the main sectors of the economy, which again would lead to an unavoidable confrontation with the United States. The influential Rafael Rodríguez (who at first refused government positions, but gave advice on economic matters) believed that Cuba could not rely on the Western capitalist countries (accustomed to regarding Cuba as their sugar-bowl) for the assistance necessary to develop an industrial economy. Che Guevara's three-month tour of Africa, Asia and Europe (mid-June to mid-September 1959) had confirmed that other Third World nations (like Cuba, importers of manufactured goods and exporters of raw materials) offered little scope for trade. Thus there were significant economic incentives for revolutionary Cuba at least to increase its options with the Soviet Union.

By this stage it is possible – the idea is corroborated to some extent by Castro's actions in December 1959 and January 1960 – see pages 72–3 – that he had already taken the decision to embark on a campaign to present the USSR with a *fait accompli* of 'socialist' reforms to enlist their total support. However the evidence suggests (see pages 75–6) that it is more likely that this decision was reached at a later date, when the force of events made it seem imperative. In November 1959, Castro must simply have felt that he had little to lose by seeing what Moscow was prepared to offer.

The Soviet Union officially accepted the invitation, but it was not until the end of January that Mikoian's imminent arrival (on 4 February 1960) was announced. Why did the Soviet leadership decide to send him? Internationally, the increasingly frequent application of the label 'Communist' to the Cuban regime throughout 1959 had introduced the issue of prestige for the Soviet Union. The fact that Guatemala in 1954 had 'returned from Communism' (and was regarded by the United States as the first country to do so)[3] increased Soviet reluctance to be perceived to be experiencing another 'loss' in

---

[3] Former US ambassador to Mexico, William Dwyer, in Susanne Jonas and David Tobis (eds.), *Guatemala* (NACLA, Berkeley, 1974), pp. 46–7, in Black: 1983, p. 5.

the area (even though they did not accept that Castro was embarking on a road towards Communism). This factor was exacerbated by Chinese criticism (at that stage, expressed privately) of the USSR's lack of revolutionary internationalism and its willingness to appease the imperialists.

More specifically, significant pressure was exerted on Moscow by the Cuban Communist Party and by Castro himself with his new policy orientation. In late 1959 Castro began to stress the class content of his revolution and referred to 'the image of the revolution' as 'the tight union of the workers and peasants', apparently precluding any future role for the national bourgeoisie. A rapid acceleration took place in the implementation of the agrarian reform. In late 1959 less than ten per cent of the expropriable land area had been touched, and only 6,000 out of a potential 150,000 beneficiaries had received their allocations. At that rate, twenty years would have passed before the reform became fully effective (Brundenius: 1984, p. 43). However, in one week of January 1960 over 600,000 hectares were expropriated, including 70,000 acres of US-owned lands. Thus Castro was demonstrating not only that he was serious in his commitment to social reform but also, more importantly – in terms of how Soviet analysts assess the viability of a regime – that his revolutionary government had the power to implement the measures that it chose. The revolution was also clearly in control of armed power within Cuba. In addition to the Revolutionary Armed Forces, Castro was sufficiently confident of support by late 1959 to organise the formation of popular militias, and was stirring up patriotic fervour by repeated assertions of the imminence of US military action against Cuba. Castro also openly courted the Communists throughout December 1959 and January 1960.

The Cuban Communists, who for the first six months of 1959 had made policy proclamations which were cautiously but unequivocally more radical than Castro's, subsequently found that they were fast being outstripped by him in the proposal of anti-capitalist measures. Recognising that they had no power and little influence with which to contain Castro's radicalisation (as Moscow wished), the skilled and experienced politicians of the PSP responded quickly to the changed situation and began asserting the advanced character of the revolution as one of their ploys for enlisting Soviet assistance. In fact their own interests – in terms of improving both their domestic position and their leverage with Moscow – coincided with Castro's in pushing for a fully socialist revolution. As early as 29 September 1959, Aníbal Escalante had publicly demanded Sino–Soviet support for Cuba. The tactic of exploiting the emerging rupture between Beijing and Moscow was an all too obvious one, particularly in the light of the appropriateness of the Chinese agrarian model to Cuba. It became a dominant element in the PSP campaign (on 9 January Escalante publicly acclaimed Beijing's position on Cuba), along with a defence of Castro's foreign policy and critical references to Khrushchev's strategy of accommodation with the United States. A conciliatory statement by Eisenhower on 20 January 1960 (which may in itself have given the Soviet leadership the impression that a little meddling in Cuba would not incur serious repercussions) was vociferously denounced by the PSP, creating an additional source of pressure on the Kremlin to make at least some show of solidarity with Castro's 'small country struggling alone'.

February 1960–July 1960

At the press conference at the end of his visit, Mikoian made it quite clear that the Soviet Union did not want a show-down with the United States over Cuba (Dinerstein: 1962, p. 69). However, Mikoian was favourably impressed with the enthusiasm and commitment of the Cuban revolutionaries and, on 13 February, he signed a trade agreement, by which the Soviet Union undertook to buy 5 million tons (m.t.) of sugar over five years, 20 per cent of which was to be paid for in hard currency and the remainder in Soviet goods, including 6 million barrels of oil per year. The USSR also agreed to lend Cuba $100 million at a yearly interest rate of 2.5 per cent.

Two points are worth noting regarding this agreement. The first is that Khrushchev's general policy of extending Soviet links with developing countries had resulted in the signing of similar agreements with various African and Asian governments. Therefore, at this stage, Soviet policy towards Castro was related to this broad objective and there is no indication that Cuba was as yet regarded as having the priority status that it later commanded.

The second point is that this agreement reflected a certain degree of complementarity between the Soviet and Cuban economies. Clearly Soviet oil was an attractive buy for the Cubans: Che Guevara stated that the landed price of Soviet crude was 33 per cent lower than the price at which the majors imported oil to Cuba from their Venezuelan subsidiaries, and the fact that it was a barter deal enabled the revolution to conserve its dwindling hard-currency reserves. Furthermore, Cuba's new arrangement with the Soviet Union reduced its dependence on the multi-nationals. What is not always made clear, however, is that the February agreement was economically quite favourable to the USSR. As was indicated above, Moscow had continued to buy Cuban sugar even after the severing of relations with Batista. In 1960 the Soviet sugar crop was hit by drought, at the same time as the authorities were embarking on a drive to raise the levels of sugar consumption. Moreover, the Soviet negotiators had clearly hoped to sell some of the sugar on the world market, which would have been highly advantageous to them, but the Cubans insisted on the insertion of a clause prohibiting re-export to their traditional markets. In addition, Moscow was at that time, after the discovery of rich deposits in the Urals, looking for outlets for a disposable surplus of crude oil. As they had done in the 1930s, Soviet organisations approached state-owned Latin American oil companies. Although Mexico rejected a Soviet offer in 1959, as indicated in chapter 1, the Soviet Union did succeed in selling oil to Argentina, Brazil and Uruguay. Soviet oil also made substantial inroads into the Italian market and, in 1960, an offer of cheap Soviet crude enabled the Indian government to extract price concessions from the major oil companies. In this context Cuba, with its exceptionally high dependence on imported oil (which accounts for approaching two-thirds of the island's total energy consumption) and its sophisticated modern refining capacity (installed by Shell, Esso and Texaco), must have looked a promising market for Soviet oil. None of this is to deny that the February 1960 agreement was partly a result of Khrushchev's 'allowing Mikoian to make trouble for the Americans in Cuba' (Bonsal: 1971, p. 156), but it is important to recognise that, whatever political considerations were involved, they were firmly backed up by a favourable set of economic circumstances. Nor was the Soviet Union at this stage inclined to be particularly generous in its terms. According to Mikoian himself, the USSR insisted that the Cubans buy Soviet goods if they wanted Moscow to continue purchasing their sugar, and adamantly refused to pay more than the world market price for Cuban produce (*Mikoian in Cuba* (Crosscurrents Press, New York, 1960), in Boughton: 1974, p. 450). As Jorge Pérez-López points out, 'since in 1960 the world market price was around 3 cents per pound, this meant that sales to the Soviet Union would be effected at prices significantly below the prevailing preferential price paid by the United States in that year – 5.3 cents per pound . . . In fact, some of the sales to the Soviet Union in 1960 were made at prices *below* the world market price. For example, a sale of 345,000 tons announced in February 1960 was made at 2.78 cents per pound, compared to a world market price of 2.90 cents per pound' (Pérez-López: 1988, p. 124).

In his concluding press conference Mikoian also made it clear that it was Havana, rather than Moscow, which was stalling on the resumption of diplomatic relations, a remark which was not quoted in the *Pravda* report (Dinerstein: 1962, p. 68). This is not surprising: the Cubans had obtained a useful economic agreement from the Soviet Union, but it was hardly a substantial enough commitment to warrant precipitating an open break with the United States by resuming relations with the USSR. What, then, prompted the change of heart that led, less than three months later, to the official announcement (on 8 May) that Soviet–Cuban relations were at full diplomatic level?

From Cuba's point of view, the significant events occurred in March 1960. On 4 March the Belgian ship *La Coubre* – carrying weapons purchased by the Castro regime – was blown up as it entered Havana Bay by a bomb allegedly planted by the CIA. At about the same time a consortium of West European banks refused to grant Cuba the credits it had requested, apparently as a result of US pressure. Moreover, as Eisenhower later publicly admitted, on 17 March Washington took the decision to prepare an invasion of Cuba (The *New York Times*, 13 June 1961, p. 18). Whilst there is no conclusive proof, it seems highly likely that this piece of information would have reached Castro's ears soon after. Thus the Cubans identified a new aggression in Eisenhower's attitude, and my hypothesis is that it was in response to these events that Castro decided to stake the survival of his revolution on enlisting the total support of the Soviet Union.

The actions of the USSR must be seen in the context of a dramatic change in the international situation, caused by the shooting down on 1 May of a US U2 spy plane flying over the heart of continental Russia. This incident acted as a powerful catalyst, forcing each superpower to reveal its true position. On 5 May Eisenhower chose to respond to the ensuing crisis by asserting the right of the United States to fly its planes over the Soviet Union if security considerations demanded such a course of action. (This belligerent insistence on Washington's right to behave as it chose in the interests of US 'security' must have aggravated Cuban fears.) Eisenhower reiterated this theme from 15–18 May at the much-vaunted Paris Conference, which had originally been intended to further cooperation and understanding between the USSR and the United States, France and the United Kingdom. It was significant that during a press conference called on 18 May 1960 Khrushchev not only denounced Eisenhower but also asserted the importance of the Cuban revolution, which had suddenly become the subject of enthusiastic and laudatory articles in the Soviet press. Now that Moscow's hopes for fruitful negotiation with the United States had been shattered, it was necessary for the Soviet Union to adopt a more aggressive stance if it were to maintain credibility as a rival to Washington. Cuba – only ninety miles from the United States – must have seemed to Khrushchev (who had to be seen to be making progress on at least one front) an irresistibly appropriate object for a Soviet response to US arrogance and intransigence.

The outcome was that at the end of June 1960 a Cuban delegation in Moscow was warmly received by Khrushchev himself, and was told by the Soviet premier that 'the Soviet Union has only to press a button in any part of the Soviet Union for rockets from that country to fall on any other part of the planet'.[4] A few weeks later, in a speech made to the All-Russian Teachers' Congress in Moscow on 9 July, Khrushchev made a specific reference to Cuba in this respect. 'Figuratively speaking', he declared, 'in case of need, Soviet artillerymen can support the Cuban people with their rocket fire should aggressive forces in the Pentagon dare to start intervention against Cuba' (*Pravda*, 10 July 1960, pp. 1-3). During a visit to Moscow made by Raúl Castro in mid-July 1960, the USSR not only arranged to supply arms to Cuba, but Khrushchev 'reaffirmed that the Soviet Union would use everything to prevent US armed intervention against the Republic of Cuba' (Soviet–Cuban Communiqué, *Pravda*, 21 July 1960, p. 1).

Khrushchev, whose 'peaceful coexistence' policy had been criticised both at home and abroad (by the Chinese Communist Party at the Congress of the World Federation of Trade Unions held in Beijing in June 1960) was taking advantage of the situation in Cuba to reassert Soviet strength. He may also have hoped that by supporting a revolution with which the Chinese felt no small degree of identification, he would be able to outmanoeuvre his Maoist critics. K. S. Karol points out that it was the same meeting of the Central Committee (on 11 July) which both endorsed Khrushchev's announcement on 9 July of virtually unlimited economic aid to Cuba and approved his decision to withdraw all Soviet economic aid from China, and argues that the Cuban affair gave Khrushchev 'an unexpected internationalist alibi' for his anti-Maoist campaign (Karol: 1971, p. 204).

[4] Broadcast statement of 15 July 1960 by Captain Antonio Núñez Jiménez, Executive Director of the Cuban Institute for Agrarian Reform, on the reception by Khrushchev of a Cuban delegation in Moscow in June 1960, *Obra Revolucionaria*, 25 July 1960, in Clissold: 1970, p. 256.

However, scrutiny of the events leading up to the 9 July announcement suggests that this decision was a result not so much of Soviet 'opportunism' as of the policies of the Eisenhower administration and the brinkmanship of Fidel Castro. The first shipment of Soviet crude petroleum arrived in Havana on 9 April 1960, to be processed at a small refinery operated by the Cuban Petroleum Institute. On 17 May the three major oil companies were informed by the Cuban National Bank that they would each have to purchase and process 300,000 m.t. of Soviet crude oil during the remainder of 1960, in order to comply with the government's new purchasing arrangements. In June 1960 the United States Treasury advised the companies not to refine Soviet crude, and they accordingly refused to do so, alleging that, without expensive alterations, their refineries would be seriously damaged by any attempt to process the Soviet product. The weakness of this argument was later shown up by the fact that 'Russian technicians readily overcame the difficulties alleged to be inherent in running the Russian product through the refineries in Cuba. There was no interruption in the availability of refinery products to consumers in Cuba' (Bonsal: 1971, p. 150).

The US move was clearly designed as a challenge to the Castro regime, but it was one which (in the words of the then US Ambassador to Cuba, Philip Bonsal, who strongly opposed the Treasury decision) would, if met, give the Cuban revolution a 'shot in the arm' comparable to the effect of the Suez Crisis on the Nasser regime. This proved to be the case: on 29 June 1960 the Cuban government – encouraged by Khrushchev's statements of Soviet support – seized the refineries operated by the multi-nationals on the grounds that they had violated the law by their refusal to process Soviet petroleum. Castro later admitted to Herbert Matthews that when he took over the refineries he did not know whether or not Moscow would supply Cuba with oil (Matthews: 1969, p. 171). On 6 July, in a move generally interpreted as a retaliation for this seizure, the Eisenhower administration cut the balance of the Cuban sugar quota. It is interesting to note, however, that US Ambassador Bonsal argues that the suspension of the sugar quota was not linked solely to the intervention in the oil refineries, but would in any case have been 'a major element in the programme for the overthrow of Castro' (Bonsal: 1971, p. 151).

Thus Cuba, which for nearly half a century had run its economy on the basis of near-total reliance on the United States, was faced with the need to find a new market for 700,000 tonnes of sugar and an alternative source of oil supplies. Moscow's decision to assume the economic burden of Cuba can be attributed to the fact that, by this stage, it had no other credible option in political terms, partly because of Khrushchev's own extravagant statements of support for the Castro revolution, but largely because of the policies pursued by the United States. Ambassador Bonsal states, 'I do not believe that the Russians would have taken sugar from Cuba which the United States was prepared to purchase. The opportunity we now presented them with was one I am convinced they would gladly at that time have done without' (Bonsal: 1971, p. 153).

That Khrushchev's decision was not without some immediate economic cost is indicated by the difficulties which ensued from the commitment to supply Cuba with its oil which, according to his memoirs, placed a sudden and unwelcome demand on the Soviet fleet:

the Cubans were obliged to turn to us for help. Life on the island was in danger of coming to a standstill. It was urgent that we organise an oil delivery to Cuba on a massive scale. But that was easier said than done. We didn't have enough ocean-going vessels in our own tanker fleet. Our efforts to provide Cuba with the petroleum products it needed put a heavy burden on our own shipping system and forced us to order extra tankers from Italy. (Khrushchev: 1970, p. 490)

The sudden influx of sugar also caused some temporary problems: 'Russian storage facilities for Cuba's raw sugar appear to have been strained to the point that some sugar spoiled. Some domestic beet production was diverted from human consumption to cattle feed to make room for Cuban imports' (Bonsal: 1971, p. 208). However, it appears that the plentiful supplies of sugar were not wholly unwelcome to Soviet leaders, who were still pursuing the consumption drive which was behind the February 1960 agreement. After the initial difficulties:

Through increased consumption per capita, through the development of markets for refined sugar among Russia's clients in Third World countries, and with assistance from other Communist countries Russia not only solved the problem of absorbing the portion of the Cuban crop formerly taken by the United States, but did so in the context both of a resumption after 1964 of the upward movement in its home production and of a contractual willingness to buy far more Cuban sugar than Castro has so far produced for the Russian market. (Bonsal: 1971, p. 208)

Deliveries of Cuban sugar, which arrives mainly in the first half of the year, load the Soviet sugar factories' productive capacities in the period when they are not processing sugar beet (Kolodov: 1984, p. 16).

It is important to bear in mind, however, that in July 1960 the Soviet leaders could have had little or no intimation of exactly how imbalanced their economic relationship with Cuba was destined to become. Their expectation that this relationship would be based, at least to some extent, on mutual advantage is indicated in an assertion, made on 21 July 1960, that:

the forces of the countries of the socialist camp are so great today and they are so strong economically that they can fully take upon themselves, *on the basis of the development of normal trade relations*, the provision of Cuba with all the necessary goods which are denied her by the United States . . . the Soviet Union is prepared to deliver oil and other goods in amounts fully meeting the requirements of Cuba, *in exchange for Cuban goods*. (Soviet–Cuban communiqué, *Pravda*, 21 July 1960, p. 1 [my emphasis])

This assumption is also implicit in the major 1964 oil and sugar agreement, the terms of which were such that 'Had Cuba been able to deliver in full its annual commitment of sugar to the USSR, this would in all probability have balanced the cost of Cuban imports from the Soviet Union. Furthermore, if world sugar prices had remained high, Moscow might even have realised a profit in its Cuban trade by reselling imported sugar on the world market' (Gouré and Weinkle: 1972, p. 75).

August 1960–May 1962

During the last half of 1960, the Soviet leaders – perhaps conscious of having over-reached themselves in political terms, retreated from their former position as staunch defenders of the Cuban revolution, and adopted a far more equivocal tone. A proposed visit to Cuba by Khrushchev was cancelled, probably as a result of a combination of the following factors: (1) pressure from Khrushchev's political opponents at home; (2) fears (both Soviet and Cuban) of inciting Washington; and (3) Castro's own worries about according too high a profile to the relationship with Moscow. However, the Cuban leader had eagerly latched on to the dramatic statements made by Khrushchev in June-July 1960. Not only were relations with the United States very tense, but in August 1960 an OAS meeting in Costa Rica issued a declaration denouncing Sino–Soviet designs to gain a foothold in the hemisphere, proving that Washington could obtain the support of Latin American countries for its anti-Cuban policies. Thus Castro was in dire need of a Soviet commitment to preserve his revolution, and in a speech given to the United Nations on 26 September 1960 the Cuban leader may have been hinting at the price he might have been willing to pay when he said, 'We understand how terrible the subordination of the economy and life in general of nations to foreign economic power is. I need only note that my country was left defenceless in Costa Rica' (Fidel Castro: 1972, p. 49).

Cuba replied to the *Declaration of San José* with the *First Declaration of Havana* which welcomed the Soviet Union's 'offer to support Cuba with the aid of rockets' (*Obra Revolucionaria*, 6 September 1960, in Clissold: 1970, p. 259). The USSR, however, mindful of the fact that Cuba had been made into a prominent campaign issue by both contenders for the US presidency, paid no heed to the wave of Cuban nationalisations of US property during August–October 1960. In retaliation for confiscation of its sugar mills and oil refineries (6 August), its banks (17 September) and the majority of its larger companies (13 October), the United States announced an embargo on Cuba on 19 October, covering all goods except non-subsidised food-stuffs and medical supplies (within a few months even these items were included). In response, Havana nationalised the remaining US properties in Cuba. In this tense situation Khrushchev, perceiving the inauguration of President Kennedy in November 1960 as a new opportunity to promote peaceful coexistence, made a point of stressing the 'symbolic' nature of the rocket pledge (interview with Cuban journalists on 22 October 1960, *Pravda*, 23 October 1960, p. 1).

So far as is known, nothing definite came out of the meeting between Castro and Khrushchev in New York in late October 1960, despite all the drama attached to the Soviet head of state's seeking out the Cuban leader at his hotel in Harlem. After the encounter Khrushchev observed that Castro was 'like a young horse that hasn't been broken. He needs some training, but he's very spirited, so we'll have to be careful' (Shevchenko: 1985, p. 106) – a revealing indication of a patronising attitude that the Russian was to have cause to regret.

It seems to have been Moscow's need to counter a challenge from Beijing which prompted the next Soviet commitment to Cuba. Castro had established relations with the People's Republic of China in September 1960 and, two months later, Che Guevara signed an agreement in Beijing whereby the Chinese bought 1 m.t. of Cuban sugar in 1961 and made a $60 million credit available for the purchase of Chinese goods and technical assistance. With the rift between Beijing and Moscow deepening, the Soviet leaders, aware that the Maoist model was not unattractive to the Cubans, made haste to better the Chinese deal. On 19 December 1960 a new Cuban–Soviet agreement was announced, by which the USSR committed itself to the purchase of 2.7 m.t. of sugar in 1961 at 4 cents per pound, along with a wide variety of economic aid and technical assistance measures. Even so, there were several passages in the ensuing joint communiqué emphasising the Cubans' appreciation of 'the sincere efforts of the Soviet Union to attain world peace'.[5]

The early months of 1961 saw an intensification of US pressure on Cuba, initiated by the rupture of diplomatic relations on 3 January, and culminating in the abortive Bay of Pigs invasion on 17 April. The Soviet leadership, no doubt extremely relieved that Castro had succeeded in crushing the invasion without having to redeem the pledges that Khrushchev had made to him, extracted maximum propaganda value from Washington's loss of face, but once again reassured the Americans that 'we have no bases in Cuba and do not intend to establish any' (Khrushchev's message to J. F. Kennedy, 22 April 1961, US Department of State Bulletin, 8 May 1961, pp. 664–6). The Soviet leaders were evidently nonplussed by Castro's assertion, on the eve of the invasion, that the Cuban revolution was a 'socialist' one. Khrushchev records that 'We had trouble understanding the timing of this statement. Castro's declaration had the immediate effect of widening the gap between himself and the people who were against socialism, and it narrowed the circle of those he could count on for support against the invasion. As far as Castro's personal courage was concerned, his position was admirable and correct. But from a tactical standpoint, it didn't make much sense' (Khrushchev: 1970, p. 492).

Of course Castro's stand, far from being just one of principle, was an attempt to enforce his claims on the Soviet Union at a time when the security of his revolution had never been more seriously threatened. It was one of a whole series of measures designed to force the pace of Soviet identification with his regime and Cuba's integration into the Soviet bloc. As early as January 1961 a US Department of State report on Cuba argued that 'Castro, aware of [growing discontent within Cuba] and of the lack of decisive support by the Soviet countries is endeavouring, through his acts of provocation, to create a crisis against Cuba that will compel the Soviets to support him and will restore him to the position of anti-imperialist hero in the eyes of his own people and the Latin American masses' (US Declassified, 1982, 001697).

At first the Kremlin refused to respond to Castro's manoeuvres.

---

[5] Joint communiqué signed in Moscow by Mikoian and Che Guevara, 19 Dec. 1960, Hoy, 20 Dec. 1960, in Clissold: 1970, pp. 260–2.

Highly conscious of the strategic risks of the defence of Cuba, sensing that Castro – who had no orthodox Communist credentials – was too ambitious and unpredictable a leader to be a wholly reliable client, and (as explained in chapter 4) already beginning to regret the extent of their economic commitment, the Soviet leadership once again retreated into caution. The most they would say in 1961 regarding Cuba's ideological status was that 'Cuba had achieved its revolution independently and had freely chosen the path of socialist development'.[6] Soviet commentaries referred to 'the USSR, the People's Democracies, and Cuba', conveniently leaving the status of the latter hanging in the air.

Castro, however, was not to be deterred, and he set about organising his revolution along lines that were acceptable to the USSR, as will be described below. In the meantime, however, the Cubans sought to gain at least a breathing space by making a little known but highly significant approach to the United States. On 17 August at 2 a.m. Che Guevara, representing Cuba at the OAS conference at Punta del Este in Uruguay, instigated a meeting with the US delegate Richard Goodwin, who gave a full account of the conversation in a memo for President Kennedy dated 22 August 1961 (US Declassified, 1978, 303A). An Argentinian, Horatio Larretta, and a Brazilian, Edmundo Barbosa Da Silva, acted as interpreters. It is worth citing Goodwin's description of what took place in some detail:

Guevara begun by saying that I must understand the Cuban revolution. They intend to build a socialist state, and the revolution which they have begun is irreversible. They are also now out of the US sphere of influence, and that too is irreversible. They will establish a single-party system with Fidel as Secretary-General of the party. Their ties with the East stem from natural sympathies, and common beliefs in the proper structure of the social order.

He said that in building a Communist state they had not repeated any of the aggressive moves of the East. They did not intend to construct an iron curtain around Cuba but to welcome technicians and visitors from all countries to come and work.

[Che went on to discuss several basic problems in Cuba at that time]: (1) There was disturbing revolutionary sentiment, armed men and sabotage. (2) The small (sic) bourgeoisie were hostile to the revolution or, at best, lukewarm. (3) The Catholic Church (here he shook his head in dismay). (4) Their factories looked naturally to the United States for resources, especially spare parts and at times the shortage of these resources made things very critical. (5) They had accelerated the process of development too rapidly and their hard currency

---

[6] Joint communiqué following the visit of Osvaldo Dorticós to the USSR, signed by Brezhnev and Dorticós, 21 Sept. 1961, Pravda, 21 Sept. 1961, pp. 1–2.

reserves were very low. Thus they were unable to import consumer goods and meet basic needs of the people.

He then said that they didn't want an understanding with the United States, because they know that this was impossible (*sic*). They would like a *modus vivendi* – at least an interim *modus vivendi*.

[Guevara then went on to mention] some things he had in mind: – (1) That they could not give back the expropriated properties . . . but they could pay for them in trade. (2) They could agree not to make any political alliance with the East, although this would not affect their natural sympathies. (3) They would have free elections – but only after a period of institutionalising the revolution had been completed. In response to my question he said that this included the establishment of a one-party system. (4) Of course, they would not attack Guantánamo. (At this point he laughed as if at the absurdly self-evident nature of such a statement.) (5) He indicated, very obliquely and with evident reluctance because of the company in which we were talking, that they could also discuss the activities of the Cuban revolution in other countries.

Goodwin came away convinced that 'Cuba [was] undergoing severe economic stress, that the Soviet Union [was] not prepared to undertake the large effort necessary to get them on their feet . . . and that Cuba [desired] an understanding with the United States' (*US Declassified*, 1981, 605A). The initiative foundered, probably largely because Kennedy found it politically unacceptable to be seen to be making any deal with the Cubans after Washington's humiliation at the Bay of Pigs. However, the incident is highly revealing of the concern felt in Cuba about the difficulties of persuading Moscow to make a substantial commitment.

In pursuance of this objective, in July 1961 Castro announced the formation of a new political party, known as the *Organizaciones Revolucionarias Integradas* (Integrated Revolutionary Organisations – ORI). Although the detailed composition of the party was not made public, it was well known that prominent members of the PSP, including Aníbal Escalante and Carlos Rafael Rodríguez, had significant influence in the new organisation. Moscow was thereby reassured that the situation in Cuba was under control. Castro's next move, designed to convince the Soviet leaders of his personal reliability, was his famous declaration of 1 December 1961 that 'I am a Marxist-Leninist, and I shall be a Marxist-Leninist until the last day of my life' (a statement which was reported in full in the Soviet press).

However, the Cuban leader's tactics were not purely conciliatory. In the *Second Declaration of Havana*, issued on 4 February 1962 in response to the suspension of Cuba from the OAS, Castro reminded the Soviet Union that there is more than one interpretation of Marxism-

Leninism. He made no concession whatsoever to Moscow's policy of peaceful coexistence and asserted the primacy of the guerrilla strategy in the fight of oppressed peoples against imperialism. Not surprisingly, the *Declaration* was warmly welcomed in Beijing. Similarly, the announcement on 8 March 1962 of the composition of the National Directorate of the ORI, which revealed that the Communist old guard would have the upper hand, was countered three weeks later by the denunciation of Aníbal Escalante for 'sectarianism', a measure which forced the Soviet Union to take a stand.

This is not to say that Castro's actions as described above can be explained solely in terms of Cuba's relations with Moscow. Clearly there were also domestic factors involved, primarily concerning Castro's needs to consolidate the power base both of the revolution and of himself personally. Nevertheless, this in itself cannot easily be divorced from the introduction of organisations on Soviet-approved lines, for the USSR to some extent provided a much-needed model for the Cuban revolutionaries. It is also clear that Castro's overriding concern with the security, both military and economic, of his revolution obliged him to conduct domestic policy with one eye on Moscow.

The Soviet Union decided to endorse the expulsion of Escalante: Castro was henceforth referred to as 'comrade' and Cuba's place in the Soviet bloc was officially acknowledged when it was listed along with the other 'socialist' states in the traditional May Day slogans. Thus from mid-1962 the Soviet Union and Cuba were committed to each other to an extent which made it extremely difficult for either party to renounce the relationship. Cuba needed Moscow's military, political and economic protection, and the Soviet Union could not afford politically to abandon its new-found ally. On the other hand, in the event of direct US aggression the Soviet Union would be confronted with the even more unacceptable choice of risking nuclear confrontation with the United States. This is the background to the event which perhaps more than any other has fuelled the arguments that the Soviet Union has 'expansionist' designs on Latin America which can only be countered by US strength.

The Cuban Missile Crisis (October 1962)

My contention is that the events of October 1962 took place in a very specific historical context in terms of the Soviet appraisal of global power relations. There is no doubt that the launching of the first earth satellite (*Sputnik*) in 1957 – which, at least in Soviet minds, symbolised the idea that socialism was the wave of the future – together with the successful Soviet testing and subsequent deployment of Inter-Continental Ballistic Missiles produced a decided shift in both Soviet and American perceptions of international relations. William Zimmerman, who offers a detailed and convincing analysis of Soviet perspectives at this time (Zimmerman: 1969), states that by far the most important aspect of the changed situation for Soviet commentators was that 'the United States had lost its privileged position of strategic invulnerability'. From Moscow's standpoint this represented 'a turning point in the development of international relations' (Zimmerman: 1969, pp. 171–2). The new strategic situation, Soviet space successes, the decolonisation process and (until 1958–9) the apparently successful reintegration of the socialist camp after 1956 all contributed to a surge of optimism within the Soviet Union that socialism was in the ascendant. Measured against 'a stagnant US economy, a not altogether successful satellite programme, and perennial crises in NATO' (Zimmerman: 1969, p. 179), these developments created high expectations expressed at the November 1960 Conference of Eighty-One Parties in the definitive formulation that 'the superiority of the forces of socialism over those of imperialism . . . is becoming ever more marked in the world arena' (Zimmerman: 1969, p. 181). Khrushchev asserted in March 1960 that 'the Soviet Union is now the world's strongest military power' (*Izvestiia*, 2 March 1960) and, although it was recognised that Soviet economic capacity was then inferior to that of the United States, it was confidently predicted that the socialist nations would have outstripped the West within a decade.

By the time that the decision was taken to challenge the United States by the installation of missiles in Cuba (probably in early July 1962) the USSR had been forced to revise its optimistic view. The decisive response by the Kennedy administration to a potential missile gap and the Sino–Soviet crisis were the two main factors forcing Moscow to scale down its claims. In the first months of Kennedy's presidency the United States not only undertook a substantial arms build up, but also began to float new ideas in strategic doctrine, most notably Maxwell Taylor's theory of flexible response. From his analysis of Soviet commentary, Zimmerman argues that in the period October 1961 to March 1962 these developments 'exacerbated the ongoing dialogue within the Soviet ruling group concerning the adequacy of the Soviet deterrent' and 'suggested grave misgivings on the part of some Soviet observers lest the defining characteristics of imperialist international relations be restored' (Zimmerman: 1969, p. 187).

By March 1962, however, the Soviet military had taken several steps – nuclear weapons' tests, the development of the 'global rocket', the redeploying of launch sites – to bolster the credibility of the Soviet deterrent, and commentators once again 'buried the myth of the invulnerability of the United States of America' (*Pravda*, 31 March 1962, in Zimmerman: 1969, pp. 189–90). The very need to do this – for the second time in four years – testifies to a certain degree of insecurity within the minds of the Soviet leaders that their recent gains in terms of strategic power could easily be snatched from them. Zimmerman points out that 'it was at this stage that Soviet authorities permitted, tolerated or encouraged Marshal Sokolovskii and his colleagues to publish an awesome picture of American military might' (*Voennaia Strategiia*, 1962) and that 'wide dissemination was given to statements declaring that never before had imperialism been so strong' (Zimmerman: 1969, p. 192). Thus it was in this context, with Soviet leaders feeling that although they possessed an adequate deterrence, it was only *minimally* adequate, that the decision was taken to install missiles in Cuba (see Horelick: 1964).

In the aftermath of the Cuban Missile Crisis and in the broader context of the continuing growth in US military strength and reappraisal of strategic doctrine, even under Khrushchev the Soviet leadership 'reverted to an appreciably more restrained description of the distribution of power' (Zimmerman: 1969, p. 205). After Khrushchev's ouster in 1964, his successors avoided the use of bold terms such as *pereves* (preponderance) or *ravnovesie* (equilibrium) which had been fashionable in the early sixties, and contented themselves with less specific formulations depicting the global correlation of forces (*sootnoshenie sil*). This was consonant with the repudiation of Khrushchev's style of conducting international relations, which was designated a 'voluntaristic and unrealistic approach to the phenomena and events of international life', fraught 'with grave consequences, and capable of giving rise either to smug over-confidence or a weakness in the face of the military threat from imperialism' (*Pravda*, 8 August 1965, pp. 3–4).

Khrushchev initially claimed (in a report to the Supreme Soviet on 12 December 1962) that by installing the missiles in Cuba he acted in response to a Cuban request; this has been contradicted not only by statements from Castro, but also by Khrushchev himself. In his memoirs he wrote, 'It was during my visit to Bulgaria that I had the idea of installing missiles with nuclear warheads in Cuba without letting the United States find out they were there until it was too late to do anything about them' (Khrushchev: 1970, p. 493).

There seems little doubt that the initiative came from Moscow. However, arguments along the lines of 'the Russians' real objective was less their alleged anxiety to protect Cuba than to alter the whole balance of global strategy to their advantage by one bold stroke' (Clissold: 1970, p. 49) would seem to raise something of a false dilemma. Undoubtedly Khrushchev wanted to challenge the Americans, and to force them to acknowledge that Soviet power was an equal match for the power of the United States. This is implied in the following passage from his memoirs: 'We hadn't given the Cubans anything more than the Americans were giving their allies in Italy and Turkey. We had the same rights and opportunities as the Americans. Our conduct in the international arena was governed by the same rules and limits as the Americans' (Khrushchev: 1970, p. 496).

However, this cannot be divorced from the fact that, in the minds of the Soviet leadership, Soviet prestige had become inextricably linked to the fate of Cuba: 'One thought kept hammering away at my brain: what will happen if we lose Cuba? I knew it would be a terrible blow to Marxism-Leninism. It would gravely diminish our stature throughout the world, but especially in Latin America. If Cuba fell, other Latin American countries would reject us, claiming that for all our might, the Soviet Union hadn't been able to do anything for Cuba except to make empty protests to the United Nations' (Khrushchev: 1970, p. 493). To this extent, Khrushchev's strategy was partially successful. Although he did not achieve any recognition from the United States that the USSR was an 'equal' power, he did secure an American guarantee not to invade Cuba, which has diminished the spectre of how the Soviet Union would respond to such an event.

From the Cuban point of view, however, the missile crisis looked rather different. Castro subsequently admitted that he had been opposed to the removal of the missiles, and his adamant refusal to allow US inspections to be carried out on Cuban territory (despite Soviet pressure) testifies to the anger and resentment that he felt over the fact that matters which vitally affected Cuban sovereignty were settled without his knowledge or consent. A revealing passage from Khrushchev's memoirs, citing a letter written by the Soviet premier to Castro in late 1962, shows his complete insensitivity to the Cubans' wounded national pride and barely conceals his irritation at what he evidently believed to be ingratitude on Castro's part. He wrote:

The main point about the Caribbean crisis is that it has guaranteed the existence of a socialist Cuba. If Cuba had not undergone this ordeal, it is very likely that the Americans would have organised an invasion to liquidate Cuba's socialist way of life. Now that the climax of tension has passed and we have exchanged commitments with the American government, it will be very difficult for the Americans to interfere. If the United States should invade now, the Soviet Union will have the right to attack. Thus we have secured the existence of a socialist Cuba for at least another two years while Kennedy is in the White House. (Khrushchev: 1970, p. 504)

Whatever Castro's feelings at being addressed in such patronising tones, they were not made public. His speech of 1 November 1962 made references to 'some differences' between the two governments, but it was asserted that 'Nothing shall come between the Soviet Union and Cuba', and the emphasis was on the Soviet arms which had not been withdrawn rather than on the missiles which had (*Cuba Socialista*, no. 16, Dec. 1962, pp. 28–30, in Clissold: 1970, p. 276). The Cuban leader could not afford to allow anti-Soviet feeling to take a hold amongst the population. Castro is reported to have said in private that 'we shall not make the same mistake twice; we shall not break with the Russians after having broken with the Americans' (Suárez: 1967, p. 175).

Nevertheless, the Russians were left in no doubt that they had blundered in their relationship with Castro. At a post-crisis discussion between Mikoian and a State Department official, Mikoian was 'clearly influenced by commitments to Castro to make a strong case on Castro's behalf' and tried to establish the idea of a protocol signed by all three countries '[attaching] a good deal of significance to Cuba being one of the signatories'. The degree of pressure the Russians felt from Castro is indicated by the fact that in the course of this discussion Mikoian raised the possibility of the reciprocal inspection of territory ('and then we would not have any trouble with Castro on getting international inspection in Cuba'), and even mentioned Puerto Rico, although he can only have expected the immediately forthcoming flat refusal by the United States (Memorandum to the Secretary of State from Mr McCloy, 25 November 1962, *US Declassified*, 1985, 002292). In what was interpreted by the CIA and the Department of State as a post-missile crisis concession, the Soviet Union agreed to turn over control of all weapons systems within Cuba (including surface-to-air installations which could be used to shoot down US overflights).[7]

---

[7] 'CIA Memorandum for the Director – Cuba a year hence', 22 April 1963, *US Declassified*, 1985, 002293, and 'Memorandum for McGeorge Bundy from Llewellyn E. Thompson', Department of State, 19 March 1964, *US Declassified*, 1977, 221C.

Peter Bourne recounts how Carlos Rafael Rodríguez, visiting Moscow in December 1962 to negotiate an economic agreement for the following year, had lengthy private meetings with Khrushchev and Mikoian, at which they expressed their surprise at Fidel's reaction and gave assurance that there had been no intention to offend him. Khrushchev declared, 'Fidel is a son to me', to which Rodríguez replied, 'That is the mistake. Fidel is not your son. Fidel is the leader of the Cuban revolution and you have treated the Cuban revolution as a daughter of the Soviet revolution, which it is not, and Fidel as your son, which he is not. You have taken liberties that you can take with a son, but not with a leader' (Bourne: 1987, p. 243). The lavish reception afforded to Fidel Castro himself when he went to the Soviet Union the following year is well known, and it was during this visit that he was guaranteed economic concessions, notably a rise in the price paid for Cuban sugar. Thus there is every indication that the Cubans, stung by the ignominious discovery that Moscow's attitude towards dependent Third World allies was not significantly different from Washington's in the context of superpower relations, managed to extract significant compensation (both material and symbolic) for the slight.

It is also interesting to note that in the aftermath of the October Crisis both Castro and Kennedy sought to exploit the low point in Soviet–Cuban relations. William Attwood recounts how, as a member of the US delegation to the United Nations and a close associate of Kennedy, he received information in September 1963, both directly and indirectly, that Castro was interested in an accommodation with Washington. Exploratory discussions were pursued with chief Cuban delegate to the United Nations, Carlos Lechuga, and Dr René Vallejo, Castro's personal physician (Attwood: 1967, pp. 142–4). President Kennedy, interviewed by Jean Daniel of L'Exprès, hinted that the United States might be willing to make some concessions. Daniel passed this on to Fidel Castro on 23 November and the Cuban leader, who was apparently convinced of Kennedy's sincerity, expressed eagerness to pursue the dialogue. During the course of their meeting, however, news arrived of Kennedy's assassination the previous day, and what seems to have been primarily a personal initiative by the President was dropped.

By the end of 1962 Castro had sound economic reasons for sustaining Cuban links with the Soviet Union, apart from his security concerns. In 1961 and 1962 the USSR had provided virtually all of Cuba's oil imports and had purchased just under half of its sugar crop (Gouré and Rothenberg: 1975, p. 52). In addition, the Soviet Union and its East European allies had given large-scale economic aid to Cuban development projects. However, mutual dissatisfaction with the nature of this aid and the way it was administered had already given both sides cause to regret their commitment. The root of the problem lay in the fact that, having cut its links with the United States, Cuba 'was forced to graft itself onto a bloc which, apart from being totally different, was already afflicted with its own specific illnesses. The operation would at best have caused a great deal of pain, even if all those concerned had given proof of great foresight and clarity of mind; in the absence of both, it became a source of enormous waste and disappointments' (Karol: 1971, p. 225).

4   The Soviet–Cuban balancesheet

There are certain widespread assumptions about the nature of the Soviet–Cuban relationship. It is commonly held that, for the USSR, the economic burden of supporting Cuba will have been outweighed by the strategic and political advantages derived from the alliance. Castro, however, is thought to have preserved his revolution at the cost of economic dependence on and consequently political subservience to Moscow. With these premises in mind, the development of the relationship is frequently analysed in terms of Castro's attempting, after the disillusionment and humiliation of the 1962 Missile Crisis, to assert Cuban independence by challenging the revolutionary credentials of the Moscow-backed Latin American Communist parties and actively promoting the armed struggle, in direct contravention of the Moscow line. He is believed to have capitulated to the Kremlin's 1967 economic sanctions with his endorsement of the Soviet invasion of Czechoslovakia the following year, and a shelving of the policy of active support for guerrilla warfare. This resulted in a rapprochement with his Soviet benefactor which paved the way for Cuba's integration into the Soviet bloc when it joined Comecon in 1972. During the rest of the decade, it is argued, Castro's need to accommodate Moscow's wishes increased in direct proportion to the ever-growing volume of Soviet economic assistance to Cuba. Havana is perceived to have acted as a Soviet surrogate in, for example, the Angolan Civil War of 1974–5, the conflict between Ethiopia and Somalia over the Ogaden in 1978, the Non-Aligned Movement from 1979 to 1982 when Cuba held the Chair, and most recently in the intensifying Central American crisis.

A close examination of the course of events (apart from other, more circumstantial evidence) lends only partial support to the above schema. It is my contention that such a framework of analysis drastically oversimplifies the nature of the Soviet–Cuban alliance, and that all of its assumptions need to be re-examined carefully. The following chapter seeks to reassess the balancesheet of the Soviet–

Cuban connection from the points of view of both governments. From the conclusions drawn, the implications of Moscow's commitment to Havana for the overall development of Soviet–Latin American relations are discussed.

Strategic consequences

For the Soviet Union, the calculus of strategic gains from its alliance with Cuba is more balanced than is often suggested. The advantages (which since the late 1960s the USSR has had the conventional means to exploit) are greatly reduced by Cuba's vulnerability to US air power. As a result of an undertaking given by Khrushchev to Kennedy during the Cuban Missile Crisis, the Soviet Union has debarred itself from stationing offensive weapons in Cuba. To date Moscow has backed down when Washington has taken steps to enforce this (for example, in 1970, when the United States accused the USSR of building a submarine base at Cienfuegos).

The USSR has modern docks and repair facilities in Cuba, airport facilities for reconnaissance aircraft, satellite stations and sophisticated intelligence equipment for monitoring US satellite and microwave conversations, US ship and air movements, and advanced NATO weapons testing in the Atlantic (Valenta: 1983, p. 293). These base facilities enable the Soviet Union to deploy a naval presence in the region. The first Soviet squadron to penetrate Caribbean waters arrived in Havana in July 1969, and such visits have since continued on a regular basis. However, as James Theberge (who is not normally inclined to underestimate Soviet capabilities) pointed out in 1974, 'a Soviet naval deployment in the Caribbean is extremely vulnerable to American power' (Theberge: 1974, p. 69). It seems likely that the Soviet Union's naval activity in the area is intended to assert its global rights as a superpower (and to provide a counterweight to US deployments in the Mediterranean and the Indian Ocean), to test US reactions and to 'fly the Soviet flag' in Latin America. To quote Theberge again, all these activities are 'of greater potential political than military significance' (Theberge: 1974, p. 70).

In practice, then, the strategic advantage of Cuba is limited and is largely reducible to the highly potent symbolic significance of the crucial challenge to US power posed by the very existence of a Communist state only 90 miles from Florida. This must be weighed against the complications of deeper involvement and possible over-exposure. In exchange for Khrushchev's guarantee against the presence of offensive weapons in Cuba, Kennedy pledged that the United States would not take direct military action against the Castro regime. This partly contained the problem of how the Soviet Union would respond in the event of a US invasion of Cuba, but Khrushchev himself regarded the promise as binding only to the Kennedy administration. The sabre-rattling of Alexander Haig in 1981 suggests that a commitment made over two decades ago would be unlikely to deter the United States from launching an attack against Cuba if Washington felt that such action could be undertaken successfully with a containable level of diplomatic backlash. The Cubans themselves have recognised that the Soviet Union is unlikely to send its own troops to fight for the Cuban revolution. Moscow has not succumbed to Cuban pressure to be admitted to the Warsaw Pact (although Cuba does have political/military treaties of friendship and cooperation with the German Democratic Republic and with Vietnam – signed on 31 May 1980 and 19 October 1982 respectively).

Nevertheless, the Soviet Union has staked considerable prestige on the preservation of Cuban Communism and the losses attendant on any US overthrow of the revolutionary regime could hardly be overestimated. Because of this, Moscow has invested immense resources in the development of the Cuban armed forces into a significant deterrent in their own right. The weakness and incoherence of the Cuban army under Batista was one of the factors which facilitated Castro's seizure of power in 1959. From this negligible base, the Revolutionary Armed Forces have been transformed into a highly trained and effective body of 160,000 (with 190,000 reserves), which has proven itself in combat in Angola and Ethiopia. The Soviet Union has, however, limited its supplies to materiel sufficient to ensure that Cuba has a powerful defensive capability but a virtually non-existent offensive potential. For example, it lacks any significant amphibious assault or sea-lift capacity. Cuba also has an agreement with the Soviet Union to the effect that it will not ship weapons received for its own defence to other countries without Soviet agreement (Domínguez: 1984, p. 177). This probably reflects not only a Soviet desire to avoid unduly provoking the United States, but also the fact that Moscow's interest in containing Castro is not far short of Washington's.

For Cuba, the Soviet Union has provided an important (probably vital) shield but, as indicated above, Castro has never obtained the ultimate security guarantees which he sought. Indeed Cuba has no formal military alliance with the USSR. The 1962 Missile Crisis brought a recognition that at any critical juncture the USSR would subordinate its ties with Cuba to its relationship with the United States. It is clear that the Cubans, not without justification, see US invasion as a possible, albeit an improbable scenario.

Alignment with the Soviet Union has complicated Cuba's efforts to strengthen its security by other means: in the 1960s, by trying to spark off revolutions in other nations of the Western hemisphere and, in the 1970s, in the wake of the failure of *foquismo*, by normalising relations with as many nations as were willing, particularly in Latin America. This strategy worked fairly well in the detente climate of the early 1970s, but it became problematic as East–West tension heightened again in the late 1970s and early 1980s. The debt crisis weakened Latin American nations *vis-à-vis* the United States and made them less willing to challenge Washington on issues such as Cuba, although Havana's high-profile support for Argentina during the Falklands/ Malvinas war has had significant diplomatic pay-offs, particularly in the wake of democratisation in the Southern Cone. Uruguay opened trade and maritime links in June 1985 and restored full relations the following October. In July 1986 Brazil renewed relations and Alfonsín's Argentina has given a far higher profile to its links with Havana, including the granting of a $600 million export credit in 1985. In the Caribbean, however, where Cuba is in direct competition with the United States, Havana has seen the influence it won at the turn of the decade drastically cut back by the 1983 overthrow of Maurice Bishop in Grenada and the breaking of relations in October 1981 by Edward Seaga's Jamaica after the 1980 electoral defeat of reformist Michael Manley, with whom the Cubans had developed close ties. Most of the Caribbean nations proved more than ready to accept the condition of cutting links with Cuba attached to aid offered under President Reagan's Caribbean Basin Initiative. Thus Cuba's attempts to build a secure network of diplomatic and trading links, especially in Latin America, are subject to fluctuations in East–West tension over which Havana has minimal control.

Economic consequences

When, on the day of Khrushchev's fall from power in 1964, Mikhail Suslov told the Central Committee that the outgoing premier had been indiscriminate and profligate in the promises he had made to other nations (Steele: 1983, p. 163), he may well have had Cuba foremost in mind. The dictates of socialist internationalism precluded Brezhnev and his colleagues from abandoning the Castro revolution and for the rest of the decade they were obliged to continue subsidising an 'ally' which showed itself reluctant to toe the Soviet line either politically or economically. The rapprochement between the Soviet Union and Cuba which took place towards the end of the 1960s is often attributed primarily to political factors, namely the decline in Cuba's export of revolution and, most importantly, Castro's (qualified) endorsement of the 1968 invasion of Czechoslovakia.

However, I would argue that the real turning point (particularly for the Cubans) was the failure, two years later, of the famous attempt to produce a '10 million ton' sugar harvest. It was the severe dislocation of the whole Cuban economy caused, in 1970, by Castro's grandiose scheme, which led to a recognition within Cuba that previous economic policies had been unrealistic and that a more conventional approach, along Soviet-approved lines, was not merely desirable but essential. In July 1972 Cuba was granted full membership of Comecon (Council for Mutual Economic Aid), a move which helped to stabilise a hitherto uneasy relationship, and gave Moscow greater long-term influence over Cuba's internal organisation and policies, as reflected in the restructuring of the Cuban political apparatus which culminated in the adoption, in 1976, of a constitution drawing substantially on its Soviet predecessor.

This new-found accommodation was achieved only at a substantial price for the Soviet Union. In December 1972 five generous economic agreements were signed, which have since formed the basis of the Soviet–Cuban economic relationship. The USSR (1) raised the purchasing price of Cuba's two main exports, nickel and sugar; (2) promised technical aid, primarily for the sugar industry, but also to help in planning and electronic computation, to the value of 300 million rubles; (3) deferred payments of the Cuban debt for 1960–72 until 1986–2011 (at zero interest); (4) granted credits (at 2 per cent interest) to cover the expected Cuban trade deficit for 1973–5, repayments of which were also postponed until 1986; and (5) arranged for a new trade agreement covering 1973–5 (Mesa-Lago: 1978, p. 21). The 1970s saw a Soviet commitment to large-scale industrial projects – such as a steel plant and a petroleum refinery – which they had backed away from during the previous decade.

The costs to the USSR of this integration of the Cuban economy into the Soviet bloc can best be indicated by citation of the CIA estimate of cumulative Soviet economic assistance to Cuba. CIA calculations are based on official Cuban and Soviet trade data, and take into account balance of payments and trade and development aid (repayable), and subsidies of sugar, petroleum and nickel (grants, which are not subject to repayment) (Blasier: 1983, p. 21). It has been argued that there are several problems with this approach. Firstly, it uses the official peso/dollar and ruble/dollar exchange rates, which distort the value of soft currency; secondly, it ignores the fact that all subsidies are tied to trade with Comecon and, therefore, the Cubans are paying inflated prices for Soviet merchandise which could not be sold on the competitive world market; thirdly, it assumes that the value of the subsidy is the difference between the world market price and the subsidised price, whereas in the case of sugar (which accounts for roughly 70 per cent of total subsidies) only a small proportion (around 14 per cent) is actually sold at the world market price. Most importers, including the United States and the European Community, buy under a quota system which fixes the price substantially above the prevailing very low rates, although still well below the Soviet price.[1]

These points are all valid. Nevertheless it is interesting to note that, according to Tad Szulc, the CIA version is not disputed by Cuban officials (Szulc: 1986, p. 549). Whatever the precise situation, the CIA figures provide a useful indication of at least the pattern of Soviet input into the Cuban economy. This was calculated at $4.765 billion in 1972 (around $400 million per annum during 1961–71). It increased steadily throughout the 1970s to reach a total of $16.66 billion in 1979 ($600 million per year in 1972, 1973 and 1974, $1 billion in 1975, $1.5 billion in 1976, $2 billion in 1977 and $3 billion in 1978 and 1979). Since then it has been at the level of $4 billion per annum, reflecting the rapidly rising energy and technology requirements of Cuba's desire to industrialise, a strategy that apparently emerged as an issue of friction before the June 1984 Comecon summit took place, which Castro did not attend (Duncan: 1985, p. 198). If so, the Cubans must have argued their case well for, in October 1984, a new agreement on economic cooperation was signed, involving substantial industrial projects and extending until the year 2000. April 1986 rescheduling arrangements have postponed repayments of Cuba's estimated $10 billion debt to the Soviet Union until 1990, and 2.5 billion rubles worth of new credits were granted for the period 1986–90, representing a 50 per cent increase over the previous five-year period. On this basis, Soviet economic assistance to Cuba over the period 1961–79 not only

[1] These arguments were presented by Andrew Zimbalist and supported by Claes Brundenius during a seminar at the Latin American Studies Association conference in New Orleans, 18 March 1988. For a detailed survey of the literature on the issue of the extent of the Soviet sugar subsidy, see Pérez-López: 1988.

exceeded total Soviet economic aid to all non-Communist developing countries, but was also greater than official US aid to Israel. It was running at approximately half of Soviet aid to Vietnam (which has a population over five times greater than Cuba's), and was roughly comparable to Soviet assistance to Mongolia, with a population of 1.7 million.

In addition to this massive economic input, the USSR has also provided military aid (free of charge up to 1971; current arrangements are not known). Accurate figures for this are not available, but clearly the total must be exceptionally high given that Cuba now has one of the largest and best-equipped forces in Latin America. Cole Blasier states that in 1979 Cuba took 5 per cent of Soviet trade, and Soviet aid to Cuba was equivalent to 25 per cent of the island's GNP (Blasier: 1983, p. 117 and p. 123). This level of commitment is probably greater than the Soviet economy can sustain comfortably, and is certainly far beyond what the Soviet Union can have envisaged in 1960. US State Department analysts considered that Moscow's provision of balance of payments relief and consumer goods shipments to Cuba during 1962 and 1963 was seen by the Kremlin as 'emergency assistance' to act as 'a temporary palliative', and that 'the USSR appears hopeful the island can be set on the road to economic recovery in a few years' (CIA memorandum for the Director – Cuba a year hence, 22 April 1963, *US Declassified*, 1985, 002293, p. 11).

Indeed, disillusionment with their new-found economic relationship came swiftly to both parties, setting in as early as 1962. The Soviet Union had not been warned, and could not have been expected to foresee, that the Cuban economy had been so dependent upon the United States that even technical faults at factories had to be sorted out by means of a telephone call to the American parent company. The adjustment process was not helped by the fact that, particularly in the sugar industry, much of the existing equipment was obsolete. Most of Cuba's sugar processing plants had been built during the nineteenth century. Thus the incoming Soviet advisers were faced with immediate and pressing technical problems, exacerbated by the fact that the two countries employed different systems of measurement. Soviet economic planners found themselves confronted with a chronic shortage not only of trained personnel but also of any reliable data upon which to base their calculations. One East European adviser to JUCEPLAN (the Central Planning Board) complained that:

We were asked to establish the maximum growth rate of an economy, without being given exact information about its productive capacity, the availability of labour, the mineral resources, the possibility of replacing sugar cane with new crops – in short, without any information . . . No other developing country gave us so much trouble . . . In Cuba, people expected miracles. Everyone felt entitled to throw up his hands in indignation when an inexperienced engineer failed to make quick repairs to an automatic cable in the nickel factory, or when some agricultural expert was unable, on the spot, to pick the ideal place for starting the cultivation of something that had never been grown in this climate. (Anonymous source, in Karol: 1971, p. 228)

Indeed, as can be inferred from the above, the Cubans were by no means ready to fall down in gratitude before their Soviet benefactors (despite the fact that, as Castro has subsequently acknowledged, it is unlikely that he could have prevented the collapse of the Cuban economy if it had not been for Moscow's support). They complained, with justification, that the industrial equipment and raw materials provided by the Soviet bloc were of inferior quality and in any case not adaptable to their US-designed and built industrial plant. Former president of the Cuban Planning Board (JUCEPLAN), Regino Botí, confirmed that the necessity of switching from US to Soviet bloc supplies caused problems in all sectors of the economy:

No sooner had we filled one breach, then we had to face a far more serious one in another sector. Our public transport system – buses, trains, trucks – ran short of spare parts, which could only be found in the United States. We tried to put Russian engines into General Motors buses, but without success; we would also have had to change the automatic transmissions for Russian manual ones. (Karol: 1971, p. 225)

It appears that many of the Soviet experts who came to help the Cubans plan their economy were over-optimistic about Cuba's development prospects and, due to a lack of understanding about the Cuban situation, irresponsible in their allocation of resources. As a result, many hasty and indiscriminate orders for equipment and raw materials were placed, which led to inefficiency and waste when it was discovered that these goods could not be used in Cuban factories. In Spring 1963 the White House stated that 'bloc aid for economic development [in Cuba] is still largely in the planning stage. It has yet to have an effect in helping to restore the economic momentum lost in the revolution' ('Current situation in Cuba', White House document, 21 April 1963, US Declassified, 1980, 322A).

It should be noted, however, that Soviet officials were not the only people to be misled by the relatively good economic results of the first two years of the revolution and the bumper 6.2 million tonne sugar harvest in 1961. Many outside experts who came to advise the new

Cuban regime shared the view that 'Cuba is a country with absolutely exceptional agricultural possibilities . . . within a relatively few years (generally from 10 to 12), it will be possible to multiply the production of many commodities by a factor of 3, 4, 5 or even more, without any great investment effort' (Charles Bettelheim, 'Memorandum sobre la planificación económica en Cuba', 19 September 1960, in Huberman and Sweezy: 1961, p. 198). In 1961 annual growth rates of 10–15 per cent were being predicted for the next decade. For example, the Polish economist Michal Kalecki projected an annual 13 per cent increase in gross material product from 1961 to 1965 in his 'Hypothetical outline of the Five Year Plan 1961–5 for the Cuban Economy' (Brundenius: 1984, p. 47). Regino Botí, head of the newly created JUCEPLAN, told a National Production Conference in August 1961 that Cuba was counting on growth rates in total material production from 1962 to 1965 of 'not less than 10 per cent (per year) and probably not more than 15.5 per cent' (Boorstein: 1968, p. 93). This was despite the fact that by spring 1961 shortages of basic goods such as toothpaste and soft drinks were already evident. Brundenius believes that 'There was a basic assumption that rapid socialisation of the means of production coupled with sophisticated planning techniques would be a sufficient panacea for the problems. Probably there was also the widespread idea that there were almost endless untapped reserves in both agriculture and industry' (Brundenius: 1984, pp. 48–9). What the Cubans, who were accustomed to Western-standard consumer goods, were really complaining about was the fact that, just at a time when they were optimistic that unprecedentedly high living standards were within reach, they were having to adapt to inferior quality merchandise which, moreover, did not come cheaply.

Some twenty-five years later, the Cubans still have their grievances. The technical problems resulting from the attempt to reorientate an entire economy away from Western goods to Eastern bloc supplies are by no means fully resolved. Castro has made little secret of the fact that he would like to be in a position to import more Western machinery and equipment, and indeed this has been acknowledged to be crucial if Cuban development is to proceed as planned. It is likely that a Cuban agency, Transimport, exists for the specific purpose of clandestinely importing US spare parts. One observer writes 'The importance of American goods and the potential profit involved is perhaps indicated by the fact that items of significant weight, such as diesel engines, have been shipped from the US to Rotterdam and then back across the Atlantic to Cuba' (Losman: 1979, p. 29). When sugar prices fell further than anticipated in 1976, twenty-two major investment projects had to be cancelled, most of which relied on credit lines from the West (Mesa-Lago: 1978, p. 46). In the previous two years, when high sugar prices enabled Cuba to earn increased supplies of foreign exchange, there was a marked decline in imports from the Soviet Union of agricultural and industrial machinery, transportation and construction equipment, foodstuffs and chemicals, and a corresponding increase in the purchase of such goods in Western markets (Mesa-Lago: 1981, p. 91 and p. 99). Cuba also took full advantage of the greater availability of Western credit lines during the late 1970s to finance similar orders. The importance of such imports is implicitly acknowledged by Moscow in its readiness to allow Cuba to sell sugar from its Soviet quota on the free market when prices are high.

One striking example of the persistent failure of Soviet goods to meet Cuban needs is in the mechanisation of the sugar harvest. In a recent study of Soviet attempts to assist in this process, Charles Edquist suggests that the 'inherent deficiencies' of the Soviet-supplied cane-cutting machines were a significant factor in the failure of the 1970 '10-million-ton' harvest. Their appalling productivity resulted in the need to deploy large numbers of 'voluntary' labourers, causing severe dislocation amongst all other sectors of the Cuban economy. Edquist also concludes that these problems remain, despite the introduction in the 1970s of a newly developed cane-cutting machine, and that 'there is still a technology gap between Cuba and producers of combine harvesters in industrialised countries' (Edquist: 1983, p. 50). What is more, he adds, that although this gap 'decreased considerably during the first fifteen years of efforts in harvester design and production . . . recently it has increased, and will continue to do so unless Cuba manages to design and manufacture more efficient machines in the near future' (Edquist: 1983, pp. 62–3). A 1985 Soviet publication stated that 'work is underway to improve and update the KTP-1 sugar cane harvester', the inference being that all is not yet well (Rodríguez Llompart (Minister-Chairman of the State Committee for Economic Cooperation, Cuba): 1985, p. 23). In 1983 it was reported that Cuba needed to import $130-million-worth of spare parts a year from the West for its sugar industry, either because they were not available in the socialist countries or because their quality was too poor. Apparently a Soviet-made chain for a sugar harvester has a working life of one year while a Western-made one lasts for three.

Problems have also emerged in the development of Cuba's second major export industry, nickel. Soviet technology has not found it easy to cope with the refining of Cuba's laterite deposits, which have a low nickel content and require a far more energy-intensive extraction process than the more common sulfide ores (Moran: 1979, p. 205). These cannot be considered mere teething troubles which have now been overcome. In 1986 it was reported that the newest Soviet-built nickel smelter at Punta Gorda (scheduled to have been commissioned in 1985) will not be up to capacity until 1990, and that a second plant at Las Camariocas (planned to become operational in 1992) was likely to be similarly delayed. Clearly there is no hope of meeting the target of 100,000 tonnes of nickel by 1992 (the 1985 figure was 33,400 tonnes) (*Latin America Regional Report: Caribbean*, 28 August 1986, p. 8; *The Financial Times*, 3 November 1986, p. 38).

Thus it is clear that integration with the Eastern bloc has proved far from optimal for the Cuban economy. The modernisation of Cuba's sugar and nickel industries has been severely hampered by the necessity of operating with Soviet equipment, and the fact that the Cubans seize every possible chance to ensure Western cooperation with other industrial projects suggests that similar problems have arisen throughout the Cuban economy. Moreover the centralised management of foreign trade has proved difficult to administer partly because of 'the low priority afforded Cuba by its CMEA trade partners' (Theriot: 1982, p. 70).

It is often suggested that a further significant disadvantage of Havana's commitment to supply the Eastern bloc is that Cuba is unable to capitalise on favourable changes in the world market price of sugar, except with a small percentage of its crop. It should be borne in mind, however, firstly that the price paid by the Soviet Union for Cuban sugar has been higher (since 1976, considerably so) than the world market price every year except for 1963, 1972 and 1974. Secondly, since the Cuban revolution the world sugar market has experienced an expansion in production coupled with a contraction of demand. One of the main reasons for the adverse trend is that the EEC transformed itself during the 1960s and 1970s from a net importer of sugar to a net exporter of over 4 m.t. per year since 1980. Moreover, the EEC has remained outside the International Sugar Organisation, greatly reducing that body's capacity to control the market and ensure profitable production. Cuban sugar exports to the EEC countries were reduced from over 800,000 tonnes in 1954–8 to about 460,000 tonnes in 1959–63 and 160,000 tonnes in 1964–8. They were eliminated altogether by 1981 (UNCTAD: 1982, p. 5). Although Japan is still a net importer of sugar it has developed a protected sugar industry, increased purchases from Australia and South Africa, and dramatically reduced Cuban imports. By 1985 a huge and growing world oversupply led to a real crisis in the sugar market, with sugar prices at their lowest for fifteen years (just over 3 cents per pound – a quarter of the level generally considered profitable). All analysts were agreed that production cutbacks were the only route to a more healthy market, since there were few signs that relief would come on the demand side. Cuba is currently aiming to increase its sugar production to 12 million tonnes by 1990. It is hard to see how this strategy could be pursued successfully in the current climate without the guarantee of greater demand from Comecon. The socialist countries are reported to pay in convertible currency for any sugar bought outside the terms of their multilateral agreements with Havana (*Latin America Weekly Report* (henceforth *LAWR*), WR-83-18, 13 May 1983, p. 8). Moreover, as indicated above, in more recent years the USSR has allowed Cuba to redirect sugar committed to the Eastern bloc on to the open market when prices are favourable (although since the USSR has sustained its role as a sugar exporter the two countries are then in competition).

Another frequent assertion is that Cuban development has been hindered by an increasing trade dependency and a continued reliance on sugar as its major export commodity and that this model, with its 'colonialist' overtones, has been imposed on Cuba by the Soviet Union. The first point to make in relation to this is that it is notoriously difficult to arrive at any reliable conclusions about the role and composition of trade in the Cuban economy because of the difficulties of undertaking statistical analysis for an economy which has only begun to produce comprehensive figures relatively recently, and because of the problems involved in taking into account the subsidised prices paid by the Soviet Union. Two authoritative analysts of the Cuban economy have arrived at diametrically opposed conclusions by taking different points of comparison. Carmelo Mesa-Lago claims that there was an increase in Cuba's trade dependency in the 1970s, whilst William Leogrande asserts that Cuba began to escape the export economy pattern during that decade. Claes Brundenius argues that both of these calculations are flawed in that they are based on price indicators, which inevitably fluctuate without relation to structural changes within the Cuban economy. I would accept his argument that a more accurate indication of structural economic development within Cuba is obtained by analysing volume of exports in relation to GDP. On this basis, he contends that 'although there was a definite rise in trade dependency between 1965 and 1970, there was a definite reduction in the trade dependency after 1970 – and the reduction was probably significant in relation to 1958' (Brundenius: 1984, p. 63). This would seem to reflect the information we have about the drive to increase sugar production from 1965 to 1970, and about the wide variety of industrial projects which the Soviet Union has been sponsoring in Cuba since the mid-1970s. An UNCTAD report to the government of Cuba in 1982 agreed that 'Efforts made to diversify exports during the 1970s enjoyed considerable success' and confirmed that progress was being made in developing Cuba's steel, manufacturing and food processing industries (UNCTAD: 1982, p. 19 and p. 22).

It is important to bear these assessments in mind when trying to determine to what extent the USSR has imposed a model of development on Cuba. I would argue that throughout the 1960s the Cubans evolved their economic policy with a stubborn independence (to the extent of failing to draw on the rich experience of 1920s Soviet Russia in addressing many of the problems that Cuba faced) and that the adoption of Soviet-style policies after 1970 was a result of a Cuban recognition that their alternative model had failed. From 1963 to 1966 Cuba, politically disillusioned with the USSR after the Missile Crisis and (as described above) unenthusiastic about the results of Soviet-style planning, underwent a period of experimentation with alternative economic models and development strategies. The debate, the polemics of which were published in journals such as *Cuba Socialista*, *Nuestra Industria* and *Comercio Exterior*, focused on many of the issues (for example, the implications of moral versus material incentives, the role of the state in the process of accumulation) which caused such controversy in the aftermath of the Soviet revolution, which were extensively discussed in China – particularly during the economic crisis that emerged in the wake of the 1958–9 Great Leap Forward – and which have to be hammered out by any government trying to build a socialist society. With reference to the role of sugar, an inter-ministerial committee set up at the end of 1962 to examine supply and balance of payments problems found that it was impossible to squeeze imports any further and that the solution therefore had to be found in exports. By 1964 'Nobody seemed to question any longer that a renewed reliance on sugar to provide the necessary foreign exchange for the importation of capital goods would be the best road toward accumulation. The focus of the debate in Cuba was on the implications of this strategy rather than on the strategy itself' (Brundenius: 1984, p. 53).

Thus it was a Cuban decision to concentrate the resources of their economy on the development of sugar production (albeit with the guarantee provided by the 1964 agreement for the supply of sugar to the Eastern bloc). The outcome of the debate was the rejection, in 1966, of the Soviet-style policies favoured by Carlos Rafael Rodríguez and other former members of the PSP, and the adoption of strategies propounded by Che Guevara (moral incentives as the most effective way of increasing production, a budgetary system of financing state enterprise rather than the self-management system used in the USSR and Eastern Europe), 'embellished with personalistic Castroite features' (Mesa-Lago: 1978, p. 9).

The case most frequently cited by those who argue that the USSR's economic leverage over Cuba is such that it can automatically induce political compliance is that of the 1967–8 slowdown in oil shipments. There is the famous remark of Soviet official Rudolf Shliapnikov, Second Secretary at the embassy in Havana, to the effect that in the event of serious disagreement all the Soviet government had to do was to tell the Cubans that repairs were going to be carried out at Baku for three weeks. The source of this remark is, it should be noted, the Cuban official newspaper, *Granma*. Clearly, Moscow's position as sole supplier of oil, not to mention any other aspects of its involvement, gives the Kremlin significant scope for the application of economic sanctions (witness the increasing desperation of the Nicaraguans in mid-1987 before they secured a Soviet commitment to renew oil shipments).

Nevertheless, when in 1967–8 the Soviet Union opted to exploit this leverage, Castro launched a successful propaganda campaign to maximise the political costs of Moscow's decision. His strategy consisted of (1) fully publicising the sanctions in order to denounce the USSR's lack of 'proletarian internationalism'; and (2) compounding this attack by demonstrating (with the trial of Aníbal Escalante and the 'microfaction' who were accused of conspiring to enhance Soviet influence within Cuba) that the Soviet Union was exploiting its relationship with Cuba in political as well as economic terms. As Carmelo Mesa-Lago points out, the illegal activities of the group reached a peak in July 1967; Castro waited six months to make the accusation, choosing the moment when he was acknowledging difficulties in petroleum supplies (Mesa-Lago: 1971). In February 1968 he also refused Moscow's request to send Cuban representation to the Budapest meeting of Communist parties convened by the Soviet Union to enlist support for a crusade against Beijing.

Castro's qualified endorsement of the 1968 Soviet invasion of Prague can be explained primarily in terms of Cuba's own security interests and Fidel's personal distrust of Dubcek-style socialism. Given that Cuba had consistently argued that the Soviet Union should come to the defence of socialism in Vietnam and, by implication, in Cuba if it became necessary, Castro would have completely undermined his own bid for Soviet support if he had denied Moscow's right to defend what it defined as socialism in a country which it regarded with far greater strategic concern. Indeed he used the fact that Brezhnev had sent troops into Czechoslovakia to apply further pressure for a Soviet military commitment to Cuba, as for example in the following speech: 'Will Warsaw Pact troops also be sent to Vietnam if the Yankee imperialists step up their aggression against that country . . . Will they send the divisions of the Warsaw Pact to Cuba if the Yankee imperialists attack our country, or even in the case of the threat of a Yankee imperialist attack on our country, and if our country requests it?' (*Granma Weekly Review*, 25 August 1968, in Robbins: 1985, p. 172). As Carla Robbins points out, at that time 'almost every major Cuban policy statement – whether a critique of Soviet policies in Vietnam or an endorsement of Soviet policies in Czechoslovakia – included a reminder of Soviet responsibilities for Cuba's defence' (Robbins: 1985, p. 186).

By that stage, Castro had exhausted the potential of the China card, which he had played quite effectively earlier in the 1960s to exercise leverage on Moscow. Following the Cuban Missile Crisis, during which Beijing staunchly backed Castro's stand, much play was made upon Sino–Cuban solidarity and Castro made serious attempts to cement links with China. Relations deteriorated after 1965 when the Chinese, because of their own shortages, refused to fulfil commitments to supply Cuba with rice and, by 1967, the hostility between the two nations was such that Cuba was in effect undergoing sanctions from China as well as the USSR and the USA.

Fundamental political realities could not be ignored, and the fact that Cuba was suffering Soviet economic sanctions at the time was probably of limited relevance to Castro's decision. (Indeed, there was no immediate resolution of the delivery problems, and the Cubans were still suffering from inadequate oil supplies until the end of the year [Szulc: 1986, p. 505].) The Cuban leader has since endorsed the Vietnamese invasion of Cambodia, despite the fact that the action was in clear violation of the principles of territorial integrity that Cuba maintained had been the basis of its support for Ethiopia's claim to the Ogaden, the Soviet invasion of Afghanistan (albeit almost a year after it took place) and the 1981 imposition of martial law in Poland. All these expressions of support have been given at no little cost to Cuba's own position within the Non-Aligned Movement; nevertheless it is almost certain that basic security considerations will result in a similar alignment in the future.

Concerning the issue of Cuba's turn away from the support of armed struggle in Latin America, it is hardly surprising that Che Guevara's 1967 death in the Bolivian jungle should have led to a reappraisal of a policy which had failed so spectacularly. Moreover the late 1960s presented several previously non-existent opportunities for Cuba to break out of its diplomatic isolation in Latin America, with the coming to power of reformist military governments in Peru and, more briefly, in Bolivia and Ecuador.

Castro's endorsement of the Soviet invasion of Czechoslovakia had no effect whatsoever on the economic policies of the Cuban government: 1968 was the year of the 'Revolutionary Offensive' (an attempt to eradicate the last vestiges of private enterprise in Cuba in order to promote a mass socialist consciousness), and the mobilisation for the 1970s harvest was on the basis of the moral incentives appropriate to the 'New Man'.

In the aftermath of the failure to achieve the 10-million-ton target Castro managed to salvage his reputation in Cuba by undertaking stringent self-criticism, in the course of which he held out the promise of increased mass participation in the development of the economy. As the implementation of a Soviet model proceeded from 1972 to 1976 there were accusations that Castro had once again 'betrayed' his people by sacrificing stated aims to the dictates of Moscow. However, in terms of Castro's political style and philosophy, there was no inconsistency in his 1971 promises of greater mass participation and his subsequent setting up of Soviet-style trade unions and a structure of 'Organs of People's Power' which, although constitutionally supreme, in fact have very little input into decision-making. Examination of Castro's speeches and writings reveals that for him democracy implies participation, but it does not imply control. It provides a channel for criticising, but not for challenging, the established system. One only has to look at the development of the 1960s Committees for the Defence of the Revolution – locally based organisations which could potentially have become the focus of genuine self-representation but which were gradually confined to the functions of a kind of voluntary social work such as ensuring that everybody had their vaccinations on time (apart from providing a convenient means of monitoring revolutionary commitment) – to appreciate that Castroism is essentially paternalistic and anti-democratic.

Thus the Cuban decision to integrate their economy into the Socialist bloc was a result not of Soviet pressure but of a belated recognition that they could not go it alone. Given that further substantial investment was necessary to realise their development plans and, indeed, to sustain the island's economy – resources which in Cuba's political predicament could only be obtained from the Soviet Union – the best option available was to achieve a position in which maximum benefit could be derived from an alliance which had become unavoidable. Fidel Castro has said:

> We are Latin Americans . . . in the future we should integrate ourselves with Latin America . . . But for there to be economic integration and political integration there must be a social and anti-imperialist revolution in Latin America . . . However, this will take time. We cannot make plans looking to an integration that may take . . . thirty years . . . In the meantime, what are we to do, a small country, surrounded by capitalists, blockaded by the Yankee imperialists? We will integrate ourselves economically with the socialist camp. (Matthews: 1975, p. 398)

There is no doubt that Moscow enjoys far greater influence and control over adjustments in Cuban economic policy now that Cuban planning is integrated with overall Comecon strategy than it did in the 1960s. Nevertheless, as has already been indicated, the economic price has been high. It is often implied that Cuba's entry into Comecon indicated Havana's acquiescence to a long-standing Soviet desire to incorporate Cuba into the Eastern bloc. The evidence suggests, however, that the decision was the product of far more complicated negotiations. It is important to bear in mind that in 1971–2 the Soviet assessment of the advantages of its relationship with Cuba must have been more negative than it perhaps is today. Throughout the 1960s Havana had clashed with Moscow on ideological issues (see pages 113–4), a dispute which stymied the Soviet Union's attempts to cultivate trade and diplomatic ties in the rest of Latin America. The advantages which the USSR derived from Cuba's presence in Africa could not have been foreseen. Cuba's consistently poor economic performance undermined its credibility as a model for other developing nations and proved an embarrassment to Moscow. Moreover, the Soviet Union has paid often disregarded opportunity costs for its maintenance of the Cuban economy.

Firstly, there is the fact that the USSR could have obtained valuable foreign exchange by selling the oil it supplies to Cuba on the open market. (Attempts to penetrate the Brazilian market with offers of Soviet oil have been dogged by the fact that Soviet production is not always high enough to enable it to be a reliable supplier beyond its commitments to other socialist states.) Secondly, the sheer distances involved in conveying goods between the two countries meant that the basic trading relationship proved expensive and vulnerable to developments over which Moscow had little or no control.

The initial problems involved in delivering oil to Cuba were exacerbated by two factors. In the first place there was an attempt by the Western oil companies, who own much of the world's tanker fleet and are customers to the rest, to organise a boycott. This might well have succeeded were it not for a deep slump in oil freight rates due to the overbuilding which followed the 1956 Suez Crisis.

Furthermore, immediately after the 1962 missile crisis the United States declared that any vessel which had carried goods to or from Cuba, North Vietnam or China would be ineligible for bunkering facilities at US ports. In 1965 Soviet shipping minister Bakaev made an explicit connection between the substantial increases in Soviet merchant shipping tonnage which occurred between 1962 and 1965 (see table 1) and the imposition of the US blockade. He stated that 'if there were no discrimination against us we would give it another thought before embarking on this build-up of the merchant navy', for it would be both easier and cheaper to hire British ships (in Fairhall: 1971, p. 132). As one observer has pointed out, many of the orders which accounted for the increases in 1962 and 1963 must have been placed before the missile crisis (Hanson: 1970, p. 48). It is clear that the Soviet Union was in any case intent upon an expansion of its fleet, both to ensure the independence of Soviet trade and because they saw potential for earning hard currency by competing for charters with Western shipping. Nevertheless, the US blockade must have acted as a vital incentive to accelerate the programme.

In the light of these developments it is worth considering the background to the slowdown of shipments of Soviet oil to Cuba in 1967–8. This has been widely interpreted as Soviet retaliation for having found itself compromised as a result of Castro's manoeuvres at the 1966 Tri-continental Conference in Havana (see pages 113–4). There is little doubt that Soviet leaders were incensed by this humiliation (which succeeded a whole series of economic and political disputes with the Cubans) and that economic sanctions were one of the most powerful weapons available for applying pressure on the unrepentant Cuban regime. There may, however, have been an element of making

Table 1. *Soviet merchant shipping: tonnage by flag*

Year	Tonnage
1939	1154
1956	2140
1957	2412
1958	2654
1959	2768
1960	3266
1961	3254
1962	3572
1963	4207
1964	5694
1965	7455
1966	8218
1967	9113
1968	9843

Source: Hanson, 1970, p. 45.

a virtue out of necessity. The USSR's oil export programme, which had expanded substantially into the mid-1960s, ran into difficulties by 1967 because of a slowdown in domestic production. Exports, which had increased nearly threefold from 1955 to 1959, and by well over 100 per cent from 1960 to 1964, rose by only 7.1 per cent in 1967 and 9.4 per cent in 1968 (Klinghoffer: 1977, pp. 69–70). Thus the Soviet Union was able to take only minimal advantage of the 1967 Arab oil embargo: in 1968 Soviet oil exports to Western states fell to 32 m.t. from 34 m.t. in 1967 (Klinghoffer: 1977, p. 70). Thus Castro was asking for more oil (he wanted a 10 per cent increase in 1968 imports and received only 2 per cent) at a time when the closure of the Suez Canal was causing transport problems not only in supplies to Cuba, but also to Vietnam. Additionally, Moscow could have earned valuable foreign currency if it had been in a position to free more oil to sell on the world market.

Keeping Cuba supplied with oil obviously presented a major challenge to the Soviet Union, and it is one which overall has been met with an impressive degree of success. In 1969 Radio Moscow announced that on average 60–65 vessels were in transit between the USSR and Cuba at any given moment, and the same broadcast stated that in 1968 Soviet vessels had made a total of 1,600 voyages to Cuba. Most produce destined for Cuba is shipped from Black Sea ports, but at the end of 1968 the USSR built a special oil jetty at the Crimean port of Feodosiia to facilitate the loading of tankers to Havana (Radio

Moscow, 14 February 1969, in Gouré and Weinkle: 1972, p. 75). By 1972 150 medium-sized tankers (i.e., approximately one tanker every other day) were needed to supply Cuba with oil. Inevitably the industrialisation which occurred in Cuba during the 1970s has required even greater supplies. The general trend is clear from the fact that by 1976 Cuban oil consumption was 200 per cent higher than in 1972, and by 1980 it had doubled again. Most Soviet ports are not equipped to handle the 200,000–300,000 ton tankers used by Western oil companies. The first Soviet supertanker, of 150,000 tons, was due to be built in the early 1970s, but is too large to be accommodated by Cuban ports. In October 1986, however, an agreement was announced whereby the Soviet Union is to finance a $30 million project for a French and a Yugoslavian company to build suitable docking facilities at Matanzas (*The Financial Times*, 29 October 1986, p. 4). Additional problems were anticipated in 1982 because of the likely coming into effect of an International Agreement on Environmental Protection specifying that petroleum and its products must be carried in large tonnage oil tankers, necessitating 'the reconstruction of Cuban ports and their oil-distribution schemes' (Burmistrov: 1982, p. 11).

Various initiatives by the Soviet Union indicate its concern at the expense of conveying oil to Cuba, and at the fact that most of the tankers return home in ballast. In 1969, for example, Soviet ships carried 7.8 m.t. of cargo to Cuba, including 5.6 m.t. of oil, but brought back only 1.3 m.t. worth (Moscow Maritime Press Service, 25 March 1970, in Gouré and Weinkle: 1972, p. 75). During his 1974 visit to Cuba, Brezhnev is reported to have asked the Cubans to reduce oil imports from the Soviet Union by importing from other Latin American countries (the *New York Times*, 22 January 1974, p. 6). In the early 1970s Soviet shipping authorities attempted to charter their tankers to oil companies operating in Venezuela for voyages to European countries, but Caracas was not receptive to this. Around the same time, an American oil company was offered Soviet tankers at low voyage charter rates, again to carry oil from Venezuela to Europe. The offer was rejected, apparently on the basis that to accept it would contravene US policy as dictated by the 1962 blockade.

In the wake of the July 1975 OAS decision that its members should be free to ignore the 1964 sanctions against Cuba, Moscow has undertaken several other initiatives aimed at cutting its transportation costs to Cuba. In 1978 an apparently promising deal was arranged whereby the Mexicans were to supply oil to Cuba (paid for by the

USSR) in return for which the Soviet Union was to fulfil Mexico's contracts in Spain. The first tanker carrying oil to Cuba from Mexico was originally scheduled to leave the Gulf port of Tuxpan on the same day, 17 May 1978, that President López Portillo flew in to Moscow on a state visit. However, a few days before the President's departure Zairean rebels operating from Angola invaded the province of Shaba. Washington promptly accused Cuba of involvement in the internal affairs of Zaire, and applied pressure on the Mexicans to ensure that the tanker failed to leave for Havana. Mexican Trade and Industry Minister José Andrés de Oteyza and Pemex director Jorge Díaz Serrano insisted that the deal was still on and that the difficulties were limited to the problems of settling on a price that all four countries could accept, since Cuba pays less than the world price for Soviet oil. Speculation suggested that such difficulties were merely convenient in view of Washington's deteriorating relations with Havana and Moscow. In any case, the deal can have only a limited impact on Cuban supply problems because the Mexicans are reluctant to furnish more than a very small part of Cuba's needs, for fear of entering into a closer relationship than they would wish to have with Havana. In late 1984 an agreement was reached whereby Soviet ships on voyages to Cuba would call at Mexican ports to pick up cargo to avoid returning home in ballast, but trade with Mexico is still relatively insignificant and it is unlikely that this arrangement will apply to more than a small percentage of trips to Cuba.

In 1978 a similar oil-swap was concluded – and went into effect – by which Venezuela sent 20,000 b.p.d. to Cuba in exchange for Soviet deliveries to refineries at Geselkirchen in West Germany, which are jointly owned by Petróleos de Venezuela and the German state company Veba. This agreement has, however, proved to be fallible. It lapsed in 1982, when the differences between Venezuela's OPEC-determined prices and those of the Soviet Union made the deal uneconomical for Venezuela's customers, although it was renewed again in August 1983.

In 1972 Cuba was still heavily dependent on Soviet vessels for the transportation of the bulk of its foreign trade, and although the tonnage of the Cuban merchant marine increased tenfold from 1958 to 1975 to make it the fourth largest merchant fleet in Latin America, in 1975 it still carried only 10 per cent of the island's trade. Even if expansion plans had been met, this figure would have risen to only 13–15 per cent by 1980 (Mesa-Lago: 1981, p. 100). In addition, Cuba is notorious for its inadequate port and storage facilities (a legacy of its former dependence on nearby United States ports): queues of ships waiting to unload at Havana Bay at times number as many as thirty, and similarly lengthy delays are involved in moving cargo off the docks to its final destination. In 1980 it was estimated that about $250 million was being lost annually because of this inefficiency. Soviet officials have stated unequivocally that: 'Any further increase in mutual trade volume depends directly on the capacities of the merchant fleet and the port facilities of the Soviet Union and Cuba' (Burmistrov: 1982, p. 11). It was not until early 1981 that plans for comprehensive modernisation were announced. Not surprisingly, Soviet technicians are said to have played a major part in helping the Cubans to pinpoint the main problems.

Perhaps because of the difficulties involved in making satisfactory alternative arrangements for the supply of oil to Havana, the Soviet Union has also invested heavily in oil and gas prospecting in Cuba, aiming to increase Cuban oil production from 270,000 tons in 1980 to 700,000–800,000 by 1985. In 1981 construction began on an atomic power station designed to save over 1.5 m.t. of petroleum products per year (Ryabov: 1984, p. 6).

In the light of its experiences with Cuba Moscow has not so far shown itself willing to admit any other developing nation to Comecon (with the exception of Vietnam, which joined in 1978) although it is known that Mozambique, and probably Ethiopia as well, have been pressing for the privileges of full membership. (The security advantage of an alliance with Vietnam is clearly so great as to be an overriding factor in this decision and, moreover, the opportunity costs are far less significant than in the cases of Cuba or the African nations.)

The Kremlin's calculation in 1972 was probably that political and ideological constraints would make it difficult for them to abandon Cuba. It was therefore necessary to ensure that an economy in which the Soviet Union had invested so much should be seen to be viable (which would inevitably require even greater levels of aid). If further substantial investment were to be made, Moscow would maximise the chances of ensuring its effective use if Cuba made a formal commitment to the integration of its economy with the socialist bloc. The Soviet leaders were probably also impressed with Castro's attitude, policies and the popular support that he still enjoyed despite the 1970 debacle. None of this suggests a power relationship fully compatible with the image of a 'subdued' Castro.

Political consequences

As indicated above, Communist Cuba is a highly significant symbolic component of the superpower relationship and it is this factor above all which constitutes Moscow's greatest advantage from the alliance. In terms of the Soviet Union's relations with the developing world, the Cuban revolution provided an opportunity to break in to that area at a time when links were virtually non-existent. However, the enhanced prestige that Moscow initially enjoyed in the Third World because of its high profile support for Cuba has been offset by perceptions of the limits to Castro's independence (for example, when Havana endorsed the Soviet invasion of Afghanistan, an extremely emotive issue amongst the Non-Aligned countries) and by a general recognition that the USSR is increasingly reluctant to send substantial economic aid to Third World revolutionary regimes unless they lie within the area of immediate Soviet security concern.

The 1962 Cuban Missile Crisis revealed that Soviet diplomats had much to learn about the handling of relations with highly nationalistic Third World leaders. Castro's wounded pride was not appeased by generous Soviet economic commitments in 1963 and 1964, and over the next few years he set out to demonstrate that his 'independence' was not to be compromised with impunity. The Missile Crisis had damaged the USSR's image throughout Latin America, and Moscow's claims to be seeking peaceful coexistence were further undermined by Castro's outspoken advocacy of guerrilla warfare and his logistical support for such endeavours in Latin America, particularly from 1964 to 1967. Fearful of being outflanked on the Left, the Soviet Union could not completely disavow the only revolutionary strategy which had actually been successful in Latin America, although both ideological conviction and state interests required that they should do so.

Moscow achieved a partial victory for its policy of non-armed struggle at the conference of Latin American Communist parties held in Havana in November 1964. In return for a clause in the communiqué calling for 'support for freedom fighters' in the controversial case of Venezuela, and also in Colombia, Guatemala, Haiti, Paraguay and Honduras, Castro pledged that he would cease supporting non-Communist extremist groups. Two years later, however, a Tricontinental Conference was held in Havana as a step towards expanding the Afro-Asian People's Solidarity Organization (AAPSO) to incorporate the Latin American nations. Initially welcomed by the Soviet Union as an opportunity to shift the balance of power in

AAPSO away from the Chinese, the Conference slipped out of Moscow's control and the Soviet Union found itself obliged to make a statement explicitly expressing 'fraternal solidarity with the armed struggle waged by the patriots of Venezuela, Peru, Colombia and Guatemala for freedom against the puppets of imperialism' (Statement by S. R. Rashidov, head of the Soviet delegation, at the Tricontinental Conference, Havana, 6 January 1966, p. 28, in Clissold: 1970, p. 161).

These words, while falling far short of the expectations of militant Latin American revolutionaries, provoked a sharp protest from the region's governments. Meanwhile Castro (who had returned from his 1964 visit to the Soviet Union convinced that Khrushchev 'would never send a single revolver' to Latin American revolutionary movements [CIA memo for the Director, 'Current thinking of Cuban government leaders', *US Declassified*, 1978, 7D]) bitterly denounced the USSR for its relations with the Christian Democrats in Chile, who were party to the 1964 OAS sanctions against Cuba. He also began preparations for an inaugural conference of the Organisation of Latin American Solidarity (OLAS) to be held in Havana in 1967. According to a Latin American Communist who was in Moscow at the time, a request from the Soviet Union to attend the OLAS meeting was flatly refused by the Cubans on the grounds that the USSR was not a member of the Third World community. This apparently incensed the Soviet leaders, and highly placed officials revealed that there was an influential school of thought which wanted to drop Cuba altogether (Rodolfo Cerdas Cruz, interview with the author, 7 November 1984).

It was also at this time that a little-known thaw in relations between Washington and Havana took place, through the intermediary of the Mexican government. US Secretary of State Dean Rusk had suggested, during a September 1966 visit to Mexico, that the Mexicans might be able to help secure the release of US citizens wishing to leave Cuba. The Cuban government agreed to a trial period of repatriation provided (1) the Mexican government supplied transit visas; (2) no government other than the Mexican made any representation or intervention in the affair; and (3) transport Havana–Mexico was on Mexican charter flights only (Department of State telegram from the US Mexican embassy to the Secretary of State, 2 December 1966, *US Declassified*, 1981, 551C). Mexican ambassador to Cuba Miguel Covián Parez believed that Castro had allowed the trial repatriation 'partly as a friendly gesture towards Mexico but also in an effort to derive positive benefits from the United States', possibly a relaxation of US pressure on Canada and Latin American states not to trade with Cuba. Nine months later the Cuban leader felt that there had been no indications that reciprocal concessions would be forthcoming, and he rejected further Mexican initiatives to renew the arrangement (Department of State telegram from the US ambassador in Mexico to the Secretary of State, September 1967, *US Declassified*, 1979, 313A). It may have been that Castro was anticipating Soviet sanctions of the kind which occurred and was hoping, once again, to play the two superpowers off against each other.

The Soviet–Cuban polemics of the 1960s gave way to a coincidence of foreign-policy interests during the 1970s. Moscow gained prestige and an inroad to Angola as a result of the Cuban role in sustaining the MPLA in power. Cuba was also extremely useful to the Soviet Union in the 1978 Ethiopian war against Somalia. It is clear, however, that Moscow can only secure Havana's military cooperation if and when Castro determines that Cuban troops should be committed. The 1975 Cuban decision to respond positively to an MPLA appeal for assistance can be attributed to several factors, the most significant of which are (1) the desire to enhance Cuba's prestige amongst the non-aligned nations and the world's left-wing forces by proving that Cuba was prepared to back up its declarations of revolutionary internationalism, which were beginning to wear somewhat thin in the light of Havana's curtailing of support for guerrilla movements, its persistent attempts to cultivate state-to-state relations with a whole variety of regimes and, most importantly, its integration into the Soviet bloc; (2) the need to stimulate revolutionary *élan* at home to counter popular disillusionment with the introduction of a Soviet-style political structure; and (3) the calculation that neither the United States nor the Latin American nations would respond with significant reprisals. By imposing the 1962 total trade embargo, Washington minimised its leverage over Cuba to the extent that it now has few sanctions at its disposal short of outright acts of war. The tentative and abortive rapprochement policy followed by the Carter administration reassured Havana that direct US action was highly improbable. Moreover, in mid-1975, the OAS had voted to allow each of its members to determine its own policies towards Cuba (in effect lifting the 1964 sanctions which had left Cuba isolated in the hemisphere). For Latin America to have reversed this new policy so quickly in response to the Angolan involvement would have been completely against the interests of those countries in asserting their independence of Washington and trying to promote a strategy of collective self-reliance. Other, lesser, considerations include the fact that Angola is an oil-exporting country: although Cuba, of course, continues to receive its petroleum at subsidised prices from the Soviet Union, prudent policy-making dictates that alternative strategies be developed. Ironically enough, some of the oil Cuba receives today does in fact come from Angola, although it is paid for by the Soviet Union which, in another of its economy measures, finds it cheaper to buy from the Gulf Oil Corporation (through a broker in Curaçao) and ship the petroleum from Cabinda rather than the Black Sea (Szulc: 1986, p. 527).

In May 1977 a serious difference between Moscow and Havana arose over policy in Angola when a *coup* attempt was made against President Neto by a pro-Soviet nationalist group led by Nito Alves, which was defeated with the help of Cuban troops. The precise level of Soviet involvement is not known, but at the very least they were aware of the proposed action and failed to warn Neto. In 1985 the indications were that Moscow wanted Cuba to become militarily involved in the internal wars of Angola, Ethiopia and Mozambique (*Latin America Regional Report: The Caribbean*, RC-85-10, 6 December 1985, p. 2). This would strengthen the stability of these Marxist regimes and increase their dependence upon Cuban troops and Soviet hardware. Cuba, however, has consistently refused to help the Ethiopian government in its battle with the Eritrean resistance movement (to which the Cubans sent some support in the 1960s), and has shown no inclination to become involved in Mozambique. 'It is a mistake to suppose that the Cubans always do what the Russians tell them', one African diplomat remarked. 'Sometimes Castro does what suits him' (*The Times*, 27 March 1984, p. 7).

Moreover, Cuba maintains that its estimated 30,000 troops are in Angola to defend the MPLA government against attacks from South Africa which its army alone cannot deter. Its policy is not to fight the South-African-backed UNITA guerrilla army unless UNITA attacks Cuban positions or patrols. Indeed, Castro is believed to be anxious to withdraw from Angola (because of domestic resistance to a sustained commitment abroad now that the glory has diminished) although he has repeatedly stated that the Cubans will not leave until Angola is secure from South African aggression. In 1984 Cuba switched some of its troops from Angola and negotiated an agreement with the MPLA government for a phased withdrawal of Cuban forces, moves which were 'viewed with deep suspicion in Moscow' (*The Times*, 27 March 1984, p. 7). In 1987–8 there were signs that the Soviet Union was reviewing its strategy in Southern Africa, particularly in the light of serious military set-backs for Angolan government forces in late 1987 and a growing sense that neither side in Angola can win. The issue was one of three regional conflicts (the other two being Cambodia and Nicaragua) discussed by Secretary of State Shultz and Foreign Minister Shevardnadze at a series of almost monthly meetings which have taken place since 1986. Informal contacts were also established in early 1988 between Washington and Havana, after Cuba had broken the ice the previous November by agreeing to renew the 1984 immigration agreement (suspended by Castro after the United States began broadcasting Radio Martí in May 1985). Cuba has now dropped its insistence that removal of its own troops from Angola could not be linked to a South African withdrawal from Namibia. Cuban participation, for the first time in early 1988, in four-part negotiations with the United States, South Africa and Angola aroused hopes that a settlement could be within reach. In August 1988 Pretoria made the dramatic offer of independence for Namibia by 1 June 1989 if Cuban troops were withdrawn from Angola by then. Since, however, this proposal leaves unresolved the whole issue of South African and CIA funding of Jonas Savimbi's UNITA guerrilla force, and of the presence of (according to the Angolan government) some 9,000 South African troops within Angola's border, it was, predictably, rejected by the Angolans and Cubans. A new round of talks began in September 1988, but there were grounds for doubting South Africa's commitment to seeing an end to the conflict.

Signs of divergence between Moscow and Havana also emerged, particularly during the early 1980s, over Central America. The Soviet Union made only the most minimal of commitments in response to Cuban 1979–80 lobbying for support for the FMLN guerrillas in El Salvador (see the detailed discussion of this issue in chapter 7). Moreover, according to then Secretary of State Alexander Haig, in the early months of the Reagan administration, 'Castro had more reason to be nervous than he knew. In my conversations with [Soviet ambassador to Washington] Dobrynin I continued to press the question of Cuban adventurism in the Americas and in Africa as well. Dobrynin's response convinced me that Cuban activities in the Western hemisphere were a matter between the United States and Cuba' (Haig: 1984, p. 131).

Despite the fact that 'It is impossible to exaggerate the degree of Cuban identification, official and unofficial, with the Nicaraguan Revolution' (*The Sunday Times*, 18 December 1983, p. 13) and, to a lesser extent, with the FMLN guerrilla movement in El Salvador, since mid-1983 security considerations have prompted Castro to adopt a relatively low profile in Central America. Castro apparently fears that the heightened US presence on the Honduran/Nicaraguan border brings to an unacceptable level the risk that Cuban personnel may become involved in direct confrontation with US forces. Havana has made it quite clear that it would not send troops to Nicaragua in the event of an American invasion. In late December 1983 Ricardo Alarcón, Deputy Foreign Minister, was quoted as saying, 'The vast majority of our people in Nicaragua are civilians and we have offered to publish all their names. But if it came to an invasion of Nicaragua it would be up to the Nicaraguans to defend themselves' (*The Times*, 26 March 1984, p. 6). Apart from the fact that any Cuban intervention in Nicaragua would be tantamount to issuing an open invitation to the United States to instigate war measures against the Castro regime, Havana's forces are already seriously over-extended in Angola.

The Cubans have, however, tried to persuade Moscow to show the Nicaraguan revolutionaries the kind of support that Castro judges it would be unduly dangerous – in terms of Cuba's security – for his own government to give. The Cuban leader apparently asked Chernenko to allow a Soviet naval flotilla to approach Nicaraguan waters to signal the USSR's backing for the Nicaraguan government, but his request was turned down. This apparent reluctance to make even symbolic gestures in support of the Sandinistas annoyed Castro to the extent that he failed to attend Chernenko's March 1985 funeral. Neither did he sign the book of condolences at the Soviet embassy in Havana, presumably to register his displeasure with Soviet policy towards Nicaragua (the *Guardian*, 25 March 1985, p. 6).

The Soviet Union and Cuba clearly had substantial differences regarding the situation in Grenada. The documents recovered by the United States in the aftermath of its invasion indicate that Moscow was reluctant to pay more than minimal attention to the New Jewel Movement (consistently down-grading their diplomatic status compared to the Sandinistas). The limited aid agreements that the USSR did sign were primarily a result of persistent lobbying by the Cubans on behalf of the Grenadan revolution. Castro was clearly deeply shocked by the killing of Maurice Bishop on 19 October 1983 and issued a strongly worded condemnation designed, according to Hugh O'Shaughnessy, 'to preclude any help being offered to the Revolutionary Military Council from Moscow' (O'Shaughnessy: 1984, p. 149). On 22 October 1983 the Grenadan Military Council formally requested Cuban military support, which was refused. There is evidence that Castro may, however, have been willing to intervene on behalf of Bishop. Lynden Rhamdany, former Grenadan Minister of Tourism, states that the Cuban ambassador in St George's contacted Bishop twice just before his murder, offering to help, only to be turned down (Shearman: 1987, p. 66). There is no doubt as to where Cuban sympathies lay concerning the leadership struggle within the New Jewel Movement. On 14 November 1983 Castro publicly extolled Bishop, condemned Coard and Austin as the 'Pol Pot group', and declared that the government in Grenada at the time of the US invasion was 'morally indefensible' (O'Shaughnessy: 1984, p. 188 and p. 231). As US troops approached Grenada, Cuban personnel were ordered to stay indoors and fight only if attacked and, on 24 October, a Cubana de Aviación plane brought an experienced military chief, Colonel Tortoló, to organise their defence. The construction workers at the controversial Point Salines airport, who were attacked on 25 October, were ordered by radio to resist, rather than surrender. This decision can be explained by Cuba's long-standing unwillingness, determined by strategic, ideological and psychological factors, to be seen to be surrendering to the United States.

The USSR, in sharp contrast, issued no condemnation of Bishop's murder, a TASS statement merely noting that 'an armed clash' had taken place 'which claimed the lives of the Prime Minister and several ministers', and giving the reassurance that the Revolutionary Military Council was '[determined] to uphold the cause of the revolution' (O'Shaughnessy: 1984, p. 148). The Kremlin 'clung to the line that it was nothing more than a falling out of revolutionaries and that the action of Austin and Coard was understandable given the need for greater discipline and ideological clarity within the party'. The Cuban stand apparently 'infuriated the Soviets who let it be known to Western journalists in Havana that they held the Cubans responsible for "losing them a country" ' (O'Shaughnessy: 1984, p. 188).

In the aftermath of the US invasion Havana recalled an estimated 1,000 of its people from Nicaragua, fearful of any provocation to a US administration which had recently had its confidence so massively boosted. In December 1984, when an abortive peace proposal called for the withdrawal of Cuban military advisers from Managua, Havana complied. Castro has also reportedly put pressure on the Salvadoran Left to negotiate an end to the civil war. According to one official of the FMLN/FDR, the Cubans told the guerrillas that their February 1984 peace proposal 'was not flexible enough, and [Havana] had specific suggestions' for making it more acceptable to the Americans (Rothenberg: 1984, p. 140). There was apparently no such pressure from Moscow. Cuba, however, because of its own security considerations and because of its identification with the Sandinista regime and the Salvadoran guerrilla movement, is keen to promote a political settlement of the region's crisis as rapidly as possible. Havana is acutely aware that any military 'solution' can only involve an escalation of the US role to the point of defeat for the revolutionary forces.

During 1983–4 the Soviet leaders, with an eye on the autumn 1984 US presidential elections, probably hoped to see Reagan drawn more deeply into the Central American quagmire, in the hope that public opinion would turn against him. (The Soviet press did not reproduce Castro's October 1983 statement that Cuba could not come to the defence of Nicaragua, despite publishing a long extract from the same press conference.) Gorbachev has pursued this policy, responding positively to President Daniel Ortega's desperate plea for oil supplies in May 1985 and ensuring that the Sandinista army has sufficient supplies to prevent the *contra* forces from developing into a serious threat to the regime's survival. He has thus succeeded, to a considerable extent, in establishing Central America as an effective counterweight to Afghanistan. As superpower relations thawed during 1987, Moscow revealed increasing impatience with the Sandinistas and has given out signals to Washington that it may be willing to make a bargain on Nicaragua (see chapter 7 for more detailed discussion). Thus Moscow's and Havana's respective interests in Central America derive from crucially different standpoints. For Cuba, the fate of revolutionary regimes in the Caribbean region is intimately linked to its own security concerns. The Soviet Union, however, sees the region primarily in the context of strategic rivalry with the United States, and in terms of the potential that it offers for exercising leverage in superpower negotiations.

Thus the Soviet Union and Cuba are by no means always in accord on foreign policy. When priorities differ and interests diverge, one of Moscow's strongest cards is its capacity to exercise a veto on any offensive action by Cuba. Cuban support for insurgency in Latin America during the 1960s was in fact far short of Havana's claims. US government sources have testified that only 'four instances of direct Cuban support to insurgent groups in Latin America' could be proven – in total no more than two hundred Cuban guerrillas and several tons of weapons for the entire decade ('Communist activities in Latin America', *Report of the Subcommittee on Inter-American Affairs*, US House of Representatives Committee on Foreign Affairs, July 1967, in

Robbins: 1984, p. 218). The reason for this is quite simply that Cuba does not have the resources (little spare foreign exchange, no armaments industry and limited transport facilities) to give substantial support to foreign military operations without Soviet backing. The Cuban military operation in Angola was crucially dependent on Soviet air and sea lift support. However, if Havana chooses to take negative action, such as withdrawing some of its troops (for example, from Angola in 1984), or refusing to commit them at all, the Soviet Union is in a far more delicate position. Clearly if Moscow felt that significant interests were threatened by a Cuban foreign (or domestic) policy decision it has a broad range of telling sanctions at its disposal. Cuba's entry into Comecon has, however, virtually eliminated the possibility that the Soviet Union would apply the ultimate sanction of cutting aid altogether. There is little doubt, however, that Castro would ensure that any public attempt to force Cuban compliance with a Soviet foreign-policy aim would receive full publicity and would carry high political costs in terms of damage to the Soviet Union's image. As discussed above, quite significant differences have occurred (over Grenada, Central America and Angola) which have provoked angry reactions in the Soviet Union, and yet the Kremlin has so far held back from any measures which might make the disputes public.

From the Cuban point of view, its connection with the USSR has enabled it to play a far more significant world role than would be expected given the country's size, population, geo-strategic situation and economic weakness. The obvious drawback is that, since the military muscle behind Cuban declarations of socialist international-ism is dependent on Soviet support, Cuba is not perceived to be, and indeed cannot be, a completely independent actor. As indicated in the sections above, Castro has established broad parameters within which to manoeuvre in his dealings with the country which many Cuban officials refer to as *el hermano mayor* (Big Brother). Indeed to increase Cuba's leverage in its relationship with Moscow, enabling it to preserve and ideally enhance the benefits of the alliance whilst increasing its own autonomy in international affairs, has become one of the major aims of Havana's foreign policy. The fact remains that the strategic predicament of the Cuban revolution determines that at critical junctures (most notably the Soviet invasions of Czechoslovakia and Afghanistan) Castro to date has always made his allegiance clear.

Since the mid-1970s Cuba's internal political system has been very closely modelled on that of the Soviet Union. Castro, however, succeeded in manipulating the reform process to bring about a greater concentration of power into his own hands, with the added advantage that his role as Maximum Leader is now formalised. In late 1985 he clearly established the position of his brother Raúl (who, incidentally, apparently has a good personal relationship with Gorbachev [Castro: 1986, p. 56]) as his intended successor, and the PSP veterans who saw their influence increase in the mid-1970s found themselves, a decade later, being removed to make way for a new generation of *Fidelista* recruits, popularly referred to as 'Castro's golden boys'.

Soviet–Cuban relations under Gorbachev

In the context of the issue of Soviet political influence in Cuba it is interesting to observe that, whereas the Soviet Union is attempting to boost productivity and economic efficiency by the process of *perestroika*, Cuba is tackling its own problems by what is known as 'rectification' (introduced in April 1986). In direct contrast to the USSR, the Cuban approach involves a turn away from material inducements (private peasants' markets were closed down in May 1986) and a rhetorical emphasis on moral incentives, a campaign which drew amply on the opportunities presented by the fact that 1987 was the twentieth anniversary of Che Guevara's death to remind Cubans that their revolutionary heritage involves the philosophy of the 'new man'. This policy is at least partly determined by the fundamental pragmatic consideration that there are simply not enough consumer goods available in Cuba to make material incentives effective. There is also considerably less emphasis than in the Soviet Union on the importance of political and cultural liberalisation (*glasnost*) as a necessary complement to economic reform. Whilst there are some signs of a revival in the arts, and there is an increasing dialogue between the church and the state, the press has so far proved relatively resistant to a change in style, despite the replacement of *Granma*'s editor in June 1987. Corruption and administrative abuse has been exposed, but this is all part of the process of self-criticism that Castro is now demanding from every worker. In late 1987 figures were released for the first time on Angolan casualties, but this may simply be intended to prepare the population for the fact that Havana is actively seeking to withdraw its troops, rather than signalling a policy decision to provide Cubans with more information.

Any assessment of how the Kremlin regards Cuba's adoption of policies which are so different from those being instigated in the Soviet Union can only be speculative. Three Gorbachev/Castro meetings in less than two years indicates that, at the very least, the USSR is keeping a very close eye on Cuban developments. As ever, both sides have their complaints about the other. One unwelcome consequence of Soviet *glasnost* for Cuba is that articles criticising Cuban economic management have begun to appear in the Soviet press. Havana ignored a January 1987 article in *New Times* by Vladislav Chirkov entitled, 'How are things, *compañeros*?', in which the author discussed misuse of Soviet aid and 'negative tendencies and abuses in public affairs, as well as errors and miscalculations' in Cuba (*New Times*, 12 January 1987, pp. 18–19). However, when a further article by the same writer appeared in August, entitled, 'An uphill task' (*New Times*, 17 August 1987, pp. 16–17), Carlos Rafael Rodríguez was stung into retorting that Cuba was undergoing 'A difficult but steady ascent' (*New Times*, 19 October 1987, pp. 16–17). Furthermore, Cuba's attitude towards *glasnost* is perhaps indicated by Rodríguez' tart observation that, 'When openly and publicly beginning this struggle [for rectification], we were aware that we were giving thereby our enemies the chance to use these arguments to shout from the rooftops for all the world to hear about the so-called "weaknesses of socialism". But it never occurred to us that they could be used in the pages of *New Times* . . . ' Nor can the Cubans have been reassured by Chirkov's discussion of 'the heavy burden' of Cuban defence expenditure which he described as 'a loss to the economy', and his assertion (*New Times*, 17 August 1987, p. 16) that 'there may be different views' on the subject of whether the United States intends to attack Cuba, although 'as far as the Cubans are concerned, they prefer to have a strong defence'.

For its part, Cuba is demanding more efficiency from its Comecon partners, arguing that failure to fulfil production targets is often due to delayed deliveries of equipment from the Soviet bloc. Indeed Chirkov did acknowledge in his August article that 'the fault does not lie only with the Cuban side – its CMEA partners are also to blame' and that 'certain ministries and departments' had failed to draw 'the proper conclusions from the decisions of the Communist party Central Committee on improving economic cooperation with the fraternal countries'. Recently Soviet economists have been arguing that the principles of *perestroika* should be applied to trade within Comecon. This would not necessarily augur well for Cuba, at least not during the (probably lengthy) implementation stage. To date, Soviet attempts to effect the decentralisation of foreign-trading operations have not proved particularly successful, largely because of a shortage of staff qualified to undertake the requisite responsibilities, even at the level of processing simple transactions (Daniel Franklin, seminar, 26 March 1988). An October 1987 Comecon meeting in Moscow brought little progress, largely because the introduction of viable measures into the organisation is crucially dependent on the successful reform of Soviet economic structures, particularly its system of wholesale pricing.

The general uncertainty as to whether *perestroika* can sustain momentum and inject enterprise and efficiency into the inert and unwieldy Soviet economy clearly places Cuba in a vulnerable position in the longer term. If the Soviet economy stalls because of the failure or defeat of reform, Moscow may simply become less and less able to sustain substantial aid commitments. In the more immediate future, Cuba is likely to continue to feel the pressure of the effects of Moscow's increased emphasis on cost effectiveness. When Castro announced an austerity programme on 27 December 1986, he explicitly stated that it was necessary to compensate for a 50 per cent decline in foreign-exchange earnings and 'cuts in Soviet subsidies' (*LAWR*, 15 January 1987, p. 10). In 1986 deficiencies in oil supplies forced Havana to spend its precious hard currency on purchases in the world market (*Latin America Regional Report: Caribbean*, 9 May 1986, p. 1). Over the past two years Moscow has cut the price it pays for Cuban sugar by about 7 per cent (Andrew Zimbalist, seminar, 18 March 1988), while keeping high what it exacts for oil (*Latin America Regional Report: Caribbean*, 28 August 1986, p. 1). In keeping with its new emphasis on material incentives, however, Moscow has reportedly agreed to give Cuba so many cents of a dollar for every litre of oil that it saves.

There is no doubt that the Cuban economy faces extremely severe problems of its own, aside from those caused by Moscow's increased parsimony. The seriousness with which Castro regards the situation is suggested by the fact that he has identified the errors of the 1970s as 'strategic', whereas those of the 1960s were merely 'tactical' (*The Financial Times*, 29 October 1986, p. 4). Many of the problems are the same as in the Soviet Union: corruption, administrative excess and low labour productivity. Complex incentive pay schemes introduced during the second half of the 1970s under the Comecon-inspired System of Development and Economic Planning were misapplied. For example, managers who had authority over state resources would often make a deal with farmers who were engaged in private trading of scarce vegetable crops, with the result that state equipment, such as lorries, tractors and fuel, was being used to further private wealth acquisition.

In 1986 the Cuban sugar crop, hit by both drought and hurricane, fell by over 1 million tonnes, and the government was obliged to purchase 145,000 tonnes of sugar on the open market to meet its Comecon sugar requirements. In the Soviet Union Gorbachev's restrictions on the sale of alcohol have boosted demand for sugar, both to cater for the booming soft drinks trade and, probably, to supply home distilleries. In 1987 the USSR, China and Japan were buying Thai sugar because of Cuba's inability to fulfil its export quotas and, in early 1988, a meeting was convened in Havana by the Cuban sugar authorities with members of the international trade and Soviet officials to discuss ways around anticipated problems in meeting its 1988 commitments (*The Financial Times*, 13 January 1988, p. 26). The 1986 fall in world oil prices drastically reduced Cuba's hard currency earnings (which had in any case been decreasing steadily since 1981) from the re-sale of Soviet crude, which fell from about $600 million in 1985 to $450 million in 1986. With little surplus sugar to sell for hard currency, Cuba suffered an overall drop in foreign-exchange earnings of about $300 million (*The Financial Times*, 21 April 1986, p. 5). Debt service commitments on Cuba's $3.5 billion foreign debt remained roughly constant, however. By early 1987 Cuba was seriously behind in payments to commercial Western banks, and faced the prospect of annual meetings with the Paris Club for several years to come. Negotiations seem to become more protracted each year, and the banks are clearly worried by the lack of an IMF shield for their exposure in Cuba. Moreover, chilled Soviet–Cuban relations in 1984–5, and the Kremlin's new-found toughness with costly aid recipients placed additional strains on Cuba's connections with creditor banks in the West. There is virtually no scope in the near future for Cuba to import the hard-currency Western equipment it so desperately wants.

Ultimately, Moscow's attitude towards Castro's 'rectification' campaign will be determined by whether or not it actually succeeds in rehauling the Cuban economy. This, of course, is the criterion by which Gorbachev's domestic opponents will judge his own reform policies. With a situation which is precarious both in the Soviet Union and in Cuba, particularly in the light of the fact that Fidel Castro has now entered his sixties, the Cuban revolution has probably entered 'a critical phase'.

Implications for Soviet policy in Latin America

In assessing the overall balance-sheet of its support for the Cuban Revolution, Moscow probably does conclude that the political benefits outweigh the economic problems. Nevertheless, Soviet officials have made it abundantly clear that they do not want, and cannot afford, another Cuba. As Victor Volskii, Director of the Institute of Latin America in Moscow, said in April 1983, 'We have never abandoned a friendly country, but it has cost us a lot to send oil to Cuba – two tankers a day for twenty years. We wouldn't like to have to repeat that on a large scale' (the *Guardian*, 28 April 1983, p. 15).

Apart from the economic burden, the Soviet Union's connection with Cuba has caused distortion in the development of ties with other Third World nations. In Latin America, the legacy has been that conservatively minded regimes have been cautious about pursuing links with the USSR, preferring to confine relations to the economic sphere. Amongst the Left in Latin America there has been strong disillusionment on two counts: firstly, political, after the Cuban Missile Crisis and secondly, economic, because the Cuban model has not proved viable. Amongst governments which on ideological grounds might be inclined to be sympathetic to the USSR there has been a recognition that for Latin American economies, historically dependent on Western imports, reliance on Soviet technology is very much a last resort measure. Even if the Soviet economy were in a position to sustain another Cuba, it would be a case of diminishing returns: their relationship with Cuba already gives them all the advantages to be gained from such an alliance in Latin America.

5   'Socialism with red wine . . . '
Moscow and Chile's Popular
Unity experiment

After the Cuban revolution no other country in Latin America presented itself as a candidate for large-scale Soviet support until the Marxist Salvador Allende led Popular Unity to victory in the Chilean presidential elections of 3 September 1970. The significance of this event lay in the fact that, for the first time in Latin America, where the Soviet Union had spent the past decade competing for ideological influence with Castroism and Maoism, the popular front tactics advocated by Moscow since 1935 had proved successful. The 'Chilean experiment' was seen as a potential model not only for other Latin American countries, where local Communist parties set about trying to organise popular fronts (most notably in Argentina, Uruguay and Venezuela), but also for left-wing forces in Europe, particularly in France and Italy. In ideological terms, Allende's Chile was a far more obvious target for Soviet aid than Castro's Cuba had been in 1960.

However, whereas in the case of Cuba an initially cautious reaction had subsequently given way to a long-term commitment, Soviet policy towards Chile was restrained throughout the three years of Allende's presidency. Although Moscow used events in Chile to fight its ideological battles, especially with the Chinese, arguing, for example, that 'it has not been the gun but the actions of the revolutionary class which have enabled the people to take over political power in Chile' (Radio Moscow, 8 January 1971, in Gouré and Suchlicki: 1971, p. 57), in practice the Soviet Union consistently sought to avoid being identified with Chile. Allende's election was hailed as 'a truly outstanding event', but not until nearly two months after it had taken place, by which time fears that he would be prevented from taking office had been allayed. Even so, the USSR sent only a low-level delegation to the inauguration ceremony. Similar caution was shown on any occasion when Soviet comments could be subject to public scrutiny, most notably at the Twenty-Fourth Congress of the CPSU in 1971, when Brezhnev would say only that 'The victory of the Popular

Unity forces in Chile was a most important event. There, for the first time in the history of the continent, the people have secured by constitutional means the installation of a government they want and trust.'[1] *Pravda* (21 April 1971, p. 5) reported a speech by Castro on the Tenth Anniversary of the Bay of Pigs invasion, pledging Cuban economic and, if necessary, military support to Allende, but failed to relay remarks he made during a three-week visit to Chile in December 1971 exhorting the Chileans to make use of the Soviet aid that, according to him, would be available to them (Grayson: 1972).

When Chile was mentioned in Soviet commentaries the emphasis was not on Allende's progress within Chile in establishing a model for socialism, but on Popular Unity's contribution to what was perceived as a broadly revolutionary situation throughout Latin America. Thus Marxist Chile was habitually cited along with the 'progressive' military governments of Peru and Bolivia as testimony to 'the multiplicity of forms within the framework of which Latin America is paving its way to true independence' (*Pravda*, 26 January 1971, p. 1). The Allende experiment was, of course, of a qualitatively different nature to the reformist military regimes, as was acknowledged in a specialised academic journal where the election of Allende was described as 'second only to the victory of the Cuban revolution in the magnitude of its significance as a revolutionary blow to the imperialist system in Latin America'.[2] While the USSR's overall policy in Latin America was certainly furthered by the portrayal of a strong anti-imperialist movement in the area, the corresponding lack of emphasis on Chile also enabled Moscow to distance itself from the failures of the Popular Unity government.

Political caution was reflected in the level of economic assistance granted to Allende. Total credits offered to Chile by the Soviet Union from 1970 to 1973 amounted to approximately $350 million, of which perhaps $260 million consisted of long-term credits and the remainder of short-term loans.[3] This figure may be compared with the volume of

[1] L. Brezhnev, *Report of the Central Committee of the Communist Party of the Soviet Union* (Novosti Press Agency Publishing House, Moscow, 1971), p. 25, in Gouré and Rothenberg: 1975, p. 99.

[2] V. G. Spirin, 'USA imperialism and Latin American reality', *SShA: ekonomika, politika, ideologiia*, no. 8 (August 1971), p. 33, in Gouré and Rothenberg: 1985, pp. 97.

[3] The precise magnitude of Soviet credits to Allende over 1970–3 remains uncertain although the broad picture is fairly clear. Soviet and US Department of State sources give comparable figures for total Soviet long-term credits 1970–2 (in effect to 1973, since no credits were granted in that year) of $260 million and $266 million respectively.

The Chilean government figure of $335 million, announced after Allende returned from the Soviet Union in December 1972, is almost certainly exaggerated in order to

Table 2. *Chile's trade with the socialist countries (US$ millions)*

	1970	1971	1972	1973
Exports	28.8	n/a	60.0	158.0
Imports	5.8	24.0	25.6	83.0

Source: Chilean Central Bank and SEREX (Foreign Trade Department of the Central Bank) in Guardia: 1979, p. 96.

concessionary credits extended by Moscow to Havana to finance Cuban trade deficits (see pages 95-7). Aid to Allende's Chile can also be compared with the $600 million loan extended to Argentina's Peronist government in 1974. Nor was the lack of aid to Popular Unity compensated for by any substantial bolstering of trade. According to Popular Unity figures, Chile's exports to the entire socialist bloc represented only 7 per cent and 6.3 per cent of total exports in 1972 and 1973 respectively. Total imports from socialist countries (of which the Soviet Union's share was 20 per cent) accounted for 2.5 per cent of all Chilean imports in 1971 and 2.7 per cent the following year, rising to 7.7 per cent during 1973. As one former economic adviser to Allende points out, 'according to these figures, the Chilean economy was not considered a special case, but followed the normal trade patterns of the socialist countries' (Guardia: 1979, p. 82). It is also interesting to observe that for the first two years of Allende's government the trade imbalance so generally typical of Soviet–Latin American commerce persisted, with Chilean exports far easier to place than Soviet goods (see table 2).

The USSR's failure to substantiate its rhetorical expressions of solidarity with the Chilean revolution can be explained by a combination of four factors, two of which pertain to the general international context in which the Popular Unity experiment took place, and two of which are specific to Chile.

Firstly, Allende's presidency coincided with the height of detente

---

lessen the impact of his failure to secure substantial assistance.

A later Popular Unity figure, published in a retrospective study, of $217 million ($102 million for complete plants and technology and $115 million for machinery and equipment) may be exclusive of $30 million for food imports granted in December 1972 while the US and Soviet estimates given above are inclusive of that figure, or there could be other, unknown, reasons for the differential. As for short-term credits, it is reliably reported that $50 million was granted in January 1972 and an additional $20 million the following December. A Popular Unity figure gives $100 million in total for 1972.

between the two superpowers: Richard Nixon went to Moscow in May 1972 and Brezhnev returned his visit the following year, shortly before the Chilean *coup* of 11 September. While this factor may initially have seemed advantageous to Popular Unity, it in fact turned out to be a very mixed blessing. Soviet ideologists, seeking to render their rapprochement with the United States acceptable to Third World countries, were quick to point out that open US intervention, at least in Latin America, was less likely during a period of superpower cooperation. Popular Unity, as the second Marxist government in the Western hemisphere, was the inevitable target of Washington's hostility, not so much because of US economic interests in Chile (although these were said to be 'considerable'), but because Allende's victory was perceived by the Americans as 'a definite psychological defeat for the United States and a decisive psychological success for the Marxist ideology' (Informe de la Comisión Church', Comité Chileno de Solidaridad, *Boletín Informativo*, no. 85 (Havana 1976) p. 6, in Cantero: 1977, p. 40). Nevertheless it was felt, both in Moscow and Santiago, that implementation of the 'Johnson Doctrine' that there should be 'no more Cubas' (which had been used in 1965 to justify an invasion of the Dominican Republic) was not a realistic policy option for the Nixon administration, nor was the open imposition of an economic blockade such as had been applied against Cuba. In an international context, any such action would have threatened the tentative framework of coexistence negotiated between the two superpowers, and on a domestic level North American public opinion, reacting against US involvement in Vietnam, was unlikely to countenance overt aggression against the democratically elected Popular Unity government.

Both these factors, however, had a corollary that worked against Allende. On the one hand, US intervention in Chile may have been confined to covert operations, but it was no less and arguably more strongly motivated than open interference would have been. Concomitant with the administration's policy of building better relations with established Communist governments was the need to reassure the US electorate of a suitably anti-Communist toughness. This was particularly true of men like Nixon and Kissinger, who had built their careers around the advocacy of hard-line foreign policies, and who were personally involved in overseeing the $8 million CIA sabotage operation in Chile, designed to 'make the economy scream'. On the other hand, as far as the Soviet Union was concerned, the prestige to be won among the world's left-wing forces by supporting Allende simply did not compare with the potential economic and political benefits of peaceful coexistence with the United States, and Moscow was wary of overplaying its hand in a country which Washington regarded as being within its 'sphere of influence'. This consideration was paramount during 1972, when the Soviet Union's need for massive grain imports from the West made it more than usually reluctant to jeopardise superpower cooperation. The USSR was always careful to distinguish between US multi-national corporations and the US government in its denunciations of outside interference in Chile. Further confirmation of Moscow's priorities was given by the fact that US involvement in the 1973 *coup* was not condemned in the Soviet press until Washington itself admitted responsibility.

Secondly, in the light of the Soviet Union's experience in Cuba (and in other Third World countries) during the early 1960s, after the fall of Khrushchev in 1964 Moscow undertook a reappraisal of its role in the developing world. This occurred at the same time as Soviet foreign policy overall was gradually being orientated along more pragmatic lines in accordance with an increased emphasis on the primary goal of attaining strategic parity with the United States. A distinction was drawn between countries which were said to be 'constructing social-ism' (a category embracing Eastern Europe and Cuba) and those which were at the earlier, more unstable stage of 'non-capitalist' or 'revolutionary democratic' development. In 1971 it was stated that:

[while] the material and technical support of the socialist countries furthers the development of the young independent countries and serves them as a socio-political guarantee of the success of their progressive reforms and as a safeguard against the encroachments of imperialism . . . assistance from the socialist countries necessarily bears the character of mutually beneficial cooperation, because the resources of one side obviously cannot satisfy the acute and growing requirements of the countries that have taken or are preparing to take the road of non-capitalist development. (Ulyanovsky: 1971, p. 28)

More explicitly, *New Times* asserted that 'to strengthen the economic might of their own country and raise the welfare of its working people is the supreme internationalist duty for Communists in power. As for assistance to the Third World, it is rendered on such a scale as will not impede the progress of the socialist community' (*New Times*, 3 March 1970, p. 23).

In this context, Soviet commentators formulated their characteri-sation of the situation in Chile in such a way as to avoid the suggestion that Popular Unity (which, after all, was not controlled by a Leninist party and was operating without the control of either the armed forces or the mass circulation media) was implementing socialism. The implication was that although Chile was set on a path towards socialism, it was as yet a relatively distant aim. For example, on 2 June 1971 *Pravda* stated (p. 1) that the Popular Unity programme 'envisages the carrying out of fundamental social, economic and political transformations and the transition to the construction of socialism'. Politburo member Andrei Kirilenko, speaking in Santiago at celebrations to commemorate the Fiftieth Anniversary of the Chilean Communist Party (PCCh) early in January 1972, said, 'The people's government has proclaimed socialist goals. The implementation of revolutionary changes in Chile is a new page in the creation of the socialist world' (*Pravda*, 4 January 1972, p. 4). The following July an article in *International Affairs* stated, 'The record of Chile shows that a number of Latin American countries can adopt a form of socialist construction' (Poterov and Godunsky: 1972, p. 35). However, this status was immediately withdrawn after the three-week 'bosses' strike of October 1972, which virtually paralysed the Chilean economy and exposed both the weakness of the Popular Unity government and the strength of its opponents. Subsequently, Allende's government was relegated to a lower division of socialist development. Instead of 'building socialism', it was said to be seeking 'free and independent development on the path of democracy and social progress' ('Meeting in the CPSU Central Committee', *Pravda*, 23 November 1972, p. 1).

In this context it is highly significant that it was in 1972 that Cuba, having joined Comecon in July of that year, became fully integrated into the 'socialist community'. Although Castro and Allende naturally felt solidarity with one another as leaders of the only two Marxist governments in the Western hemisphere, they were in effect competing for Soviet aid. It was probably the same meeting of the Politburo on 18 December 1972 that both decided against giving a favourable hearing to Allende's request for massive economic aid to Chile, and which authorised the 1972–6 economic package rewarding Cuba for its economic reforms and its full membership of Comecon. Although any assessment of the extent to which these decisions were linked can only be speculative, it is hard to imagine that they were wholly coincidental.

Thirdly, the development of relations between the Soviet Union and Chile is in any case hindered by the absence of a sound material base: the Soviet and Chilean economies are simply not very compatible. The USSR is self-sufficient in Chile's major export, copper (indeed there were some intermittent Soviet copper exports to the West) and, like Chile, has long since relinquished its role as a grain exporter. In the early 1970s both countries were significantly dependent on grain imports for their urban food supplies. Allende clearly hoped that the Soviet Union would buy Chilean copper for re-export to other Comecon countries, particularly Rumania, which imports substantial quantities of this mineral and has since entered into a supply agreement with the Pinochet government. From Moscow's point of view, however, such a commitment made neither political nor economic sense, and they refused to undertake it, despite the fact that the Chileans were experiencing severe difficulties in marketing their copper in the face of attempts by expropriated US multi-nationals to block deliveries. A sale of 8,000 tons was made in 1972, and an agreement was signed committing the Soviet Union to buying 130,000 tons of copper from 1973 to 1975, plus $87 million worth of copper products. Given that the Chilean copper mines were at that time producing over 700,000 tons per annum, the bulk of which was available for export, this agreement could hardly have been of substantial assistance to the industry even if it had been fulfilled. In fact, purchases in 1973 amounted to only 6,000 tons of copper and 19,000 tons of copper concentrates (*Vneshniaia torgovlia*, 1973, pp. 312–13).

Finally, the reluctance of the USSR to enter into the unequal relationship which would have ensued with Chile was compounded by the instability of the Allende government. At first, Soviet leaders may well have felt that they had grounds for optimism about the prospects for Popular Unity. The coalition, which was made up of six parties,[4] owed its existence largely to the work of the Chilean Communist Party. The Communists were instrumental in the writing of the programme adopted by the Popular Unity parties in December 1969, which bore a marked resemblance to the programme approved by the Communists' own Congress during the previous month, and in the securing of Allende's nomination for presidential candidate when many of his own Socialist Party would have preferred a more radical figurehead.

The history of the PCCh shows that it has long since proved itself worthy of Moscow's confidence. It is probably the best-organised and effective Communist party in Latin America (outside Cuba) and certainly has the strongest electoral showing, consistently taking well

---

[4] These were the Communist Party, the Socialist Party, the Radical Party, the Movement for Unitary Popular Action, and two independent minority groupings, the Social Democratic Party and Independent Popular Action.

over 10 per cent of the vote from 1960 to 1973. Apart from a period in
the late 1920s when the party was criticised by the Comintern for
taking too moderate a line (see page 39) it has had no major disputes
with Moscow and, indeed, in the 1960s was one of the staunchest
defenders of the Soviet position on revolutionary tactics in Latin
America during the bitter polemics with Castro. Its commitment to
constitutional avenues to power, maintained since 1935, is not only
indicative of its tradition of faithful adherence to the official Moscow
line, but also reflects its own experiences within the Chilean political
structure which have convinced Communist leaders that power could
be won through participation in the parliamentary system. The 1935
Seventh Comintern Congress popular front policy was skilfully implemented in Chile, where Communists secured an election victory in
alliance with Radicals and Socialists in 1938. The Popular Front
remained in power for the next fourteen years consistently supported
by the Communists (although not the Socialists). In 1946 Communists
participated at ministerial level in the government of Radical President
González Videla. During their five-month period in office PCCh
membership rose considerably and their strength within the labour
movement reached its height. It seemed, however, that the Communists tried to move too quickly. Their rapid headway provoked the
Liberal Party to leave the coalition, and Radical President Videla,
disturbed by PCCh inroads into his own party's support base, took
measures in 1948 to outlaw the Communist Party. This was a very
serious blow which taught a whole generation of Communist leaders
some valuable lessons in how to conduct alliance politics, with the
result that in subsequent coalitions (the Popular Action Fronts of 1952,
1958 and 1964, and Popular Unity) the Communists sought to promote
their own position only when such manoeuvres seemed unlikely to
threaten the overall unity of the alliance. Thus by 1970, the PCCh had
developed the organisational strength and the ideological maturity to
act in the circumspect way that orthodoxy deems necessary.

Nevertheless, Soviet officials would have been far happier if the
PCCh had exercised firmer control within Popular Unity. The Communists' main partner, the Socialist Party, had never committed itself
unequivocally to constitutional government, and lacked the ideological cohesion imposed on the PCCh because of its links with the
CPSU. The history of Communist–Socialist Party relations in Chile is
one of intense rivalry and only uneasy cooperation. The socialists have
strong nationalistic tendencies which exacerbate their suspicions of
the Communist Party's connections with Moscow. Throughout

Popular Unity's period in office Soviet leaders were concerned about the instability of the coalition. Despite assertions in the Soviet media that 'The Chilean experience most convincingly confirms that the unity of popular and anti-imperialist forces, cemented by the unity of the proletariat – and, in the case of Chile, by the cooperation of . . . the Communists and the socialists – guarantees the successful advance of the liberation movement . . . '(*Pravda*, 25 September 1971, p. 4), an article by a specialist indicates that Moscow was fully aware of the difficulties involved in holding the coalition together. It said, 'Among the participants . . . there are differences in their understanding of democracy, in their assessment of the essential rhythm for the trans-formation [of Chile] and of the tactics in the anti-imperialist struggle. The inclusion of new masses in the active social process gives rise to the strengthening of anarchism, to the appearance of adventuristic slogans and actions. All this complicates the problem of maintaining unity' (Zorina: 1971, p. 63).

The overriding Soviet preoccupation was Allende's failure to secure power beyond the executive base. In an article in the October 1971 edition of *Kommunist*, leading ideologist Ponomarev observed that Popular Unity still faced 'major trials' because 'the creation of a popular government does not mean as yet that the working-class has assumed full power' (Ponomarev: 1971, p. 61). Soviet analysts seem to have been divided amongst themselves on the question of exactly how Allende should have set about consolidating his position. Ponomarev cited a passage from the resolution of the preceding PCCh Congress, stating that either the process of change in Chile would deepen, or the counter-revolution would win (Ponomarev: 1971, p. 61), implicitly urging the revolution to move at a faster pace. However, another article reviewing Allende's first year in office devoted much attention to opposition activity and advocated caution: 'Popular Unity . . . rejects attempts to nudge it into an adventurist forward leap, bypass-ing the stage set forth in its programme' (Pravda, 4 November 1971, p. 4).

Although Soviet ideologists failed to resolve the theoretical disputes about how Popular Unity was to expand its support base, Soviet and East European ambassadors to Chile, according to Washington's representative in Santiago, maintained a basic scepticism about the possibility of achieving socialism in a consumption economy, and complained privately that 'Chileans don't like to work' (Davis: 1985, p. 75). The Soviet leaders' concern was proved justified at the begin-ning of 1972 when it became clear that the problems they had identified were having a direct effect on the nature of Santiago's requirements of Moscow.

On taking office Allende had made it quite clear that he neither wanted nor expected Chile to become dependent upon Soviet aid to the extent that Cuba had done. It is true that in one pre-election interview, Allende stated his belief that 'our country would not be an oasis. International solidarity is today a fact' (*Ercilla* [Santiago], 4 February 1970, in Gouré and Suchlicki: 1971, p. 54), thereby hinting that he was hoping that the USSR would step in with substantial aid in the event of any sustained attempt to isolate Chile. However, at this early stage Allende's main foreign-policy goal was to diversify away from the United States, and initially the socialist bloc was only one of the areas to which he made overtures. A Socialist rather than a Communist was appointed to the Foreign Ministry, and Allende stood by an early decision not to buy Soviet military equipment, although it was reported that in 1971 the USSR had offered a $300 million credit for such purchases (Theberge: 1974, p. 80). A former economic adviser to Allende has stressed that Popular Unity's early efforts in the socialist countries 'centred fundamentally on obtaining grants of long-term credit for the purchase of machinery and industrial plant' (Guardia: 1979, p. 82). The results of Foreign Minister Clodomiro Almeyda's May 1971 visit to the USSR, which was the first major diplomatic meeting between the two governments, went some way towards answering those needs. The Soviet Union renewed an untouched credit of $57 million granted to Allende's predecessor, Eduardo Frei, and made further sums available to finance the building of a lubricant oil plant and a prefabricated housing plant. They promised to consider Chilean requests for assistance in the construction of chemical industry facilities and a fishing port. Agreement was concluded on the latter project the following September, and the Soviet Union arranged to lend Chile fishing trawlers. While these agreements hardly suggest any overwhelming Soviet enthusiasm for becoming involved in Chilean development, at this stage there may not have been too great a discrepancy between what the Chileans wanted and what the Kremlin was prepared to supply.

However, by the beginning of 1972 the gap had begun to widen. Popular Unity found itself increasingly unable to satisfy the consumer demand which its policies had stimulated during the preceding year. Allende once observed that 'The political model towards socialism that my government is applying requires that the socio-economic revolution takes place simultaneously with an uninterrupted economic expansion.' He was aware that the Chilean working classes, long accustomed to having their demands ignored, would not be inclined to make further sacrifices, even if by so doing they would be helping to sustain a government 'representing their own interests'. 'Many Chileans', he observed, 'are convinced that a socialist government is supposed to make each citizen a lottery winner' (Nogee and Sloan: 1979, p. 343 and p. 345). To survive politically, Popular Unity needed both to sustain production and to ensure effective distribution.

From the outset it was clear that, because of the domestic political situation and the flight of capital occasioned by the election of a self-proclaimed Marxist, the resources needed to finance the necessary economic expansion would have to be raised externally. Allende sought to do this firstly by compensating for the reduction in US investment with development credits from other nations, the socialist countries among them, and secondly by the expansion of the copper industry, which accounts for the vast bulk of Chile's foreign-exchange earnings. In formulating these plans, Popular Unity could not have been expected to predict that world copper prices would fall during 1971 from 64.2 cents to 49.3 cents per pound and remain at that level or slightly below until well into 1973. However, former Popular Unity ministers have since admitted that they made several fundamental errors of judgement concerning external financing. Firstly, it was not foreseen that the United States would succeed in blocking virtually all short-term credits, although the likelihood that Washington would find the means to implement all measures short of an open embargo ought surely to have been taken into account. Secondly, whilst Popular Unity economists did anticipate a rise in demand for imported foodstuffs and raw materials, they under-estimated its extent, particularly in the crucial year, 1972. The consequences of these miscalculations were already beginning to be felt at the end of 1971, with Chile's foreign-exchange reserves largely exhausted, a foreign debt approaching $2 billion, the onset of shortages in the shops and a flourishing black market.

As a result of all this, Chilean requests to the USSR for short-term credit to finance imports became increasingly urgent throughout 1972, particularly after May when the economic situation reached crisis point as inflation slipped out of government control. Thus, during the course of 1972, two reappraisals were underway simultaneously. The Chileans seem to have undertaken a drastic upwards revision of their expectations of the Soviet Union (perhaps encouraged by Fidel Castro's December 1971 visit to Chile, perhaps spurred on by desperation). At the same time Soviet evaluations of the viability of the Popular Unity experiment were scaled down as strikes and opposition mounted.

The Popular Unity government may have experienced one moment of false optimism at the beginning of 1972, when a Chinese credit to Allende of $67 million made Moscow especially vulnerable to left-wing criticism for failing to support Chile. Beijing was enthusiastic about Allende insofar as he was anti-imperialist, but the Chinese were naturally dubious about the un-Maoist means by which he had assumed power. Chou En-lai's remark that Allende had 'won the government but not the power' indicates that Soviet leaders were not alone in their scepticism about the viability of Popular Unity. Nevertheless, the People's Republic of China is deficient in copper and (also in contrast to the USSR) is in a position to export agricultural produce. (Significantly, Beijing did not sever ties with Chile after the 1973 *coup* and has since contracted to buy copper from the Pinochet dictatorship.) This economic complementarity led to the signing of a trade agreement in April 1971, involving sales of $65-70 million worth of copper from 1972 to 1975, in exchange for Chinese rice, tea, soy beans and light industrial goods. Beijing cultivated goodwill for itself in Santiago by the granting of $2 million in hard currency to repair damage caused by the July 1971 earthquake, and a further major agreement was signed the following November providing for the sale of 60,000 tons of Chilean nitrates to China during the first six months of 1972.

In this context Allende did not hesitate to put pressure on the Soviet Union by timing the announcement of the January 1972 credit from Beijing to coincide with the arrival of a high-level state planning delegation from the Soviet Union. At this stage, Allende was probably in the strongest position he ever occupied for extracting concessions from the Kremlin. The economic crisis had not yet broken (inflation at 40 per cent in the twelve months up to June 1972 was running at much the same level as the average annual rate throughout the 1960s). Moreover the Soviet Union had derived several political benefits from the existence of the Allende government, at minimum cost to itself. Allende's first foreign-policy act had been to establish relations with Cuba, which was hailed in Moscow as a crucial blow against the OAS blockade ('The blockade is broken', *Izvestiia*, 17 November 1970, p. 2). Chile had also given the Andean Pact group a more radical temper, which led to the adoption at their June 1971 Lima Conference of 'anti-imperialist' measures restricting foreign investments. This lent weight to the Soviet propaganda campaign for concerted Latin American action against the United States via an organisation which could potentially challenge the OAS. In similar vein, the closure of three small US military posts in Chile bolstered the Soviet campaign for the elimination of all US bases in Latin America.

This time, Allende's strategy was partially successful. The USSR, which had previously met all requests for short-term loans to finance imports of food and spare parts with a flat refusal (Turrent: 1983, p. 74), granted a $50 million credit in hard currency to contribute towards 'Chilean imports from Western countries'. In assessing the significance of this it should be borne in mind that short-term loans from the Soviet Union to developing countries are almost always bilateral and tied to the purchase of Soviet goods. More importantly, 1972 was the year in which detente facilitated an increase in Moscow's imports of technology and capital goods from the West, and in which the USSR bought massive quantities of grain on the open market. The Soviet Union therefore had strong incentives to conserve its own supplies of hard currency, and the sacrifice was almost certainly made in order to avoid being outflanked by the Chinese, who had recently stepped up diplomatic initiatives in Latin America.

Over the next few months the Soviet leaders, preoccupied with Nixon's forthcoming visit to Moscow, made only nominal gestures towards Chile, designed to preserve the appearance of a flurry of activity, whilst avoiding any substantial commitments. On 3 March an agreement involving cultural, sporting and scientific exchanges was signed, and weekly flights were inaugurated between Santiago and Moscow a few days later. Meanwhile, the rapidly deteriorating economic situation in Chile, and its adverse political effects, were given full coverage in the Soviet press. The Chilean Communists sought to put pressure on the Soviet leaders by sending ever more pessimistic reports about the precarious position of Popular Unity. In April 1972 they warned that, 'The Popular government is running with great difficulties and dangers. The class struggle is becoming fiercer and constantly more acute' (*Pravda*, 19 April 1972, p. 5).

Nevertheless, the next major encounter between Soviet and Chilean officials, which took place in Moscow at the end of June 1972, achieved very little. Carlos Altamirano, who headed the Chilean delegation, was an unfortunate choice as envoy (one which was probably dictated by overriding domestic political pressures). Not only was Altamirano secretary of the Socialist Party and one of the most vociferous advocates of a more radical course for Popular Unity, but he had also visited

China during the previous March and was inclined to a sympathetic view of the situation there. However, the vagueness and generality of the joint communiqué issued after the June visit to Moscow can be attributed primarily to the Soviet Union's desire to distance itself from Chile at the height of detente. Indeed, the US envoy to Santiago (from November 1971 onwards) reports that when the Soviet ambassador called on him that June, having delayed six months in returning the North American's initial protocol call, 'what Basov wanted to talk about was US conditions for an economic settlement with Chile' (Davis: 1985, p. 131). No more short-term credits were forthcoming from Moscow, despite the fact that Chile needed them, according to Altamirano, 'with dramatic urgency' (Altamirano: 1977, p. 237). The one agreement which was concluded, involving an unspecified degree of assistance to the copper industry, was referred to only in passing in a very brief article in *Izvestiia* a few weeks later (*Izvestiia*, 21 July 1972, p. 1).

The whole issue of aid for the development of the copper industry highlights the inherent limitations of Popular Unity's relationship with the Soviet Union. Allende stated publicly on several occasions that Chile needed Soviet assistance in this respect. Initially, Soviet experts considered the possibility of 'building a special plant to supply the mines and factories with all the necessary parts and with some of the equipment formerly imported from the United States' (Radio Moscow, 5 June 1971, in Gouré and Rothenberg: 1975, p. 142). However, Chile's US-designed and built copper mines could not be adapted to Soviet equipment without lengthy and extremely costly delays in production. Credits offered by the USSR for the purchase of machinery and equipment for the copper industry were scarcely taken up by the Chileans. Similar technical difficulties explain why Chile paid $5.5 million cash for a Boeing 707 in 1972, even though the Soviet Union would have made credits available for the purchase of *Iliushin* jets. The necessity of retraining pilots, setting up new maintenance facilities and stockpiling new spare parts made the Soviet deal ultimately uneconomical. Former Popular Unity member Sergio Bitar explained the problems the Chileans had with Soviet credits as follows:

The limited utilisation of Soviet resources can be attributed to Chile's reduced capacity to absorb bilateral credits. These could not be used immediately because of ignorance of the suppliers and of the quality of the products. This happened with machinery, spare parts, medicines and foodstuffs.

Moreover the socialist countries' negotiating methods obstructed the use of credits. The negotiations were conducted at two levels: firstly, the political and secondly, the technical. At the first stage, results were rapid, owing to the expression of political will to collaborate. But thereafter the negotiating apparatus of the socialist enterprises came into operation, and that apparatus is trained to conduct tough negotiations. Frequently the conversations were broken off, causing disappointment on the Chilean side, until they were reopened thanks to political efforts. Nor do the socialist countries have organisations which specialise in providing economic aid to meet emergencies, such as exist in the United States. (Bitar: 1979, pp. 194–5)

Despite its commitment to expansion of state control over the economy, 'the Chilean government recruited few planning experts from Eastern Europe. Those experts and technicians they did bring to Chile did not generally work out well, because of professional weaknesses, cultural differences, and lack of fluency in Spanish' (Davis: 1985, p. 81).

Between June and December 1972, when Allende made his ill-fated trip to Moscow, no further significant diplomatic exchanges took place between the two governments. This raises the question of what sources of information the Soviet leaders had at their disposal in order to assess developments in Chile. One vital contact was obviously the Chilean Communist Party. Delegations from the PCCh were frequently in Moscow to attend state functions and conferences and were always received by Brezhnev. The CPSU sent a delegation headed by Andrei Kirilenko (the only Politburo member to visit Chile whilst Allende was in power) to the fiftieth anniversary celebrations of the PCCh in January 1972. Major state visits to Moscow by Popular Unity representatives were always preceded by discussions with Luis Corvalán and other PCCh leaders. The Soviet Union also made efforts to develop a relationship with the Socialists, both to help them gauge the mood of the coalition and in the hope that they might gain some influence.

Moscow's contacts in Chile were not, however, confined to formal party-to-party relations. Undoubtedly embassy staff and TASS correspondents must have played an important role, although little is known about these activities. In 1972, the Soviet Union also increased its informal presence in Chile in order to gather first-hand intelligence without indulging in too many open contacts which could be interpreted as close identification with Allende. To this end, at least three correspondents from the *New Times* were sent out to Chile in the course of the year. However, Soviet officials received what they probably regarded as their most reliable information from one man –

diplomat and journalist Alexander Alekseev, who travelled to Chile in 1972, officially as a TASS correspondent, but in fact with instructions to carry out informal consultations 'with the governing parties, but above all with the executive'.[5] Alekseev was well-suited to this task, having played the role of mediator between the Soviet Union and Cuba in the early 1960s.[6] There is no doubt that Alekseev was very highly regarded in Moscow and his analysis of events in Chile would have conditioned the views of the Soviet leadership.

A further important possibility, although one for which there is no substantive confirmation, is that the USSR's assessment of the Chilean situation was coloured by reports from Havana. Cultural and linguistic ties, as well as political connections, made it easier for Cubans to obtain information in Chile than it was for Soviet representatives (indeed, Allende's daughter was married to a Cuban intelligence officer). Castro's own assessment of prospects for the Chilean road, informed by a three-week tour of the country in November 1971 (originally scheduled for ten days), was not optimistic. During the course of a highly provocative farewell speech delivered in Santiago's National Stadium on 2 December 1971 (a text which, incidentally, was omitted from the Chilean edition of Fidel's speeches in Chile) he argued that 'The reactionaries and the oligarchs here are much better prepared than they were in Cuba . . . they have all the weapons they need to wage a battle on every field in the face of the advance of progress. A battle on the economic field, on the political field, and on the field of the masses – I repeat – on the field of the masses.' Introducing a remark attributed to a US official to the effect that 'the days of the popular government in Chile are numbered', Castro was unequivocal in his analysis of the rationale behind such an assessment: 'I say that such confidence is based on the weakness of the very revolutionary process, on weaknesses in the ideological battle, on weaknesses in the mass struggle, on weakness in the face of the enemy' (Castro: 1972, p. 210 and p. 213). Thus if Cuba did play a mediating role, it might well have had significant repercussions on the Soviet–Chilean relationship. It was suggested above that Castro may have led the Chileans to expect too much of the Soviet Union in terms of aid: misunderstandings could equally well have been created

[5] J. E. Vega, former Popular Unity ambassador to Cuba, in an interview with Isabel Turrent, 30 September 1977, in Turrent: 1983, p. 102.
[6] In his memoirs, Khrushchev records that: 'When the Cuban leaders needed something from us, they would more often address themselves to Alekseev than to our ambassador' (Khrushchev: 1970, p. 490). In 1962 Alekseev replaced the former ambassador, Kudriatsev, whom the Cubans found very difficult to deal with.

in the other direction. However, this remains a matter for further investigation.

By the time that Allende was due to arrive in the Soviet Union, early in December 1972, Soviet leaders had seen all their grounds for caution amply confirmed. As the Politburo viewed the situation, they were faced with a government which had failed to consolidate its power, in a country with a chronically weak economy and import requirements (nearly all in hard currency goods) which were rapidly becoming 'virtually insatiable'. The Chilean perspective, however, was somewhat different. Allende's decision to go on a tour of friendly Latin American countries (Mexico, Peru and Cuba), New York (where he intended to make a speech to the United Nations denouncing the US 'invisible blockade' of his country) and the USSR, to 'negotiate a closer relationship with Moscow', reflected a consensus within Popular Unity that the deepening economic crisis called for drastic remedies and that Chile needed 'a rapprochement with the socialist camp, and with the USSR in particular'.[7] Former Popular Unity member Sergio Bitar confirms that Allende went to Moscow 'in order to obtain immediate supplies of liquid currency' and that he hoped to secure 'a high level of funds with which to confront the critical situation' (Bitar: 1979, p. 193).

The indications were that Chile had high hopes of the visit: Bitar states that 'the support of the socialist countries was considered a certainty by many political leaders, who thought that, in an emergency, they could count on receiving what was needed' (Bitar, 1979 p. 193). (US ambassador Davis suggests, however, that Allende himself may have gone to Moscow 'with doubts about the Soviet response' [Davis: 1985, p. 130].) Only a few hours before a joint Soviet–Chilean communiqué was issued announcing the results of the negotiations, Chile's representative at the United Nations, Hernán Santa Cruz, said that it would contain 'a very categorical statement' on Soviet cooperation with Chile and that the USSR was ready to 'expand its economic aid to Chile' (the *New York Times*, 9 December 1972, p. 12). In the event the communiqué could not have been less categorical. It expressed Soviet 'understanding' (rather than 'support') for Popular Unity's efforts at 'implementing social and economic transformations'. There was no mention of new credits and only a reference to general proposals for 'assistance from the Soviet Union to the Republic of Chile in the construction of industrial enterprises, in the expansion of the power-engineering base, in the fields of agri-

[7] Luis Maira, interview with Isabel Turrent, 31 January 1978, in Turrent: 1983, p. 104.

culture and fishing, and in the training and instruction of specialists' (*Pravda*, 10 December 1972, p. 1 and p. 4).

While this might seem to be a fairly lengthy list, the fact remains that Soviet officials had clearly not committed themselves to any specific projects. In any case, judging by the Soviet record at that stage, the Chileans would have been unwise to place too much faith in these proposals. At the end of 1972 the only concrete results of previous agreements were the pre-fabricated housing plant and the fishing cooperation. Moscow was still reviewing plans for an oil refinery and the fishing port that the Chileans wanted to build near Valparaíso (the *New York Times*, 7 December 1972, p. 10).

A few weeks after Allende's visit it was reported that the Soviet Union had agreed to provide $27 million worth of wheat and other agricultural products, and a $20 million hard-currency loan. Nevertheless, Chilean expectations 'remained unsatisfied' and these 'very modest results . . . created confusion within Popular Unity' (Bitar: 1979, p. 193). It seems that the Soviet leadership had been reluctant to give even this much. Apparently Allende was sharply criticised during the first round of talks for his inability to consolidate power and bring the country firmly under his control.[8] Sergio Bitar states, 'In the first meeting in the Kremlin, Brezhnev made a speech in which he emphasised that, from his point of view, the principal international problems were Vietnam, Egypt and Cuba; after which came four or five other countries, and then Chile. Secondly, Brezhnev stressed that the Soviets could not see stability, that the Popular Unity government was fighting against the centre and that it was failing to amass forces' (Bitar: 1979, p. 194). President Podgornii was reported to have told Allende that 'We understand your difficulty and concerns but we also know from our own experience that, if a people's power knows how to draw to its side and unite all democratic and genuinely patriotic forces – the working class, the peasantry, the middle classes – and if it is consistent and purposeful in realising its proclaimed programme no reactionary force will be able to stop the working people from following its chosen role' (Nogee and Sloan: 1979, p. 362). It was also reported that Allende was advised to seek accommodation with the United States, perhaps even showing flexibility over the issue of compensation for the expropriation of North American copper interests (Davis: 1985, p. 130).

When it became clear that no agreements were likely to be concluded, Allende utilised the only means of applying pressure still open

[8] Ibid., p. 113.

to him and threatened to cancel the rest of his tour of the USSR, which was to have incorporated a visit to Kiev. Anxious to avoid the adverse publicity which would have ensued, Soviet leaders consented to a further round of negotiations, which were conducted by Soviet and Chilean technical experts whilst Allende and his official hosts continued with the original itinerary.[9]

Whatever the exact level of assistance which was agreed during those talks, it is certain that it was both far below Chilean expectations and completely inadequate for their needs. A former Popular Unity adviser stated, 'The forecast made at the end of 1972 of import needs for 1973 estimated that $500 million of agricultural goods and raw materials for industry would have to be financed from the socialist camp in order to maintain the level of employment in industry, and sustain the consumption levels per inhabitant for basic goods which had been reached in 1971' (Guardia: 1979, p. 84). (In fact, figures for estimated import requirements were beginning to look somewhat meaningless for the beleaguered Chilean economy, and the country's true needs were certainly greater than the above estimate suggests.)

Allende apparently returned to Chile convinced that 'the USSR's policy had become a low-profile one with no prospects', and that there was no longer any possibility of obtaining substantial Soviet support.[10] Communist Party General Secretary Luis Corvalán implicitly confirmed this sober reassessment of what Moscow was prepared to provide when he said, shortly after Allende's return, 'We are sure of and will continue to be sure of the aid of the Soviet Union and of the socialist camp in general. But we cannot expect our problems to be solved from abroad' (Muñóz: 1984, p. 15).

During 1973, with the exception of a brief burst of enthusiasm over the results of the March congressional elections, when Popular Unity increased its share of the vote to 43.4 per cent, Soviet commentaries reflected in full the intensification of the class struggle in Chile and the difficulties faced by Popular Unity. A CIA officer, testifying after the *coup*, stated that 'We did have some quite reliable reporting [in August 1973] indicating that the Russians were advising Allende to put his relations with the United States in order, if not to settle compensation at least to reach some sort of accommodation which would ease the strain between the two countries. There were reports indicating that . . . they were in effect trying to move Allende toward a compromise agreement' (Davis: 1985, p. 131). No further credits were granted, and the development projects which were undertaken (agreements were

[9] Ibid.   [10] Isabel Turrent, from an interview with Luis Maira, ibid., p. 120.

made in July 1973 to expand Topcopilla Electric Plant, which supplies the Chuquicamata copper mine, and to construct a wheat mill in Valparaíso) were simply indicative of the need to use up previously granted credits.

The Soviet leadership clearly preferred to allocate all the resources that they had available for Latin America to the integration of Cuba into the socialist system, rather than to direct any portion of them to carrying out a rescue operation for Chile's politically and economically unstable attempt to pursue the 'peaceful road' to socialism. In retrospect it seems unlikely that, whatever the Soviet response had been in December 1972, Popular Unity would have succeeded in serving its full six-year term of office. The rupture of relations after the 11 September *coup* and Pinochet's abrupt termination of economic links only served to confirm the wisdom of Moscow's policy of caution; any further commitment by the USSR to Allende would only have resulted in heavier economic losses when the break eventually came.

In the aftermath of the *coup* the Soviet Union, constrained by its desire not to provoke the United States, confined its response to general condemnations of the repression carried out by the Chilean armed forces, particularly against the Communists, and calls for unity within the Chilean democratic camp and solidarity from their counterparts throughout the world. The Communist bloc's campaigns in the United Nations to focus attention on human rights abuses in Chile were led not by the USSR (although it may well have been the instigator), but by other East European leaders. The existence of the Pinochet regime, which rapidly became an international pariah, has in fact proved not inconvenient for Moscow. Especially after the 1976 military *coup* in Argentina, Soviet propaganda presented conditions in Chile as by far the most repressive in the Southern Cone, leaving the military governments of Brazil and Argentina – countries which (in stark contrast to Chile) offered potentially valuable opportunities for commercial exchange – to stand, by implication, as comparatively benign dictatorships.

The failure of the Popular Unity experiment provoked a further down-grading of the revolutionary potential of Latin America, which seemed to be confirmed by the shift to the right which occurred across the continent from 1973–6. The reformist military government in Peru, which had evoked so much Soviet optimism about the progressive tendencies of the military and the possibility of promoting an alternative to the Brazilian model, drifted rightwards from 1975 onwards. In Bolivia General Juan José Torres, who had come to power in

October 1970 with active worker and student support, was over-thrown the following August by right-wing General Banzer, who proceeded to consolidate a seven-year rule. Therefore in the mid-1970s scope for ideologically motivated policy-making was severely constrained and the Soviet Union was left free to pursue initiatives, dating back to the 1960s or earlier, towards the economically and politically significant regional powers: Argentina, Brazil, Mexico and Venezuela. In this context it is worth speculating as to how Moscow might have responded if Allende had become President not of Chile, but of grain-exporting Argentina, and not at the height of detente, but in the midst of the 1980–1 grain embargo.

6 The Soviet Union and the major Latin American powers

Relations between the USSR and the four major Latin American powers have never been based on ideological affinity. (The Soviet Union has shown great interest in the Mexican revolution, which antedated the Bolshevik uprising by seven years, but the two systems are founded on very different political and ideological premises.) However, the Argentine and Brazilian economies offer the Soviet Union potentially greater economic complementarity than it can find with virtually any other Latin American country. This is reflected in the fact that these two nations are by far the Soviet Union's largest trading partners in Latin America (excluding Cuba). A more limited scope for exchange exists between the USSR and Mexico, and very little at all with Venezuela. (Soviet–Venezuelan trade is still negligible and not recorded in Soviet statistics.) Mexico has some interest in cultivating relations with the Soviet Union as part of its overall foreign-policy strategy of asserting independence from the United States, and Argentina, which fiercely resists Washington's attempts to draw it into the Pan-American orbit, has also at times revealed a political motivation for its approaches to Moscow. However the interest on the Latin American side has been fundamentally economic (almost exclusively so in the cases of Brazil, Argentina since 1976 and Venezuela). It is the varying degrees of economic complementarity which reflect and have been the main determinant of the extent of Soviet relations with each of these countries. The following chapter concentrates on the development of the Soviet Union's links with Argentina, in order to highlight how the fundamental constraints on Soviet–Latin American relations outlined in Chapter 1 have affected even this, Moscow's most important Latin American trading partnership. The analysis then proceeds to consider Soviet relations with (in decreasing order of importance) Brazil, Mexico and Venezuela, in order to show how and why the pattern has been similar and indeed is likely to recur throughout the region.

For primarily political reasons, Soviet–Argentine relations rested on an uneasy basis until 1973 when President Perón, taking advantage of the prevailing climate of detente and the fact that the Soviet Union had recently witnessed the fall of Allende, sought to expand the Soviet connection in a bid to give some substance to Peronist assertions of Argentine nationalism. The USSR, confronted since 1972 with the need to import massive quantities of grain in order to make up the deficiency in its own agricultural output, did not hesitate to respond to overtures from a country which was not only a major regional power but also one of the world's principal grain-exporting nations. Perón's commitment to state control over foreign trading facilitated a major series of long-term economic agreements, which stimulated a three-fold increase in the volume of trade between the two nations in as many years (although Argentine sales to the USSR still accounted for less than 10 per cent of total exports). When the new-found stability in Soviet–Argentine commercial relations looked as if it might be threatened by the right-wing military coup of March 1976, the Soviet Union made haste to indicate that commercial expediency would take precedence over ideological distaste. The Argentine generals in their turn recognised that their country's economy was in no state to accommodate anti-Communist gestures which might jeopardise a promising export market. Both parties saw their policies vindicated in 1980 when the US-inspired embargo on shipments of grain, meat and dairy produce to the USSR, introduced by President Carter in response to the Soviet invasion of Afghanistan, presented Argentina with the opportunity to become the USSR's principal source of grain supplies for well over a year. (The embargo was lifted by President Reagan in April 1981.) In 1980 eighty per cent of Argentina's grain exports went to the Soviet Union, and a long-term supply agreement was signed in July of that year. At this stage it may well have seemed to Soviet leaders that the possibility of developing a mutually beneficial and stable trading relationship, first suggested by the 1974 agreements, had been confirmed. Three years later, however, Soviet officials were clearly doubtful that such a relationship could be achieved and it appears that, even with so much at stake for both sides, they have been unable to overcome the difficulties which hindered a major commitment in the past.

Moscow's hopes of establishing satisfactory commercial links with Argentina date back to the 1920s, when initiatives in Latin America were directed primarily at the River Plate nations and Mexico. Argentina was not only the most advanced country in Latin America and therefore, according to Comintern thinking, the one with the greatest revolutionary potential, but also an important source of food supplies to Great Britain, which was still regarded by the Soviet Union as a potential aggressor. In the 1920s Comintern officials upheld the staunchly pro-Moscow Argentine Communist Party (PCA), the first in Latin America to join the Third International (in 1920), as their greatest achievement in Latin America. This was largely because of the influence of its founder Victorio Codovilla, an Italian who had migrated to Argentina before the First World War, and quickly became the Comintern's principal adviser on Latin America. As a member of the first Latin American Secretariat in Moscow and treasurer of its counterpart in Buenos Aires, the South American Bureau, Codovilla served as a key link between Moscow and South America. After the 1930 *coup* Codovilla spent his eleven years of exile working for the Comintern in Moscow and subsequently served as one of their agents in Spain during the Civil War. He returned to Argentina permanently at the end of the Second World War and continued to dominate the Argentine Communist movement for many years. The party itself has, however, remained marginal to Argentine politics, initially because of a persistent factionalism and latterly because of the influence of the Peronist movement, which captured much of the Communists' potential support base. PCA activities have never interfered significantly with Moscow's state-to-state relations with Argentina.

It was pressure from Great Britain, rather than Comintern activities, which deterred Argentina from establishing diplomatic relations, but in recognition of the small but growing volume of trade with Moscow (involving Soviet imports of Argentine agricultural products, such as wool, hides and quebracho extract, in return for very limited Argentine purchases of Soviet machinery and equipment) the Argentine government authorised the establishment in 1927 of a branch of the Soviet trading office, Iuzhamtorg, in Buenos Aires. However, as was admitted in two *Izvestiia* articles (2 August 1928 and 24 July 1929, in Clissold: 1970, pp. 74–6 and 79–81), trade was hindered by the difficulty and expense of shipping goods from Argentina, the problems encountered by Soviet manufacturers in providing adequate packaging for goods which had to cross the Equator and, already, by the serious imbalance in favour of the Latin American republic. Trade, which fluctuated quite dramatically from year to year (see table 3), was in the event brought to a halt by the economic dislocation of the Great Depression and by the anti-Communist climate prevailing in Argentina after the 1930 *coup*. This event thwarted a potential agreement on

Table 3. *Soviet trade with Argentina 1923–1930 (thousands of rubles)*

	Exports	Imports
1923–4	0	4,674
1924–5	0	37,099
1925–6	3	36,304
1927	1,157	89,672
1928	2,737	29,836
1929	12,947	98,928
1930	12,864	60,522

Source: *SSSR i Latinskaia Amerika*, p. 83, in Clissold: 1970, p. 9.

Soviet oil sales to Argentina of 250,000 tons per annum for three years, with an option for Buenos Aires to reduce the volume of imports, or even cancel the contract, if its own national production increased (Fuchs: 1965, p. 125).

In the immediate post-war years most Latin American governments fell into line with the US diplomatic offensive in the area (intended to establish a *de facto* zone of influence to counter the *de jure* control the Soviet Union had consolidated in Eastern Europe), which culminated in the signing of a mutual defence treaty in Rio de Janeiro in 1947 and the formation of the Organisation of American States the following year. However, the easing of the Cold War in the 1950s and the growing realisation in Latin America that Washington's objectives in forming the OAS had been very different from those of most Latin American governments (who had hoped for substantial development aid) contributed to a sense that Latin America should not ignore the now vast markets of the socialist bloc.

In 1946 the newly elected government of Colonel Perón re-opened relations with the Soviet Union despite the fact that Perón was labelled a 'fascist' by the world Communist movement because of his leading role in the 1943–6 military regime which had resisted US pressure to declare war on the Axis powers until the Allied victory was imminent. A PCA manifesto published on 21 October 1945 designated Perón 'Number One Enemy of the Argentine People' (Gillespie: 1982, p. 10). Secret negotiations had in fact been held between the two sides in November 1945, probably in Montevideo, through the mediation of Brazilian President Getulio Vargas (Rapoport: 1986, p. 252). Perón's overture was motivated by a desire to exploit Cold War hostility to promote his own particular variant of Argentine nationalism, the so-called 'Third Position', which was essentially a strategy to introduce a counterweight to US influence in South America. It was clearly intended as a direct challenge to Washington, with whom relations were at an all time low in the post-war years, ostensibly because of the military government's refusal to break with the Axis, but fundamentally because of Argentine reluctance to take its US-determined place in the Pan-American system. The cut off of US aid from 1946 to 1950 and the severe curtailing of trade prompted Perón to seek access to the alternative markets of the socialist bloc. As economic crisis deepened during the early 1950s, he took measures to explore the potential of the Soviet market and a series of trade agreements were signed from 1952–1954.

Two factors of this early relationship are pertinent to subsequent developments. Firstly, Moscow demonstrated that it was willing to overlook ideological considerations in its relations with one of the major South American powers. After all, Perón had initiated diplomatic relations at a time when most other Latin American countries simply acquiesced to US pressure to sever ties with Soviet Russia. His government was one of only three in Latin America (the others being in Mexico and Uruguay) to maintain relations throughout the Cold War period.

Secondly, despite the existence of political will on both sides, and the fact that the mutual opportunities offered by trade were heralded by optimistic media commentaries in both countries, the development of relations was thwarted by economic factors. Argentina's reluctance to replace US or European imports with inferior quality Soviet goods led to the USSR's being wary of committing itself to a trading pattern which might be imbalanced. In August 1953 an agreement called for $75 million trade each way over the following year and the USSR granted Argentina a $30 million credit. By mid-1954 Argentina had exported $46.5 million worth of agricultural products to Moscow (mostly hides and wool), receiving in turn $28.9 million worth of Soviet manufactures. Complaints were made about the quality of many of these, which were said to have an extremely short working life. In 1954 a further attempt was made to consolidate trade between the two countries, with a slightly less ambitious agreement setting a target of $54 million trade each way. The $30 million credit, which remained unused, was reduced to $4 million.

Similar problems continued to hinder the expansion of commercial relations throughout the 1950s and 1960s. In 1958 (a year during which world market prices for Argentina's agricultural exports were falling) a much-vaunted agreement was signed involving a $100 million Soviet credit (at 2.5 per cent interest) to Argentina for the purchase of oil equipment, to be repaid with traditional exports such as wool, hides and quebracho extract, over a period of seven years, payments to begin three years after the shipment of the Soviet machinery. Even under these generous terms, only $30 million of the credit was taken up, presumably because the equipment available did not meet Argentine needs. A team of Argentine oil experts who visited the USSR in 1952 had found it to be 'clumsy and not interchangeable with the US oil rigs in use' (Philip: 1982, p. 407). Economic relations were also disrupted by the frequent interventions of the vehemently anti-Communist armed forces in Argentine politics during these years. Moscow kept trying, offering a total of $45 million in credit – the only Soviet credits granted to any Latin American country apart from Cuba in the period 1955–65 – to the more receptive civilian presidents Frondizi (1958–62) and Illia (1963–6), but the sheer instability of Argentine politics precluded any long-term commitments.

Events of the 1970s indicated that political resistance within the Latin American countries to trade with the USSR had been eradicated to the point where it can no longer be considered as a satisfactory explanation for the restricted nature of relations. The onset of Perón's second presidency, which lasted from September 1973 until his death on 1 July 1974, marked the beginning of a new period in Soviet–Argentine relations. Both parties had strong incentives, both political and economic, to overcome past difficulties. Peronist enthusiasm for the expansion of relations with the Soviet Union had much the same doctrinal basis as in the 1950s: in the words of Economy Minister José Gelbard, they wanted to use 'trade as a tool of sovereignty' (Milenky: 1978, p. 156). The only difference, twenty years on, was that the strategy was more likely to be successful because of the consolidation of the Cuban revolution and its challenge to US hegemony within the Western hemisphere. From the Soviet point of view, Peronist nationalism, once regarded as a 'fascist' phenomenon, now fitted in very well with Moscow's broad policy in Latin America of undermining US preponderance whilst seeking to cultivate its own ties when appropriate opportunities arose. In this context, it was highly significant that Perón's election came only a fortnight after the Chilean military had intervened to crush the Popular Unity experiment. Clearly Perón's Argentina was in no sense a substitute for Allende's Chile in political terms. It offered no model for the construction of socialism, but it did give Moscow the chance to compensate for the setback in its relations with Latin America caused by the fall of Popular Unity. Radio

Moscow said that Argentina had 'shown other countries in South America how to strengthen their independence and how to free themselves from the shackles of the multi-national corporation', and Brezhnev singled out Perón for special commendation in a speech made to the Supreme Soviet on 14 June 1974 (Milenky: 1978, p. 156).

The political factors pointing to the opening up of relations between the two countries were underscored by crucial economic motivations. At that time Buenos Aires was having difficulty selling its agricultural produce in traditional markets – by 1974–5 the European Community had virtually sealed itself off with protectionism – and balance of payments crises, deepened by 1973 oil price rises, had curtailed opportunities in Latin America and other Third World areas. For an Argentine industry that could produce relatively sophisticated consumer goods the hitherto closed markets of the Soviet Union and Eastern Europe must have looked very promising, particularly under a government whose main economic policy emphasis was on the expansion of the industrial sector. There was also the possibility of securing Soviet technology and equipment for the various hydro-electric schemes intended to solve Argentina's energy problems. In addition, Perón's initiation of diplomatic ties with Cuba and his granting of a $1.2 billion credit in August 1973 opened up what was soon to become Argentina's largest Latin American market.

From Moscow's point of view, the Argentine initiative towards Cuba was important in further undermining the US blockade against the island, which had already been challenged by Allende and reformist military President Velasco of Peru. Argentine Economy Minister José Gelbard's announcement that branches of US corporations in his country would have to cooperate in view of Argentina's new trade policies towards Cuba prompted Chrysler-Fèvre, General Motors Argentina and Ford to press the US Treasury for the necessary authorisation to sell vehicles to Cuba. (US companies have been prohibited from trading with Cuba since early 1962 by one of a series of measures carried out in retaliation for Cuba's nationalisation of American-owned corporations.) Washington finally acceded to the demand in April 1974.

However, for the Soviet Union, the most compelling incentive for a rapprochement with Argentina was the prospect of an additional source of grain. In 1972 it became clear that the Soviet leadership had taken a decision to compensate for the disastrous shortfall in its own harvest with massive imports, rather than further weakening long-term capacity to feed its population by premature slaughtering of livestock. Practically all of the USSR's purchases on the international market, in what became known as the 'Great Grain Robbery' of 1972, had come from the United States, and the Kremlin was anxious to diversify the sources of such a politically sensitive commodity.

In the light of the circumstances outlined above, both parties made certain political gestures to pave the way for a closer relationship. In the Soviet Union there was a subtle shift of ideological emphasis in Perón's favour. The November–December 1972 edition of *Latinskaia Amerika* published an article by an Argentine Communist denouncing Perón and Peronism as anti-Communist and anti-Soviet allies of the national bourgeoisie (pp. 66–79). In December, however, the Soviet foreign-policy magazine *New Times* declared that while Perón had 'persecuted Communists and other progressives cruelly' during his first administration, the subsequent military regimes had been 'even crueller' (Number 49, December 1972, p. 24). In Argentina, persecution of the PCA had largely been stopped by the previous military government of General Alejandro Lanusse (1971–3) who had signed, although not ratified, a trade agreement with Moscow in 1971 in the belief that Argentina needed to diversify its exports. Peronist President Hector Cámpora, inaugurated on 24 May 1973, moved quickly to legalise the PCA, which then sought an electoral alliance with the Peronists. Despite Perón's rejection of this proposal and his purge of Marxists from the Peronist movement, he received Communist party backing for his candidacy in the September 1973 elections, as did Isabel Perón in 1974 and the Peronist candidate Luder in 1983.

All these factors help to explain the highly successful visit of Economy Minister Gelbard to the Soviet Union and Eastern Europe in May 1974. Gelbard was accorded the honour of being received by Brezhnev, Kosygin and Podgornii, and returned to Argentina with more solid evidence of Moscow's regard: the Eastern bloc signed fourteen long-term trade and economic cooperation agreements and offered $950 million in credits, $600 million of which was granted by the USSR. This Soviet offer is well over twice the most commonly accepted estimates for Soviet long-term credits to Allende (see pages 128–9), and made Argentina the recipient of the largest Soviet credit granted to any developing country in 1974. Specifically with the USSR, the most important accord was a ten-year compensation agreement, renewable for five years and covering up to 30 per cent of total sales, with uncompensated sales to be paid at an interest of 4.5 per cent per annum for the public sector and 5 per cent for the private sector. (This was the standard rate at this time for Soviet credits to Third World nations with which it was interested in doing business, but with which it had little political sympathy. In comparison, credits to Allende were offered at a concessionary rate of 2–3 per cent.) The 1974 agreements, together with the Peronist commitment to state control of foreign trading, stimulated a three-fold increase in volume of trade between 1973 and 1976. Moreover, in 1973, a Soviet–Argentine Chamber of Commerce was founded on the initiative of private Argentine companies. This was the first such organisation in Latin America to be recognised by the Soviet Chamber of Commerce, and the fifth in the world (López: 1983, pp. 55–64). Once again, however, the relationship was highly imbalanced: Argentina's exports to the USSR outnumbered its Soviet imports by a factor of 20 to 1 in 1976 (see table 4). Even so, the Soviet market absorbed only about 10 per cent of Argentine exports in that year.

Historical precedent suggests that the March 1976 *coup* led by General Jorge Videla should have led to an abrupt reduction of trading links between Argentina and the USSR and even, in the light of the virulence of the new regime's anti-Communism and the severity of its campaign against 'subversion', a complete breach in relations. However, the Soviet Union issued no condemnation of the *coup* and indeed published a PCA statement which gave critical support to Videla, noting that 'many of the goals proclaimed in the programme of the military junta reflect, to a certain extent, the people's vital interests' (*Pravda*, 28 March 1976, p. 5). Trade was down on 1975 levels in 1976–7 but this was probably due to the Soviet Union's reduced need for grain imports rather than to any political considerations. In August 1976 the Argentine weekly *El Economista* apparently reported that the USSR had offered to buy all of Argentina's surplus wheat over the next ten years, with prices to be adjusted in line with international quotations (*Latin America Economic Report*, 13 August 1976, p. 127). Nothing came of what was clearly no more than an exaggerated rumour, but this report does suggest that the Soviet Union had taken the earliest opportunity to express a strong interest in sustaining imports of Argentine grain.

In 1976 an 'agreement' was made between the Videla government and the PCA to the effect that the latter would use its influence to protect the international image of the government in return for being allowed to remain relatively unmolested by the security forces. In accordance with this understanding, the Soviet Union vetoed attempts by the Carter administration to secure United Nations condemnation of Argentina's appalling human-rights record. In ideo-

Table 4. *Soviet trade with Argentina 1960–87 (millions of rubles)*

	Turnover	Exports	Imports
1950	0.1	0	0.1
1960	32.1	12.6	19.5
1961	27.4	9.5	17.9
1962	16.0	7.2	8.8
1963	17.4	0.8	16.6
1964	21.9	4.0	17.9
1965	86.7	18.3	68.4
1966	103.3	6.7	96.6
1967	25.1	4.3	20.8
1968	28.7	2.9	25.8
1969	29.1	6.1	23.0
1970	29.9	1.7	28.2
1971	32.3	1.9	30.4
1972	24.7	1.8	22.9
1973	76.7	4.5	72.2
1974	137.5	6.0	131.5
1975	304.4	10.7	293.7
1976	230.7	8.5	222.2
1977	206.3	13.4	192.9
1978	331.2	22.4	308.8
1979	313.5	24.8	288.7
1980	1192.5	30.4	1162.1
1981	2402.9	30.6	2372.3
1982	1292.9	27.5	1265.4
1983	1325.5	25.9	1299.6
1984	1129.9	25.6	1104.3
1985	1292.3	62.4	1229.9
1986	222.6	50.7	171.9
1987	404.8	30.6	374.2

Sources: *Vneshniaia Torgovlia SSSR* and *Foreign Trade* (Moscow).

logical terms this tacit support for a regime which defined a terrorist as 'someone who spreads ideas that are contrary to Western and Christian civilisation' (Gillespie: 1982, p. 229) was 'justified' by a somewhat far-fetched analysis of the Argentine political situation which cast Videla in the role of a bulwark against the extremism of a minority group of *Pinochetistas* within the armed forces. The Soviet leaders also took care not to offend Argentine political sensibilities in other respects. For example, in August 1979 the Moscow film festival showed a Swedish film on the life of an Argentinian political refugee. After Argentine officials had stormed out of the performance, those responsible for screening the film were hastily despatched to the embassy to make profuse apologies. More significantly, the Soviet concern Technoexport was instructed in 1978 not to bid for contracts to supply equipment for the Brazilian-dominated hydro-electric project, Itaipú, at a time of heightened tension and rivalry between Argentina and Brazil.

Although the Argentine Communist Party was by no means left completely free of persecution under the military dictatorship, it was generally subjected only to petty harassment such as the raiding of bookshops and publishing houses. At the state-to-state level Videla did not appear to be inclined to repeat the mistake of his predecessor Onganía who, in 1966, had cut off a promising oil-for-grain deal for the sake of being seen to take a suitably anti-Communist line. Throughout 1977, while political relations with the USSR remained cool, Videla took several steps towards the implementation of a stable pattern of trade. An Argentine trade mission to Eastern Europe was headed by a relatively minor official, the undersecretary for international economic relations, but he had been given the authority to grant Energomashexport the contract to supply generators and turbines for the Yaciretá hydro-electric complex. The Soviet offer was 30 per cent below those of its US and West European competitors, with a considerably lower interest rate for credits, of which up to 80 per cent were repayable in kind. In October 1977, Soviet and Bulgarian fishing vessels which were allegedly transgressing Argentina's 200-mile fishing limit were rounded up by the Argentine navy with the use of force. This 'victory' over Communist personnel was loudly applauded by the conservative elements within Argentina, at whom it was primarily directed. Peru and Ecuador, which try to impose comparable fishing restrictions, regularly escort trespassing US tuna boats away from their coastal waters with minimum fuss. The Argentine political theatricals were probably intended as a smoke screen for the fact that in August 1977 the 1974 Gelbard agreements had been given the force of law. The Argentine generals had clearly accepted the tacit Soviet offer to conduct their relationship on purely commercial terms and by 1978 Argentina had overtaken Brazil as the USSR's foremost trading partner in Latin America.

The fact that both governments were prepared to make political compromises is testimony to the importance of grain for both their respective economies. Since 1972 the USSR has played a crucial, although always somewhat unpredictable, part in the world grain trade. Its yearly purchases increased overall during the 1970s, albeit erratically, to reach a peak of 46 m.t. in 1981–2, making Moscow easily the world's largest importer of grain. The rationale behind Brezhnev's 1972 decision derived from the pressures exerted by the conflict between the Soviet Union's then commitment to provide nearly 8 m.t. of grain to Eastern Europe, Cuba, North Korea, North Vietnam and Egypt, and its need to respond to the demands of its own population. Having experienced a virtual doubling of income levels in the previous decade as money wages rose by 70 per cent and retail prices remained unchanged since 1962, the Soviet people were keen to enjoy the better diet which had been promised in the Ninth Five-Year Plan (1971–5). Brezhnev's policy may well have been influenced by the bloody rioting in Poland over Christmas 1970 in resistance to government attempts to increase food prices. The priority attached by the Soviet authorities to raising the level of meat content in people's diets is indicated by the fact that there was no increase in wheat use for direct human consumption, seed or industrial use throughout the 1970s: the expansion was wholly in animal feed (International Wheat Council, *Market Report*, 24 July 1980). Nevertheless it is still the case that Soviet citizens eat not only less well than people in the United States or the EEC countries, but also less well than their counterparts in Eastern Europe (Abouchar: 1981, pp. 277–8). The reason for this lies in the fact that, despite the impressive achievements of Khrushchev and Brezhnev in overcoming the neglect of the Stalin years and doubling grain production between 1955 and 1972, Soviet agriculture is still beleaguered both by unreliable climatic conditions (from 1979 to 1982 the USSR suffered four bad harvests in a row – see table 5) and by a chronic inefficiency.

The Soviet Union has always played some part in the world grain trade, despite being an autarkic nation until the 1950s. Small transactions were undertaken, sporadically in the 1930s and on a steady basis in the 1950s. These activities enabled the Soviet Union to build up contacts with the largely US-owned multi-national companies which dominate the world grain trade. The bulk of transactions on the international market are handled by only five of such corporations: Cargill, Continental, Bunge and Born, Louis Dreyfus and André, all of which are still controlled by the families of those names. For many years the company most active in Argentina was Bunge and Born, which had a substantial stake in the Argentine economy. However, after Juan and Jorge Born were kidnapped by the Montoneros in 1974 (they were released for a world record ransom of $60 million) and the extent of the company's involvement in Argentina had been brought fully under the glare of publicity, Bunge and Born transferred some of

Table 5. *USSR: grain production and grain imports 1976–88: June–July years (millions of tonnes)*

	1976–7	1977–8	1978–9	1979–80	July–Dec. 1980
Production	223.8	195.7	237.2	179.2	
Imports:					
Argentina	0.3	2.7	1.4	5.1	0.7
Australia	0.5	0.3	0.1	4.0	0.9
Canada	1.4	1.9	2.1	3.4	2.5
EEC	0.2	0.2	0.2	0.9	0.1
USA	7.4	12.5	11.2	15.1	12.2
Others	1.2	1.3	0.6	2.5	0.0
Total	11.0[1]	18.9[2]	15.6	31.0	16.4

	Jan–June 1980	1980–1	1981–2	1982–3	1983–4
Production		189.0	149.0	176.0	200.0
Imports:					
Argentina	4.8	11.2	13.3	9.3	6.9
Australia	3.0	2.9	2.5	1.0	1.5
Canada	1.0	6.9	9.2	9.0	6.3
EEC	0.7	1.1	2.2	4.1	4.4
USA	3.1	8.6	15.4	6.2	10.4
Others	2.0	4.1	3.4	3.9	2.7
Total	14.6	34.8	46.0	33.5[2]	32.2

	1984–5	1985–6	1986–7	1987–8[3]
Production	170.0	192.0	210.1	211.3
Imports:				
Argentina	8.1	2.3	1.8	2.0
Australia	3.2	3.4	1.4	0.5
Canada	8.4	5.2	8.2	5.5
EEC	8.8	6.7	6.9	5.9
USA	22.3	6.9	4.6	14.5
Others	5.2	5.7[2]	6.2	5.6[2]
Total	56.0	30.2[2]	29.3	34.0[2]

1. Not rice or pulses.
2. Includes other grains, mostly rice.
3. Forecast.
Sources: International Wheat Council, *Market Report* 1976–88; breakdown of 1979–80 figures from Ghoshal: 1983, p. 189.

its investments to Brazil, and Cargill is now probably the more heavily involved in Argentina.

The hallmark of the world grain trade is the secrecy with which most of its deals are conducted. Since each company is selling the same commodity, supply and demand of which are both unpredictable because of climatic conditions, grain traders need good personal contacts and a 'feel' for prospective business if they are to secure the valuable contracts. The Soviet Union, notwithstanding its highly centralised internal production and marketing system, gives Exportkhleb, the official grain trading agency, licence to use whatever commercial muscle it can to satisfy Soviet import-export needs. Its procurement practices are in many respects identical to those of the most sophisticated privately owned grain companies. When the USSR first became a major importer of wheat in the 1960s most of its business got tied down in purchasing agreements with Canada and Australia – agreements in which the respective governments participated in the negotiations and private traders played only a limited part. By the 1970s, however, Exportkhleb had evolved a highly effective strategy based on the use of its monopoly position to play governments and companies off against each other. In this context, the fact that the incoming Argentine military government returned grain marketing (which had been brought under state control by Perón) to the private sector may not have been perceived as a disadvantage in Moscow, despite the usual Soviet preference for trading with state-controlled organisations.

The grain embargo

The Argentine government's refusal to support Carter's 1980 grain embargo can be attributed to the fact that there were no political considerations sufficient to outweigh the overwhelming commercial incentives. Despite the efforts of successive governments, notably the Peronists, to pursue a policy of import-substitution industrialisation, in 1976 the vast bulk of Argentina's export earnings were still concentrated in the agricultural sector. General Videla's regime sought to promote the existing imbalance. One of its main economic priorities was to effect a re-distribution of resources away from industry and into agriculture, in an ill-fated attempt to exploit Argentina's 'natural' advantage in grain production, the aim being to use foreign-exchange earnings from grain exports to purchase the manufactured goods and raw materials that the country needed.

At the onset of the embargo Argentina had already shipped most of a 1 m.t. order for wheat to the Soviet Union. Grain production in the USSR in 1979–80 was 179 m.t., falling 48 m.t. short of the planned target. Total import requirements were estimated at between 32 and 35 m.t., of which 25 m.t. were to have been purchased from the United States. Under a long-term supply agreement signed by the two superpowers in 1975 the United States was contracted to supply a minimum of 8 m.t. of grain per annum from 1976 to 1981 and the Carter administration announced that it would honour this commitment. Thus the embargo applied to some 17 m.t. of grain. In fact, in terms of 1979–80 imports, it was less, because while the grain trading year is reckoned from July to June, the US–USSR agreement ran from October to September, and between 6.4 m.t. and 7.3 m.t. of US grain had already been shipped from July to September 1979. In theory the maximum quantity of US grain the USSR could import from July 1979 to June 1980 was 14.4–15.3 m.t. (the lowest estimates are given by the International Wheat Council; the higher figures are from Ghoshal: 1983, p. 189). Thus the shortfall to be made up was closer to 10–11 m.t. than to the oft-quoted figure of 17 m.t. Even so, Argentina, which in 1978–9 exported a total of 18 m.t. of grain, found itself with the enticing prospect of being able to dispose of a substantial proportion of its 1979–80 grain exports at extremely favourable prices. At the political level, President Carter, by making Argentina a prime target of his human rights campaign, had minimised his leverage over the highly nationalistic Argentine generals, who bitterly resented what they regarded as outbursts of American hypocrisy. By championing the principle of non-interference in the affairs of other countries, the Soviet Union had skilfully presented an image of itself which stood in marked contrast.

On 7 January 1980 Argentina suspended export registration of all grains and oilseeds. During the following two days intensive talks were held amongst government ministers with a view to determining Argentina's position with regard to the embargo. Preliminary discussions were chaired by Economy Minister José Alfredo Martínez de Hoz and attended by David Lacroze, President of the National Grain Board (JNG), Jorge Zorreguieta, Secretary of Agriculture, Commodore Raúl Cura, Secretary of International Commerce, Alejandro Estrada, Secretary of International Economic Negotiations and his deputy, Juan Dumás. Martínez de Hoz presumably communicated the results of these deliberations to subsequent sessions with the President and the Minister of Foreign Relations, Brigadier Carlos Washington Pastor, where the final decision was taken. On 10 January Argentina announced that, although it would send a representative to the meeting of leading grain exporters convened in Washington by the United States for 12 January 'in order to participate in the analysis of probable developments in the grain trade', it would not suspend grain sales to the USSR (*La Prensa* (Buenos Aires), 11 January 1980, p. 1). With a sly reference to Carter's suspension of military aid to Argentina because of its human rights abuses, David Lacroze stated that the refusal to join the boycott 'was a question of principle by which the Argentine government expressed its view that economic blockades were not appropriate measures to bring about solutions to political problems' (*La Prensa*, 11 January 1980, p. 3).

To the consternation of the North Americans, this remained the Argentine position throughout the series of carrot and stick blandishments with which they attempted to induce compliance. At first the statement that 'the Argentine government has not announced this measure with the intention of trying to replace the United States in the Soviet market' (*La Prensa*, 11 January 1980, p. 3) and that the dictates of the market would decide the destinations of Argentine grain apparently led US officials to believe that Videla was open to persuasion. The true message evidently came over loud and clear in Moscow, however. TASS glossed over a fairly strongly worded Argentine condemnation of the invasion by saying that despite the fact that Argentina did not share the 'internationalist position' adopted by the Soviet Union in defence of the Afghan revolution, the two governments could 'cooperate advantageously' (*La Prensa*, 12 January 1980, p. 2). President Carter's special envoy to Buenos Aires, General Andrew Jackson Goodpaster, the head of the US military academy at West Point, had few concessions to offer and left Argentina empty-handed only a day or so before export registrations were reopened (on 29 January) for all grains except wheat and a delegation from Export-khleb, led by its director Victor Pershin, flew in.

Not surprisingly a second US mission, led by Under-Secretary for Commerce Luther Hodges, which arrived in March promising US 'participation' in the Argentine economy in the form of a $1.2 billion credit from the US Export-Import Bank, fared little better. During the US visit the National Grain Board revealed that Argentina had sold the Soviet Union 1 m.t. of wheat and 3 m.t. of maize during the first two months of 1980. By late April a long-term supply agreement was in preparation, which was signed on 10 July in Buenos Aires. It provided for minimum sales of 4 m.t. of maize and sorghum and 0.5 m.t. of soya beans at international price levels each year until 1985. A similar agreement, worth at least $1 billion per annum to Argentina, was drawn up in late 1980 covering sales of beef. Buenos Aires undertook to supply 60,000–100,000 tonnes yearly until 1985.

The Argentine authorities defended their grain deal by saying that an embargo could not succeed in any case because private companies inevitably find ways to break boycotts of this kind. Indeed one of the US administration's major difficulties in enforcing the embargo lay in its inability to control the activities of the US-based grain multi-nationals. By the beginning of August 1980, Argentina had sold the USSR 5.5 m.t. of grain, Australia had sold 3.7 m.t., Canada had announced its intention to drop out altogether and the embargo was looking decidedly shaky. Thus it is hardly surprising that the Argentine decision was said to be 'much appreciated' by the Soviet authorities. The embargo had been effective only to the extent that an estimated $1 billion had been added to the Soviet grain import bill.

After the lifting of the grain embargo by President Reagan on 28 April 1981, it was thought that the Soviet Union would be unlikely to return to the US market without significant inducement. In May 1981 the only Soviet response to the Reagan administration's proposals for a new long-term agreement was that any such accord would have to include a clause giving financial guarantees against any further embargo, a condition which the Americans declared to be 'unacceptable'. Although talks between the United States and the USSR in Vienna in August 1981 led to a one-year extension of their existing grain agreement, taking it up to September 1982, in December 1981 the United States formally announced that negotiations on any new agreement had been shelved because of the Polish crisis.

Throughout 1981 the USSR assured Argentina that it was regarded as the priority supplier and as late as November 1982, despite the fact that 1981–2 exports to the Soviet Union were way down on Argentine expectations, grain traders were predicting that the next season's figures would attain previous high levels. However, speculation throughout 1981 and 1982 that Argentina would permanently replace the United States as the USSR's major grain supplier was brought to an end by the announcement in July 1983 of the signing of a new long-term agreement by the two superpowers. Minimum annual purchases of US grain by the Soviet Union were fixed at 9 m.t. for the next five years and Moscow has an option to buy a further 3 m.t. without consultation with the US authorities. The balance of advantage in the grain trade had clearly shifted from Washington to

Moscow, as on the one hand the US embargo had proved more economically damaging to US farmers than to the Soviet authorities, and on the other Soviet import requirements began to diminish because of somewhat improved harvests. In the light of Yurii Andropov's remark that at this time relations with the United States were 'tense in virtually every field' (*The Financial Times*, 26 August 1983, p. 26), the conclusion must be that the United States enjoys significant commercial advantages over Argentina as a source of the USSR's all-important grain imports.

Soviet concerns about Argentina as a grain exporter derive from two factors: (1) the unreliability of supplies, and (2) the costs of the operation.

The clearest instance of the disruption of Argentine grain shipments occurred during the Falklands/Malvinas War of May/June 1982. Once the British naval blockade had been extended to only twelve miles off the Argentine coast some interruption of trade flows was bound to occur, and the ports of Bahía Blanca and Quequén, which together account for 29 per cent of total grain exports, were particularly badly hit by the blockade. Difficulties were exacerbated by the refusal of Lloyds of London to issue insurance cover to vessels bound to or from Argentina. There were unconfirmed reports in the local press that sixty Soviet chartered vessels were waiting in Uruguayan waters, held up by worried owners unwilling to let them sail on to Argentina. On 14 May 1982 the British Ambassador to the Soviet Union was summoned to the Ministry of Foreign Affairs to hear a forceful protest against the way 'the British government continues to expand its zone of military operations in the Atlantic Ocean, arbitrarily declaring vast expanses of the high seas to be closed to other countries' ships and aeroplanes' (*Pravda*, 15 May 1982, p. 4).

While it might be argued that this was only an isolated incident and not in itself sufficient to discourage Soviet grain buyers, Argentine supplies are never very reliable. There are two main reasons. Firstly, Argentina's port and storage system has been operating at well above full capacity since the 60 per cent increase in grain exports which occurred in 1981, and is therefore endemically prone to breakdown and delays. Argentina has twelve loading ports, which can handle a maximum of 3 m.t. of grain per month. Both the Paraná, on which seven of the ports are located, and the River Plate are particularly prone to silting, which means that dredging work continually has to be carried out. Estimates of the country's total grain storage capacity vary from the 2.9 m.t. given by the Ministry of Agriculture to the 1.7

m.t. given by unofficial sources. Whatever the true figure, the important point is that the majority of the silos and elevators are installed at inland ports; only 16 per cent are located in the major export ports of Buenos Aires, Bahía Blanca, Mar del Plata and Quequén. The whole system appears to be more vulnerable than it need be to the year to year fluctuations brought about by changing climatic conditions.

Doubts about the ability of the Argentine port system to function reliably can only have been intensified by a ten-day go-slow in May 1983 by the 6,000 JNG employees who operate Argentina's major ports. It was estimated that the stoppage had cost $400,000 per day and had left a backlog of 300,000 tonnes of grain, which would take several months to clear. At Bahía Blanca, which handles 30,000 tonnes of grain a day at that time of year, fourteen ships were queueing waiting to load and 3,000 railway wagons piled high with grain had accumulated outside the port. There was still heavy congestion in mid-June and ships were having to wait an average of 20–25 days before docking. In 1987 the Soviet Union was negotiating with the Uruguayans to load Argentine grain onto Soviet cargo ships from Montevideo to avoid Argentina's long loading time and thereby save 'millions of dollars' (*LAWR*, WR-87-16, 23 April 1987, p. 4).

Secondly, the agricultural sector itself is not geared to reliable production. Output has increased overall in recent years, but the country's harvest is always heavily dependent on favourable weather conditions – to much the same extent as the Soviet crop, being subject to both drought and flooding. These natural difficulties were compounded by the policies of the 1976–83 military government. Uncertainty and inefficiency were greatly exacerbated by the erratic, short-term economic measures of a regime which could not decide whether it preferred to stimulate production with subsidies or to cream off much of the revenue generated by the agricultural sector by the imposition of high import taxes. President Alfonsín, announcing a series of support measures for Argentine agriculture in April 1984 (including the reinvestment of export taxes generated by greater surpluses back into the farming sector), vowed that 'Argentina will never again turn its back on the countryside' (*Latin America Commodities Report*, 20 April 1984, CR-84-08, p. 2). However, the lack of leeway within the debt-ridden Argentine economy means that the substantial investment needed to compensate for years of neglect is unlikely to be available in the near future.

In addition to these supply problems, there are four factors which contribute to the high costs of purchasing grain from Argentina.

Firstly, Argentine grain was selling at $20–30 per long ton above US price levels throughout the embargo and remained comparatively expensive until well into 1982. The fall in price at the end of that year was connected with a corresponding fall in quality, and Soviet officials were apparently unhappy about this aspect of 1983 wheat shipments. Secondly, transportation costs are also high. Since mid-1980 freight rates on the Argentina–Black Sea run have always been at least $10 per long ton higher than on the corresponding United States run, and the differential has often been far greater. In addition, the United States is in a position to grant concessionary rates for shipping, whereas any such deal with Argentina would be of negligible advantage, since so little of the grain is carried in Argentine vessels. Although the Soviet Union has a shipping agreement with Argentina, signed in 1974, to the effect that transportation of cargoes was to be shared equally between them, the Argentine merchant navy is ill-equipped to carry out its pledge. As of 1982, it had only six bulk grain carriers. To transport, say, 10 m.t. of grain using 20,000 tonne carriers, 500 journeys would be needed. Given that grain exporting from Argentina is largely concentrated in the first six months of the year, and each journey takes about one month, this means that at least 100 vessels would be needed, and probably more, because Argentine ports can only accommodate small- or medium-capacity carriers. It is thought that the Soviet Union uses chartered vessels to carry half of its grain purchases from Buenos Aires (*Latin America Regional Report: Southern Cone*, 21 May 1982, p. 1). The extent to which transportation costs are seen as a problem by the Soviet Union is suggested by the fact that a special mission was sent to Buenos Aires in November 1980 to discuss ways of reducing this expenditure.

The third problem lies in Argentina's inability to provide credit facilities, a situation which is unlikely to change in the short or even the medium term. This factor may be particularly significant at any time when gold and/or oil prices are declining and when the Soviet Union is experiencing cash-flow difficulties, as happened at the beginning of 1982.

Lastly, and perhaps most importantly from the Soviet point of view, there is the problem of the ubiquitous trade imbalance. This issue was raised by Vice Minister of Foreign Trade Boris Gordeev as early as May 1981 and has been reiterated by Soviet officials ever since. This is hardly surprising for, in 1981, Soviet imports from Argentina exceeded exports to Buenos Aires by a ratio of 80 to 1. Clearly Argentina found its 1 billion ruble trade surplus with the USSR highly satisfactory, not only economically but also politically in that it neatly matched Argentina's deficit with the United States. For the Soviet leaders, however, their loss on Argentine trade was a significant contributory factor to their deficit with Latin America as a whole, which has fluctuated between 200 million and 1,400 million rubles in recent years. This in turn must be seen in the context of the Soviet Union's global trade balance, which has varied from a credit of 4 billion rubles to a deficit of 2 billion rubles (Blasier; 1983, p. 50). Thus Argentina alone has contributed heavily to the negative side of the Soviet balance of payments.

In May 1983 Soviet negotiators proposed setting a target of $300 million for Argentine imports from the USSR during that year, to consist primarily of railway and oil production equipment and hydro-electric turbines (all to be supplied to Argentine public enterprises). Argentina's failure to achieve even 10 per cent of that figure provoked a tougher stance by Soviet officials when it came to renegotiating the grain supply agreement in late 1985. They apparently threatened not to renew it (*The Financial Times*, 23 January 1986, p. 6), and lent credence to this by deciding that, because of the current high prices of Argentine produce, they prefer to buy their meat from the EEC. The 1980 grain agreement, unlike its counterpart on meat supplies, has been renewed to cover 1986–91, but the USSR has insisted on a protocol committing Argentina to minimum purchases of Soviet goods of $70 million in 1986, $80 million in 1987, $100 million in 1988, $120 million in 1989 and $130 million in 1990 ($500 million in total). An unofficial part of the deal was that the Soviet Union is guaranteed the contract to supply equipment for the hydro-electric installation at Piedra del Aguila. Moscow has been pressing for this for several years and has modified its proposals from the original offer to supply all the equipment from Soviet factories to the final agreement, which is that the Soviet share of the contract will not exceed 40 per cent, the bulk of the equipment to be produced at Argentine plants using Soviet technology. Several other proposals for joint Soviet–Argentine ventures are being put forward by the USSR, involving *Niva* cars, tractors and road-construction machinery, and Soviet trade articles assert that 'the future belongs to such forms [of cooperation]' (Kuznetsova and Manenok: 1986, p. 24). Indeed, it seems the only way of overcoming the resistance of Argentine state companies to the acquisition of Soviet equipment.

While there may have been a political motive for this resistance under the 1976–83 military government (which appointed conservative officers to run the public sector), the prospects for Soviet exports hardly seem much better under the current democratically elected administration. Argentina is in a deep economic crisis requiring ruthless austerity and the most frugal use of foreign exchange. In this context infrastructural investment projects and those with high capital intensity and long gestation periods are most likely to be cut back, an obstacle which is openly acknowledged by Soviet officials, who have reported 'protracted negotiations' on the supplies of equipment for such projects (Kuznetsova and Manenok: 1986, p. 25). Although in 1985 the Soviet Union had some success in selling road-construction equipment and tractors (worth $36 million) directly to the local governments of the remoter Argentine provinces, it is likely that these deals were a response to pressure from Buenos Aires to buy Soviet goods to ensure the renewal of the grain agreement. The stipulations of the new agreement will ensure some increase in Argentine purchases from the USSR; however, Buenos Aires will wish to sell as much of its grain as possible for hard currency, rather than for Soviet equipment of doubtful quality and low compatibility with existing plant. One Moscow source apparently leaked the information that the increase in Argentine exports from the Soviet Union in 1985–6 was primarily due to a Buenos Aires purchases of $120–140 million worth of Soviet oil, to be resold to the Scandinavian countries (Radio Noticias Argentinas, Buenos Aires, 19 October 1985, in *Summary of World Broadcasts [SWB], Weekly Economic Report*, SU/W1362/A/1, 25 October 1985).

Argentina is either unable or unwilling to purchase Soviet industrial machinery and equipment, and it no longer needs Soviet oil, which has been a contributing factor to the somewhat more balanced nature of Moscow's trade with Brazil. In 1981 the Soviet Union sold Argentina nuclear fuel in the form of 5 tons of heavy water to supply one of Argentina's three nuclear reactors (*LAWR*, WR-80-14, 4 April 1980, p. 11) and, in March 1982, it was announced that Buenos Aires was sending 100 kilograms of uranium to Moscow for 20 per cent enrichment (a level unsuitable for the development of nuclear weapons) (Vacs: 1984, p. 35). Argentina, because of its failure to ratify a nuclear non-proliferation treaty, has found difficulty in having uranium processed in the United States. However, the USSR is also reluctant to supply nuclear materials to a nation which has made no binding commitment to forswearing the development of nuclear weapons and it is unlikely that Moscow would be keen to extend cooperation in this area.

The only other obvious way to reduce the trade deficit would be for Argentina to purchase arms from the Soviet Union. Before the transfer of power to a civilian government late in 1983, there were various rumours that such a deal might be underway. According to a recent study of the Falklands War (Rice and Gavshon: 1984) the Soviet Ambassador to Argentina, Sergei Striganov, offered arms to the Argentine generals shortly after the collapse of the peace shuttle undertaken by then US Secretary of State Alexander Haig. In return, the Soviet leaders wanted 'fishery installations' at Ushuaia, near Cape Horn; this terminology was apparently understood by the Argentine authorities to be the normal diplomatic euphemism for a military base. The motivation said to lie behind the request was that the Soviet Union was laying contingency plans to exploit a possible closure of the Panama Canal resulting from instability in Central America. Further Soviet conditions for the supply of arms were the immediate and permanent withdrawal of all Argentine military advisers from Central America; a guarantee of abstention by Argentina on all anti-Soviet votes in the United Nations on issues such as Afghanistan; and immediate cessation of support for General Torelio's right-wing military government in Bolivia. The Argentine government evidently found these conditions unacceptable and it appears that, despite a high-level exchange of military delegations dating back to 1979, the generals in Buenos Aires have to date declined all offers of Soviet arms. There is an unconfirmed possibility, however, that post-Falklands rearmament may have included two Soviet-built nuclear submarines (Dabat and Lorenzano, p. 151; no source given). Eduardo Crawley plausibly argues that the Argentine military do not want to buy Soviet equipment partly because of the experience of the Peruvian armed forces, who have had problems with spare parts and quality, and partly because Argentina's most likely enemies, Chile and Great Britain, are already equipped with materiel to pit against Soviet weaponry (Seminar given at St Antony's College, Oxford, 1 March 1985).

The Soviet Union's recent experience with Argentina highlights all the difficulties it has found in trading with Latin America, and reveals the hopelessly one-sided nature of the apparent complementarity between the two countries. Equally, the Argentine press has devoted much attention to the potential hazards of relying on Moscow as its single large purchaser. Although the USSR is likely to continue importing grain within the foreseeable future, there is no reason to assume that the level of imports will remain as high as it was in the early 1980s. The desire to achieve economic independence from the West was forcefully stated by Brezhnev when presenting a major new agricultural expansion plan in May 1982 and this drive to expand production has continued under Andropov and Gorbachev. Indeed the champion of *perestroika* is a trained agronomist who was responsible for agriculture from 1978 until he became General Secretary in 1985. He therefore has a particular interest in improving the efficiency of the notoriously wasteful Soviet agricultural sector. In mid-1986 a 'superministry' (*Gosagroprom*) was created to oversee the restructuring of Soviet farming and since then a whole series of reform measures have been introduced, including production bonuses for farm managers, increased self-management by collective farm leaders and initiatives to promote contact between scientific and research institutes and collective and state farms. During the course of President Alfonsín's October 1986 visit to Moscow, Soviet officials apparently emphasised that their aim is to be self-sufficient in grain production by 1990 (*Latin America Weekly Report*, WR-86-42, 30 October 1986, p. 5). As one commentator has remarked, there are no inherent reasons why Soviet farmers should not fatten meat as successfully as farmers in the United States: 'Information on breeding and feeding is available in every bookshop. It is certainly known in the Soviet Union. It is certain to be applied here before too long' (*The Financial Times*, 7 October 1984, p. 61). The same logic applies to grain yields. A 1986 Economist Intelligence report predicted that Soviet wheat production was likely to increase modestly over the next five years, and that the world's grain exporters would find themselves fighting for declining markets (China, a second major grain importer, is also boosting incentives to produce grain) unless they cut back on production (*The Financial Times*, 30 October 1986, p. 36). In this economic climate Argentina's plans to double its annual grain exports by the end of the century would seem to be somewhat problematic.

Even in the context of decreasing grain imports, the Soviet Union is certain to want to keep its options open with Argentina as an important alternative source of supply. However, 1982 imports plummeted to about two-thirds of the record 1981 figure, and fell even further in 1984 despite higher than average Soviet imports and a record wheat harvest in Argentina. While the figures picked up slightly in 1985, in October 1986 the Argentine journal *Clarín* was complaining that the Soviet Union had ordered less than 10 per cent of the quantities it had agreed to buy over a period of five years from January 1986, that is, less than half of the purchases they had been expected to make in 1986 (Varas: 1987, p. 37). This situation is related to the fall in world oil prices (which leaves Moscow short of hard currency) and the August 1986 US decision to sell subsidised wheat to the Soviet Union, a move which occasioned the hasty despatch of a mission of Argentine diplomats and economists to Moscow (SU/ W1405/A/1, 29 August 1986). As a leading Buenos Aires grain trader recognised, '. . . the Russians don't have any money. They are driving very hard bargains and buying at the cheapest they possibly can' (*The Financial Times*, 16 May 1986, p. 40). In September Moscow snapped up 1 million tonnes of cheap EEC wheat. Argentina, which needs to maximise its trade surplus ($4.6 billion in 1985 but only around $3 billion the following year) to continue servicing its $50 billion plus foreign debt, simply cannot offer even remotely comparable concessions on its major export earner. Despite the obvious attractions of Argentine produce, it seems improbable that the volume of trade between Buenos Aires and Moscow will recapture 1981 levels except in the event of an isolated contingency similar to the grain embargo.

Brazil

In 1961 President Jânio Quadros announced that 'Brazil cannot ignore, without wrongfully restricting itself, the reality, the vitality and the dynamism of the socialist states' (de Olivera: 1962, p. 71). Two years earlier President Kubitschek, presiding over severe economic difficulties caused by a contraction in Brazil's export markets, had taken steps to explore the potential of trade with the Soviet Union, and a trade agreement was signed providing for deliveries of goods worth $25 million on each side, planned to rise to $37 million in 1961 and $45 million in 1962. Brazil was to sell coffee, also cocoa beans, vegetable oil and raw hides, in return for Soviet oil and petroleum products (at prices much lower than those quoted by the North American suppliers), wheat, machinery and equipment, metals and chemical goods. This agreement promoted the first commercial exchanges to take place between the two nations.

The left-of-centre Goulart, who took office in September 1961, quickly re-established relations with the Soviet Union, an event to which *Pravda* devoted an entire page (*Pravda*, 25 November 1961, p. 6). In 1962 the Brazilian government founded a special commission (COLESTE) to coordinate relations with the Eastern bloc. As discussed in chapter 3, the Soviet Union sold oil to Brazil in the early 1960s, buying coffee and cocoa in return. A long-term bilateral trade agreement was signed in 1963 and Soviet oil technicians came to give advice on prospecting. Despite the strongly pro-Washington orientation of the military regime which came to power in the 1964 *coup*, Brazil evidently felt that economic incentives were powerful enough to warrant relations with the USSR, although all links with Cuba had been abruptly severed. In 1965 Roberto Campos, the economist who master-minded the Brazilian 'miracle', spent twelve days in the Soviet Union and on his return commented favourably on the possibilities for Brazil to expand exports to the Soviet Union, noting that Brazil was heavily in debt to many of the Western countries and that their markets showed signs of reaching saturation point. In August 1966 a protocol was signed in Rio de Janeiro on the granting of a credit of $100 million for the supply of Soviet machinery and equipment. The Soviet leaders were so anxious to woo Brazil at this stage that they agreed to Brazilian demands (subsequently an issue of great contention) that 25 per cent of their sales to Moscow should consist of manufactured goods. However, by 1969, only $4 million of this credit had been activated.

Nevertheless, Soviet–Brazilian trade responded favourably to a series of positive developments in the late 1960s and 1970s and it emerged that the Brazilian economy may well be more compatible with the USSR than any other in Latin America. It certainly has by far the greatest range of exports of all Latin American countries. From 1967 onwards Brazilian foreign policy embarked on a gradual shift away from an overwhelming emphasis on ties with the United States. This was prompted mainly by doubts about the tangible benefits to be gained from the relationship with Washington (aid had fallen off, access to US markets had not greatly improved and the United States was unwilling or unable to satisfy Brazilian needs in areas such as nuclear technology or arms supplies). It also reflected Brazil's interest in taking advantage of alternative options emerging onto the inter-national scene (detente, the growing economic power of Western Europe and Japan, and the development of Third World cooperation), and the fact that import substitution industrialisation policies had led (as in most other parts of Latin America) to increased, rather than diminished external vulnerability, thus making the need to boost exports a priority.

In this context, some not insignificant sales of primary products were made, mostly involving the export of Brazilian coffee and cocoa in return for oil. In February 1967 COLESTE was reorganised. In March 1968 an agreement was reached whereby the USSR was to sell

Brazil $26 million worth of oil in return for 110,000 tonnes of wheat. In October 1970 Brazil exported 1,200,000 sacks of coffee to Moscow, at world prices, and in 1972 10 per cent of Brazilian sugar exports were destined for Odessa. Two years later incoming President Ernesto Geisel announced a more explicit emphasis on direct national interest in the formulation of foreign policy, with a 'near total ending of ideological constraints' (Hurrell: 1986, p. 199). The 1973 oil crisis had revealed the weaknesses behind the Brazilian 'miracle' and placed energy requirements at the centre of policy-making. Moreover, sharp rises in the cost of Western capital goods prompted Brazil to re-evaluate the worth of Soviet equipment.

Thus if Soviet trading officials were optimistic about their trade with Argentina at the beginning of the 1980s, they must have held equally high, if not higher, hopes for the prospects of Soviet–Brazilian exchange, which were much-vaunted by both sides in 1980–1. It was in Brazil that the first Soviet hydro-electric turbine in Latin America went into operation, in March 1977 at Capivari. Brazil's then Minister of Mines and Energy expressed satisfaction with the Soviet project. 'We have useful experience of cooperation with the USSR in the construction of hydro-electric power stations', he noted in 1979. 'We welcome the further participation of Soviet firms in the development of our power industry' (Viktorovna and Yakovlev: 1980, p. 64). In the same year, Brazil turned to the Soviet Union for oil, about 80 per cent of which had to be imported. Moscow supplied 10 per cent of Brazil's oil imports during 1974 and 1975. This combination of oil and turbines seemed to provide the solution to the problem of the enduring trade imbalance.

In the late 1970s US protectionism together with a reassessment of Brazil's international position resulted in a strong trend towards diversification in foreign policy. This political shift was closely related to a determined effort to boost exports, develop new markets and steer equipment imports away from the United States, with which its deficit in 1980 was an estimated $1.5 billion. In late 1979 the *Conselho Nacional de Comercio Exterior* (Concex) explicitly acknowledged that 'the only way to export more to Eastern Europe was to buy more from that area, and recommended that imports should be diversified to permit this' (*Latin America Weekly Report*, 17 April 1981, WR-81-16, p. 5). Thus attempts to win Comecon markets were seen as part of an overall and long-term economic strategy, and the Soviet response to Brazilian overtures suggests that they believed that a moment of breakthrough had arrived. For example, the USSR offered loans, in US dollars, under highly advantageous conditions, to help finance Brazil's development plans (*Latin America Regional Report: Brazil*, 13 March 1981, RB-81-03, p. 1).

In April 1981 the Soviet–Brazilian Commission, which had been functioning since 1965 to deal 'primarily with matters of commerce' was upgraded to the Soviet–Brazilian Intergovernmental Commission on Trade, Economic, Scientific and Technical Cooperation, reflecting the Soviet belief that there were 'real prospects . . . for cooperation between the two countries' (Ishchenko: 1983, p. 50). Moscow was probably also encouraged by the fact that in 1980 Brazil signed a ten-year trade deal worth $1 billion with Poland, based upon an exchange of Brazilian iron ore for Polish coal. The culmination of these developments was the 1981 visit of Minister of Economy Delfim Neto to Moscow and the signing of a series of agreements worth about $2 billion in total. These involved Soviet participation in several large-scale projects, including the Ilha Grande hydro-electric station, oil prospecting in São Paulo state and the extraction of ethanol from timber, in addition to commitments to buy Brazilian agricultural products in exchange for Soviet chemicals. There was also talk of joint Soviet–Brazilian ventures for civil construction and engineering projects abroad, aiming to complement Brazilian engineering ability with Soviet equipment (a shortage of engineers in the USSR means that Moscow is not always keen on the construction side of foreign contracts). Great potential was seen for collaboration in Angola and Mozambique, because of the Portuguese connection and Soviet influence.

Notwithstanding all the fanfare with which the 1981 deal with Brazil was announced, a year later the only project going well was Coalbra, a new state-owned company producing ethanol from timber on the basis of Soviet technology. Despite Brazil's promises, little had been done to promote orders for Soviet industrial equipment. The USSR had gone ahead with its purchases of soya beans and cocoa (the 1982–6 agreement provides for Soviet purchases of 0.6 million tons of soya beans, 0.4 million tons of soya oil-seed meal, 0.5 million tons of corn (from 1983), 4,000 tons of vegetable oils, and 10,000 tons of cocoabeans), but the dramatic increase in Brazilian imports from the USSR in 1982 is almost entirely attributable to the 1981 agreement on oil supplies. Brazil imported 168.7 million rubles' worth of oil in 1982, R97.8 million in 1983 and R85.2 million in 1984 (*Vneshniaia torgovlia SSSR*, 1982–4).

As with Argentina, the problem is that the Soviet Union has less to

Table 6. *Soviet trade with Brazil 1960–87 (millions of rubles)*

	Turnover	Exports	Imports
1960	22.6	14.2	8.4
1961	38.1	16.5	21.6
1962	59.3	27.1	32.2
1963	65.6	26.5	39.1
1964	55.0	21.6	33.4
1965	54.4	24.9	29.5
1966	52.4	24.9	27.5
1967	42.0	10.8	31.2
1968	37.4	12.4	25.0
1969	54.8	10.9	43.9
1970	23.2	2.4	20.8
1971	43.7	2.0	41.7
1972	72.9	7.1	65.8
1973	125.8	9.3	116.5
1974	202.0	90.0	112.0
1975	396.1	93.3	302.8
1976	445.5	76.1	369.4
1977	314.0	104.4	209.6
1978	165.1	34.9	130.2
1979	179.9	19.9	160.0
1980	275.0	22.1	252.9
1981	550.2	16.3	533.9
1982	595.4	179.9	415.5
1983	697.4	106.4	590.6
1984	467.8	95.3	372.5
1985	450.3	70.3	380.0
1986	224.6	24.6	200.0
1987	232.4	42.8	189.6

Sources: Foreign Trade (Moscow) and *Vneshniaia Torgovlia SSSR.*

offer Brazil than vice versa. Clearly Brazil, as one of the major Third World arms exporting nations, is not interested in purchasing Soviet weaponry, and indeed, in 1978, made a small sale of tank cannons to the USSR (*Latin America Economic Report*, 19 May 1978, p. 146). The significant difference between the two South American powers in this respect is that Brazil needs to import oil. However, Moscow's unwillingness to make price concessions on what is its second largest foreign-exchange earner has proved a disappointment to Brazil, and the Soviet Union's own production difficulties, its commitments elsewhere and its desire to make rapid foreign-currency gains mean that it cannot be a reliable source for such a heavily indebted nation. As part of the 1981 package a new oil agreement was signed and, by the end of the year, imports of 20,000 bpd (about 10 per cent of Brazil's imported petroleum) – at international prices – had been resumed. One of Itamaraty's strategies for overcoming Brazil's economic difficulties has been to arrange countertrade transactions to cover necessary imports such as petroleum. In March 1985 one such deal, worth $750 million over the next four years, was signed with the USSR, involving the exchange of Brazilian foodstuffs and manufactured goods such as steel products and oil platforms for Soviet crude. However, Brazilian imports of Soviet oil, even at this relatively low level, have only a limited future. In response to the 1973 price rises, an ambitious energy programme was drawn up by the Brazilian government. Local oil production, which in 1979 accounted for only 13.8 per cent of Brazil's domestic consumption, now supplies over half the nation's needs, and large new discoveries mean that self-sufficiency is within sight in the next decade (*Latin America Regional Report: Brazil*, RB-85-06, 5 July 1985, p. 5). The longer term prospects for Soviet oil exports to Brazil are clearly not promising, and any concerted effort to reduce the trade imbalance will have to centre on increased purchases of Soviet machinery and equipment, which have clearly not been forthcoming so far.

A second potentially significant Soviet export item to Brazil is hydro-electric equipment. Moscow is clearly very keen to participate in hydro-electric schemes. Having been excluded from the contract for the Itaipú dam, to be built in collaboration with Uruguay and Paraguay (whose President Stroessner vetoed the participation of the USSR), the USSR made an extremely generous offer to buy Brazilian agricultural products worth $2.5 billion in return for contracts to supply $1 billion worth of hydro-electric equipment. Such initiatives have been thwarted largely by resistance from powerful lobbies of Brazilian industrialists, who argue that they can manufacture the equipment needed for Brazil's development. For example, in November 1980 a Czech mission visited Brazil to sign a contract to supply half of the equipment for three cement factories. Brazilian manufacturers adamantly maintained that they could supply nearly all the necessary equipment and that they would accept, at most, a 25 per cent share being given to the Czechs. Government officials argued that the Eastern European markets must be won 'even at the cost of sacrifices' (*Latin America Regional Report: Brazil*, 2 January 1981, RB-81-01, p. 5), but the deal was called off. Moreover the recession in Brazil has resulted in a surplus of energy rather than the expected shortage, and the government has postponed the starting date for one of the major projects in which the Soviet Union is participating, the Ilha Grande hydro-electric dam, from 1989 to 1991.

There is little doubt that both sides expected too much of the 1981 negotiations. Brazil clearly hoped that the Soviet Union would be an important new market for its manufacturing industry, demanding that Brazil should export manufactured goods to the value of its imports of Soviet machinery and equipment. The Soviet negotiators had clearly not anticipated such requests and displayed overall 'a remarkable ignorance of Brazil's industrial weight', initially believing that they could sell turnkey hydroelectric installations. 'Soviet officials made no secret of their amazement and disappointment when Electrobrás, the state electricity company, said that it was only interested in purchasing some turbine generators. As a result, the composition of the Soviet negotiating mission was immediately changed . . .' (*Latin America Weekly Report*, 12 June 1981, WR-81-23, p. 8).

The USSR, reluctant to see an increase in the existing trade imbalance, insisted on adhering to the terms of the Soviet–Brazilian agreement of 1975 which stated that manufactures would account for only 30 per cent of the value of Soviet equipment. They are making increases in purchases of Brazilian manufactured goods dependent upon a concerted Brazilian effort to rectify the trade imbalance and buy more Soviet industrial equipment (Gladkov: 1975, p. 16). The indications are that Soviet officials are in principle willing to buy Latin American manufactures: a 1975 *Foreign Trade* article stated, 'Purchases of industrial products in Latin America enable the Soviet Union to make broader use of the advantages of the international division of labour, and to meet the growing requirements of its economy and population more fully. This applies to certain types of manufactures and semi-finished goods, in the first place those that are not produced or are underproduced in the Soviet Union' (Gladkov: 1975, p. 14). However, it is one of the few bargaining counters at the disposal of Soviet officials when trying to negotiate a reduction in the trade deficit and it is hardly surprising that they have used it.

Brazil's lack of cooperation has also prompted the Soviet Union to take a tougher line on terms for development projects: for example, they have been pressing for higher interest rates of 7.25 per cent a year on the credit of $120 million offered to Electrobrás to finance the import of five generators for the Ilha Grande hydroelectric installation. Brazil was reluctant to make concessions and discussions on Soviet participation in the Ilha Grande project ended in deadlock at the end of 1981.

One Brazilian official closely involved in the 1981 negotiations with the USSR told Latin American Newsletters that Delfim Neto had deliberately exaggerated the potential of links with the Soviet Union in order to gain leverage with the international commercial banks by demonstrating that Brazil had alternative options at its disposal (*Latin America Weekly Report*, 23 July 1982, WR-82-29, p. 9). Whatever the degree of truth in this assertion, by the end of 1982 it was clear that the debt crisis had forced Brazil to postpone its strategy of diversification and to reorientate policy towards Washington. One observer writes that 'There has been an almost constant dialogue between Brazilian and American officials, politicians and bankers concerned with the debt, involving both direct American government action – as with the provision by the American Treasury of a $1.2 billion bridging loan in December 1982 – and indirect management', and 'the historic decline in the share of Brazil's exports going to the American market was reversed: 48 per cent in 1953; 17 per cent in 1981 but around 30 per cent in the first half of 1984' (Hurrell: 1985, p. 64). It is unlikely that Brazil will become drawn back into the kind of close relationship which Washington enjoyed following the 1964 military *coup*, and is eager to re-establish. US protectionism hits an increasing proportion of Brazilian manufactures, and the Brazilian government, primarily concerned with economic and financial issues, resents Washington's attempts to exploit economic vulnerability to induce political compliance on questions such as US policy in Central America. The Brazilian government's main strategy for circumventing US and EEC protectionism, within the IMF-established constraints of the need to increase trade surpluses, has been to develop trade with its major oil suppliers, China, Iran, Iraq and Nigeria, which also offer valuable markets for Brazilian manufactured goods. Brazilian officials are particularly excited by the prospects for trade with China. Beijing is keen to import steel and manufactured goods such as televisions which, being less sophisticated than the Western varieties, are cheaper and more appropriate for China's needs. In 1985 the Chinese government signed a contract for a major purchase of military aircraft from Brazil (*The Financial Times*, 5 November 1985, p. 5). Moreover, China has been prepared to sell its oil at reduced rates, and traditionally pays cash on delivery for imports, which is clearly a very attractive proposition for Brazil. As long as the Brazilians are able to promote trade on terms such as these, they are unlikely to make many concessions to Moscow. Moreover, longer term structural factors suggest that until the Brazilian economy rests on a firmer foundation, both the resources and the political will to develop a stable trading relationship with the USSR will be lacking.

Mexico

Mexico, like Argentina, was the object of early Soviet interest, both because its recent revolution made it seem fertile ground for Comintern activity and because of its proximity to the major enemy of the new Soviet state. Mikhail Borodin, who went to Mexico in 1919 to set up a Communist party, also hoped to negotiate a trade agreement. Although he was unsuccessful, Mexico did have an economic interest in developing relations with the USSR. The pre-revolutionary Russian regime had purchased some Mexican produce, for example cotton, but the transactions had been carried out through an intermediary and the Mexicans were anxious to cultivate direct links. In 1924 diplomatic relations were established and envoys exchanged, although the Mexicans, probably in order to avoid provoking the United States, withheld the recognition of the Soviet Union which Moscow had been seeking (Sizonenko: 1972, p. 19). The differing emphasis given by the two countries to the status of their mutual relations is suggested by the fact that whereas the Soviet ambassador to Mexico was the flamboyant revolutionary and feminist Alexandra Kollontai (1926–9), the Mexicans sent a former ambassador to Norway to act as their representative in Moscow (Sizonenko: 1972, p. 23).

In 1924 the first Mexican exports arrived in the Soviet Union, and in 1926 very small amounts of Soviet produce (105,000 rubles' worth of wood, hides, linen and hemp) began to flow in the other direction. Soviet purchases of Mexican goods (non-ferrous metals, chemical products and cotton) reached their peak of 2.757 million rubles' worth that year (Sizonenko: 1972, p. 29). There was talk of signing a trading agreement during 1927, but relations rapidly deteriorated due to the inopportune attempt by the Comintern in 1929 to exploit political uncertainty in Mexico, culminating in Mexico's severing of all links in 1930.

The Mexican government re-established relations with the Soviet Union in 1943 and has maintained them ever since, although the activities of the Mexican Communist Party have intermittently been a source of tension. Mexico, faced with a history of intervention and lost territory, formidable development problems and the necessity of finding a strategy of accommodation with its economically crucial northern neighbour, has traditionally maintained a low-key foreign-policy stance, committed to non-interference in the affairs of other countries and designed to maintain correct but distant relations with all governments regardless of orientation. However, there has been a steady underlying trend towards a more open and assertive approach to foreign relations, for reasons which will be discussed below. A tentative movement in this direction was made by President López Mateos (1958–64) who, in 1959, invited Anastas Mikoian, vice-president of the Council of Ministers, to attend a Soviet trade exhibition which was held in Mexico City. In 1964 a Mexican delegation, headed by the Director of the National Bank of Foreign Trade, went to the Soviet Union. The Mexican state oil company, Pemex, ordered ten oil turbo-drills and on its return the delegation recommended that Mexico should conclude a trade agreement with the Soviet Union (*Comercio de México con Europa Central*, Mexico, 1964, p. 45, in Sizonenko: 1972, p. 95). In 1968 the Minister of Foreign Trade himself visited Moscow, and a cultural and scientific cooperation agreement was signed. Further development of relations was hindered, however, by the strongly domestic orientation of the Mexican administration which presided over the dramatic threats to political stability represented by the student-led protests at the 1968 Olympic Games and the subsequent massacre of demonstrating students at Tlatelolco in Mexico City.

In the early 1970s President Echeverría, in response to a combination of domestic and international pressures, used the opportunity that oil offered to diversify his country's financial and economic ties. Having been personally involved in the violent repression of 1968, as president he needed to make overtures towards disaffected groups, particularly amongst the left and the young (Poitras: 1981, p. 104), who were questioning not only the existing political system but also the regime's development policies. Growing dissatisfaction within Mexico about the imbalance of the 'special relationship' with the United States was another significant factor pushing Echeverría towards a rethinking of Mexico's traditionally isolationist foreign policy. It is important to bear in mind that his initiatives towards the Soviet Union were a minor constituent of a broader political strategy and did not necessarily imply any lasting commitment to the development of relations with Moscow.

In 1973 Echeverría went on a much heralded state visit to the USSR, in the course of which agreements on trade and on the supply of machinery and equipment were signed. This year also saw the first session of a Soviet–Mexican Joint Commission. Echeverría subsequently announced that Mexico would like to participate in Comecon as an observer. In August 1975 a mutual cooperation agreement was signed between Mexico and Comecon, an agreement which was ratified by the Mexican government the following year.

Echeverría's hand-picked successor, López Portillo, was committed to maintaining Mexico's new assertive foreign policy, albeit in a more low-key style. The high point of Soviet–Mexican relations transpired in May 1978 when he travelled to Moscow on a state visit, to be received by Brezhnev, Kosygin and Gromyko. Portillo described his conversations with Brezhnev as 'exceptionally fruitful' (SWB, SU/5824/ A1/3, 27 May 1978). At the end of this visit the Soviet Union signed Protocol Number 2 to the Tlatelolco Treaty on the prohibition of nuclear weapons in Latin America. Agreement was also apparently reached on the adoption of measures to permit the achievement of an appropriate level of trade turnover and economic cooperation. Shortly afterwards, a five-year maritime transport agreement was signed, aimed at promoting a regular service between the two countries. In 1981 a Soviet exhibition was held in Mexico City, in the course of which twenty-five Soviet enterprises went to Mexico with specific proposals on the exchange of technology concerned with agricultural and technical machinery, food processing and, possibly, nuclear power (SWB, SU/6666/A1/2, 6 March 1981).

It is clear that the Mexicans, as well as the Brazilians, had a mistaken idea of what they could expect from trade with the Soviet Union. An article in Comercio Exterior in 1968 said, 'The Soviet Union may be an extensive market for Mexico's growing exports of manufactured goods. It is clear that the economic-industrial power of the Soviet Union offers a broad range of possible supplies to meet Mexico's import demands' (Comercio Exterior [Mexico], 1968, Number 6, p. 47). However, although Mexico's trade with Comecon has increased tenfold from the very low base prior to the 1975 agreement, Soviet–Mexican trade, as can be seen from table 7, has been highly erratic, showing no sign of settling into a stable pattern. The only noteworthy deal which has gone through is the import of Soviet tractors in knock-down form to Mexico, where they are assembled with some of the parts being supplemented by local manufacturers. However, there have been reports of the usual complaints about the quality of the Soviet merchandise and the difficulties of adapting the machinery to local conditions.

Table 7. *Soviet trade with Mexico 1970–87 (millions of rubles)*

	Turnover	Exports	Imports
1970	1.0	0.7	0.3
1971	9.5	0.3	9.2
1972	8.4	0.6	7.8
1973	0.6	0.5	0.1
1974	2.4	1.1	1.3
1975	6.1	4.4	1.7
1976	18.0	6.9	11.1
1977	2.9	1.2	1.7
1978	13.4	2.4	11.0
1979	5.5	4.8	0.7
1980	13.8	11.9	1.9
1981	22.7	4.0	18.7
1982	27.8	7.8	21.0
1983	11.6	2.9	8.7
1984	16.1	1.7	14.4
1985	20.3	4.2	16.1
1986	11.2	4.0	7.2
1987	28.8	5.6	21.0

Sources: Foreign Trade (Moscow) and *Vneshniaia Torgovlia SSSR.*

Venezuela

Venezuela in effect had no official links with the USSR until 1970 (Caracas succumbed to US pressure to establish relations just before the end of the Second World War – March 1945 – but broke the connection in 1952) and it is only very recently that serious attempts have been made to put the relationship on a firm footing. Venezuela's President Raúl Leoni was one of the signatories to the Declaration of Bogotá of 16 August 1966 (along with Colombia, Chile, Peru and Ecuador) which stated that it was important to study openings for trade with the Eastern bloc. Relations were eventually re-established in 1970 by President Rafael Caldera. At the time Venezuela was experiencing economic difficulties because of a drastic reduction in US imports of Venezuelan oil. Caracas apparently turned to Moscow in the hope of obtaining help and advice on the penetration of alternative oil markets (Sizonenko: 1972, p. 149). Rafael Caldera, speaking at a press conference on 16 April 1970, when the announcement was made, said that the establishment of relations with Moscow was 'a necessity for Venezuela because there are matters relating to the market for our oil, the world regulation of petroleum and numerous other affairs which we have to discuss with [the USSR]' (*El Nacional* (Caracas), 17 April 1970, in Sizonenko: 1972, p. 150). In 1975 the Venezuelan Foreign Minister went to the USSR and signed an agreement on cultural, scientific and technical cooperation and, in the following year, Carlos Andrés Pérez, another oil-conscious Third-World-oriented president, travelled to Moscow on a state visit, returning with an agreement on economic and industrial cooperation. Very little transpired, however, apart from the arrangements for Venezuela to supply oil to Cuba in return for Soviet deliveries to Venezuelan clients in Europe, and it is only within the last three years (see below) that further developments have occurred.

Gorbachev's Latin American policy

Since Gorbachev took over the General Secretaryship of the CPSU in April 1985, there have been signs of a new Soviet initiative in Latin America, directed particularly at the major regional powers. The Soviet Union is primarily looking for a visible economic presence in the area. It is interesting to note that Gorbachev was the Politburo member responsible for agriculture when the embargo-breaking grain and meat deals were signed with Argentina in 1980–1. Opportunities have been opened up by the post-1983 democratisation process in the Southern Cone, and by the post-Falklands backlash against the United States throughout Latin America. During the Malvinas war, the Argentine Communist party strongly backed the military initiative and explicitly pledged the support of the USSR and the socialist camp. Whilst the Soviet Union did enhance its prestige in Latin America by its verbal backing for Argentina in the course of the conflict (arguing that, whatever the motives behind the military invasion of the islands, the restoration of national sovereignty was 'objectively an anti-imperialist act'), Moscow in fact abstained on the UN Security Council resolution condemning the use of force to recover the islands; thus its support was not unlimited.

Relations with Argentina, which were distinctly cool at the end of 1983 (the USSR sent a relatively low-level official to attend President Alfonsín's inauguration), have thawed to the extent that the first visit of an Argentine Foreign Minister to the USSR took place in late January 1986 when Dante Caputo went to Moscow and President Alfonsín made the same journey the following October. Despite his failure to secure the economic guarantees he sought, Alfonsín signed a joint communiqué emphasising the importance of Moscow's recent proposal to eliminate all nuclear arms by the year 2000. The USSR has also secured, by a two-year agreement signed on 28 July 1986, extended fishing rights off the Argentine coast, in return for heavy licensing fees and an Argentine share in the proceeds of the catch. A large area of the seas included in the agreement covers the 150-mile protection zone declared around the Malvinas/Falkland Islands by the British government, which refuses to accept that the agreement has any basis in international law. The Soviet Union, by implicitly denying recognition to the exclusion zone, gave Argentina an important boost to its campaign to win diplomatic recognition of its claim to sovereignty over the islands.

In December 1985 the Brazilian Minister of Foreign Affairs paid what was described as a 'milestone' visit to Moscow, where he was received by Gromyko and Shevardnadze and signed the first Soviet–Brazilian inter-governmental agreement on economic and technical cooperation (covering the power, chemical, pharmaceutical and mining industries). Even so, a Soviet commentator subsequently presented a sober assessment of what could be achieved in relations between the two countries, saying that '. . . despite the political will displayed at the talks in Moscow and the increased intensiveness and dynamism of Soviet–Brazilian relations, a good deal of time and consistent effort will be required to accomplish the task of further expanding and diversifying the relations between the USSR and Brazil' (Vanin: 1986, p. 40).

The crisis in Central America, together with the more assertive role of the regional powers Mexico and Venezuela in the early 1980s, heightened the importance of good political relations with these countries. The Soviet Union has praised the foreign policy of the Miguel de la Madrid government, particularly with respect to Central America (Rotislav Sergeev, Soviet ambassador to Mexico, May 1984, in *América Latina – Unión Soviética*, Facultad Latinoamericana de Ciencias Sociales [Santiago de Chile], II:1 [October–November 1984], p. 3). In May 1983 the Mexican ambassador to the Soviet Union, Horacio Flores de la Pena, was granted an audience with Gromyko to discuss the Central American question. Consultations also took place in early November after the US invasion of Grenada. In 1983 the Venezuelan Minister of Foreign Affairs, José Zambrano, visited the Soviet Union and held consultations with Gromyko on the Central American situation, and, in August 1983, Yurii Fokin included Venezuela as the last stop on his tour of Nicaragua, Panama, Cuba and Mexico. However, Mexico's own economic difficulties are making it increasingly difficult to sustain an assertive Central American policy, as was exemplified by the de la Madrid government's 1985 decision to suspend Mexican oil supplies to Nicaragua. Moreover, the August 1987 Central American Peace Plan has shifted the emphasis away from the Contadora countries, particularly as the five Central American signatories have recently approached Spain, Canada and West Germany about verification.

Efforts have been made to develop trade with Venezuela, with the signing of the first trade agreement between the two countries in March 1985. Further attempts to sell Soviet goods in Mexico were made with an exhibition of Comecon products held in Mexico City during 9–23 November 1984, and the signing of a trade protocol between the Soviet Union and Mexico for 1984–5, which aimed to raise the volume of trade to $40 million. As can be seen in table 7, however, less than half of this target was achieved. During Foreign Minister Shevardnadze's visit in October 1986 further commitments were made to increase trade and to establish consultations on the oil industry.

The USSR has certainly become more sophisticated in its diplomatic dealings with Latin America since 1985, with greater attention being paid to the public relations aspects of its representation in the area, as has happened more generally in Soviet foreign policy. In yet another attempt to improve its trade balance with debt-ridden Latin America, Moscow has cut back on goods purchased on a cash basis and launched a drive to increase its exports to the region by means of joint ventures, barter and counter-trade deals. For example, the Soviet Union is involved in a joint undertaking with Brazilian and West German companies to build a large new flat steel works in Brazil's northern state of Maranhão. It is too early to assess the longer-term impact of such projects. However, Gorbachev's initiative will be subject to the same constraints that have operated in the past, and the prospects for any substantial increases in Soviet influence with the Latin American powers look slim. Moscow continues to shape its policy in the region according to developments in its relationship with Washington: it was Shevardnadze, rather than Gorbachev (as originally planned), who visited Argentina, Brazil and Uruguay in September–October 1987, apparently to avoid provoking the North Americans. All four Latin American governments may have an interest in using their relations with Moscow as a foil to the United States and a concession to domestic left-wingers, but they also have their own motivations for keeping the USSR at a distance. Latin American foreign policies are primarily geared towards supporting their nation's development strategy and managing the relationship with Washington. Apart from the desire to affirm their status as fully fledged members of the international community by maintaining relations with the 'other superpower', these Latin American states have no ideological and few political incentives for cultivating links with the USSR. Neither Mexico nor Venezuela have found any significant economic inducement to compensate for the absence of political interests. Argentina and Brazil clearly do have economic interests at stake, but to date both have preferred to confine their relations with Moscow to the purely commercial level. Moreover, even within that limited sphere, they have opted to do only the minimum necessary to ensure that the Soviet Union maintains its imports of agricultural produce. Trading agreements have not been translated into political goodwill or even into stable economic relationships as easily as Moscow might have hoped or Washington has feared.

7   The USSR and the Central American crisis

Since President Reagan moved into the White House early in 1981 his administration has insisted on presenting the current upheavals in Central America, which the overwhelming majority of observers have attributed to the endemic poverty and inequality of the social structures of these countries, in terms of the worldwide geopolitical struggle between East and West. For example, former Secretary of State Alexander Haig told a Senate committee, 'This situation is global in character. The problem is worldwide Soviet interventionism that poses an unprecedented challenge to the free world. Anyone attempting to debate the prospects for a successful outcome in El Salvador who fails to consider the Soviet menace is dealing with the leg or the trunk of the elephant' (Steele: 1983, p. 222). Thus Central America was defined by President Reagan's advisers as a test-case of US capacity to overcome the ambivalence and vacillation which characterised its foreign-policy making in the wake of the Vietnam debacle. Alexander Haig argued that 'it is in just such sensitive areas [as Central America] where Soviet vital interests are not directly engaged – as they are, for example, in Poland – that opportunities for amelioration of conflicting superpower policies are most promising' (Haig: 1984, p. 122).

The attention of the incoming Reagan administration was initially focused on El Salvador, where insurgents had recently launched an intensive campaign designed to emulate the Sandinista seizure of power in 1979. The public posture of the White House was that the FMLN (Farabundo Martí National Liberation Front) guerrillas would be unable to sustain their position were it not for shipments of arms through Honduras sponsored by Managua/Havana/Moscow. To what extent is this assertion valid? It is known that Cuban and/or Nicaraguan arms were received by the FMLN in 1980, supplies of which were stepped up from November onwards with a view to the January 1981 'Final Offensive', intended to present the newly inaugurated US president with a *fait accompli*. Indeed this proved to be the last real opportunity for the Salvadoran Left to win power through their military actions alone. The Reagan administration has publicly committed itself to 'winning' in El Salvador and in all probability a military victory for the guerrillas would spark off a US intervention of sufficient strength to prevent their taking power, thus ensuring a revolutionary defeat.

It is generally agreed that Cuba and Nicaragua curtailed arms deliveries in March 1981. Evidence of Cuban/Nicaraguan aid to the FMLN since then is conflicting and inconclusive. However, four points should be made. Firstly, there is only minimal and much-disputed evidence of Soviet involvement in supplying the FMLN, even in late 1980 and early 1981. The US Government White Paper entitled 'Communist Interference in El Salvador', published in February 1981, has been severely criticised, not least by a former US government adviser on Cuba, who declared that the paper revealed 'shoddy research and a fierce determination to advocate the new policy, whether or not the evidence sustained it'. He went on to say, 'Some of the supporting documents turned out to be forgeries. Others were of such vague origin as to be worthless. None of the documents linked the USSR to the supply of guerrilla forces in El Salvador' (Smith, Wayne: 1982, p. 162).

The paper in itself confirms that Soviet policy was one of restraint. According to this document, the Soviet Union agreed to give practical assistance to the FMLN at a meeting in Havana in December 1979, organised by Castro. However, Moscow did not switch completely to support tactics until the spring and summer of 1980, which then amounted only to the training of a few dozen recruits. Salvadoran Communist Party leader Schafik Handal travelled to the USSR and Eastern Europe in June–July 1980, but was said to be disappointed with the low level of his reception, particularly in the Soviet Union, where he met only Mikhail Kudachkin, deputy chief of the Latin American section of the Central Committee's International Affairs department. Handal apparently negotiated deliveries of US-made weapons from Ethiopia and Vietnam, and some East European countries agreed to provide communications equipment, uniforms and medical supplies. The only commitment made by the Soviet Union was to help in arranging the transfer of these supplies to Cuba.

Indeed, as discussed in chapter 4, the evidence we have (including that presented in the previous paragraph) suggests that Cuba and the Soviet Union diverged on the issue of supplies to the Salvadoran guerrillas. In 1980 Moscow, still suffering the diplomatic backlash (including the US attempt to enforce sanctions) to its December 1979 Afghanistan invasion, was reluctant to involve itself in the affairs of a Third World country in which the USSR had no security concerns and which was rapidly becoming the focus of US definitions of its own national interest. Moreover, Soviet specialists were unconvinced of the likelihood of FMLN success. Besides, partly in response to a general shift in the international Communist movement at this stage, other Latin American Communist parties were revising their position on armed struggle, most notably the Chilean Communists. A decision to render significant material support to the high-profile Salvadoran insurgents could have sparked off fears of a general Soviet revolutionary offensive which in turn could have seriously damaged Moscow's relations not only with Latin American governments (two of which, Argentina and Brazil, were crucial to Soviet success in circumventing Carter's grain embargo), but world-wide.

Secondly, since 1982 the United States has controlled an extensive military apparatus along both the Honduran/Nicaraguan and the Honduran/Salvadoran borders designed to stop gun-running. US radar installations cover both Honduran and Salvadoran airspace and US officials in the two countries 'map every acre of guerrilla territory with radar and infra-red computer-analysed photographs' – none of which 'has produced a single consignment of incoming Cuban/Nicaraguan arms' (Nairn: 1984, p. 33).

Thirdly, since 1983 the Sandinistas have been preoccupied with the threat of direct US military action against them (particularly after Grenada) and are unlikely to run the risk of pre-empting this. As detailed in chapter 4, Cuba has also pursued a consistently cautious strategy since 1981 in recognition of President Reagan's desire to go to 'the source' of insurgency in Central America. Fourthly, by 1983 the FMLN had established and has since sustained its capacity to present a military (and political) challenge which the Salvadoran armed forces alone cannot overcome, despite intensive training and heavy arming by the United States. This would not have been possible if the guerrillas had been solely or primarily dependent on materiel from Cuba/Nicaragua, even if the quantities involved were at the levels alleged by the US administration. The conclusion must be that, even if Havana and/or Managua have managed to get arms supplies through to the insurgents, it is highly unlikely that they could have been sufficient to influence the direction of the civil war.

Since, by its success in creating a *cordon sanitaire* around El Salvador, Washington effectively disproved the logic of its own analysis, US officials switched the emphasis of their argument to the contention that it is Nicaragua's (and Cuba's) influence as a revolutionary model which gives other left-wing movements the self-confidence to sustain momentum. Thus, the very existence of such regimes is defined as a threat to the security of the United States. Of course, there is little doubt that if the Sandinistas were to be overthrown, it would be a blow to the morale of the FMLN, just as the toppling of Somoza severely jolted the confidence of the Central American Right. Moreover, ill-judged and over-confident Sandinista rhetoric in the euphoric aftermath of the revolution to the effect that the Nicaraguan success had triggered a revolutionary wave throughout Central America (Cerdas Cruz: 1986b, p. 188) simply played into US hands.

However, the basic immutable fact that by its existence a government can be a source of inspiration to other groupings of a similar political orientation bears no necessary relation to the conduct of that regime's policies or to its forging of international alliances. In the early years, despite occasionally defiant and provocative speeches, Nicaragua did send out consistent signals that it wanted to maintain a workable relationship with the United States, although of course on the basis of redefining the previous 'imperialist' connection. Apart from the security issue, most Sandinista officials are well aware that access to the US market would make for a far healthier economy than would integration with the socialist bloc. However, as was the case with Cuba in 1959, both sides' distrust of each other in 1979–80 was such that relatively minor instances of diplomatic blundering or over-zealous responses by junior officials in both governments were taken as indications of a high-level policy decision to be obstructive. Carter's failure to take decisive steps to prevent the Nicaraguan revolution also made the Sandinistas over-play their hand in a way that was easily exploited by the ideologically motivated Reagan administration. As the Republican President stepped up the pressure on Nicaragua, the assertion of an 'inevitable' connection between a revolutionary regime and the Soviet Union, translated into a policy position for the United States, again served only to contract political space (as happened in Cuba) to such an extent that it became a self-fulfilling prophecy.

To support this argument, the remainder of the chapter looks firstly at the Soviet Union's policies towards Central America in the broad context of its relations with the United States, and goes on to consider the nature and extent of Moscow's commitment to Nicaragua.

The Soviet interest in Central America

The build-up of Soviet interest in Central America can be described as a series of five stages: during the first stage, before late 1979, despite a significant rise in guerrilla activity during 1977–8, the Soviet Union displayed little interest in the region, which had long been an area of low priority for them. Historically, Moscow had suffered three defeats there: El Salvador in 1932, Costa Rica in 1948 and Guatemala in 1954, and Soviet analysts indicated considerable scepticism about the probability of success for the insurgents of the 1970s. Even after the triumph of the Nicaraguan revolution in July 1979, Moscow placed heavy emphasis on the likelihood of US intervention.

However, the failure of the Carter administration to take decisive action regarding events in Nicaragua, together with the Sandinistas' success in consolidating their revolution, led to the rising and exaggerated optimism which characterised Soviet commentary on Central America through 1980 and early into 1981. Moscow's own December 1979 commitment of troops to Afghanistan provided both an incentive to extract maximum propaganda value from events in Central America and a constraint on significant Soviet involvement. This second stage also saw the unification of the guerrillas in El Salvador and the March 1980 decision of the Communist Party of El Salvador (PCES) to support the armed road, which was indicative of a new Communist strategy in response to a changing perception of the balance of forces within the region.

The third stage, which lasted from late January 1981 until perhaps a year later, witnessed the initial Soviet response to the policies of the incoming Reagan administration. Soviet leaders undoubtedly perceived the dangers of their being drawn into a confrontation in Central America as having been markedly intensified after the Republicans took office. President Reagan proved himself determined to redeem his original campaign pledge to make Central America a major issue in East-West relations and to stamp out 'Communism' in America's backyard. However, the Soviet Union refused to accept the challenge implicit in Washington's 17 January 1981 announcement that a $75 million aid package for Nicaragua was to be suspended, allegedly because Managua was supplying arms to the left-wing guerrilla forces in El Salvador. At the 26th Congress of the CPSU in February 1981 the Soviet leadership, wary of provoking Reagan, and with its previous optimism somewhat crushed by the failure of the January 1981 FMLN 'final offensive' in El Salvador, seemed to be doing all it could to play down the Central American issue. Very little mention was made of the area, Salvadoran Communists were conspicuously absent from the gathering and Brezhnev offered Reagan a summit meeting. Privately, Soviet ambassador to Washington Anatoli Dobrynin 'remained unresponsive' to Secretary of State Haig's probing about Moscow's intentions in Central America, 'pleading ignorance of events in that part of the world' (Haig: 1984, p. 108). Apparently the Soviet leaders were hoping that Reagan would turn out to be 'another Nixon', whose initial bellicosity gave way to a more flexible and pragmatic policy once he had settled in at the White House. They are thought to have abandoned such ideas by mid-1981. However (as detailed below), Moscow seems to have taken few, if any measures to step up its own involvement in Central America at this stage. What the Soviet Union did do during 1981 was to increase its military shipments to Cuba: according to US officials more was sent in the first eight months of 1981 than in any year since 1962. In addition, various high-ranking Soviet officers visited Cuba in a symbolic display of solidarity, measures which are clearly indicative of Soviet priorities in the region as a whole.

The fourth stage, from early 1982 until 1984, involved a Soviet shift away from an almost wholly defensive position towards a more equivocal stance, although its policy remained fundamentally a low-profile one. Soviet aid to Nicaragua, both military and economic, increased markedly in 1982 (from a very low base, however). This shift was almost certainly occasioned by the Reagan administration's introduction, in November 1981, of a 'covert' operation to destabilise the Sandinista government. Faced with US intransigence and the issue of whether or not the Nicaraguan revolution could be preserved, Moscow readjusted its policy in order to accommodate two basic aims: firstly, to avoid humiliation in Central America and, secondly, to make life for the United States as hard as possible in the region, particularly in the light of its own continuing difficulties in Afghanistan.

In 1982 the Falklands/Malvinas war overshadowed events in Central America and may have led the Soviet leaders to hope, temporarily, that Washington would be forced to moderate its position because of the steady erosion of support in Latin America for its Central American policies. On the contrary, however, the administration's position became more firmly entrenched during 1983, despite the fact that CIA involvement in Nicaragua had been exposed by the media in November 1982. However, Soviet aid to Nicaragua showed no significant increase on 1982 levels. Tension heightened throughout 1983, particularly in the last three months, along with a general deterioration in superpower relations marked by the Korean airliner disaster, the US invasion of Grenada and, probably most importantly in Moscow's eyes, the deployment of US missiles in Europe.

Since 1984 (stage 5) Soviet bloc aid has increased dramatically, following Daniel Ortega's June 1984 consultations with Chernenko, which were described by Managua radio as 'a very significant meeting' which was 'very useful and fruitful for our people' (*SWB*, SU/7674/A1/2, 20 June 1984). This followed an escalation of US pressure on the Sandinista regime, in particular the autumn 1983 *contra* attacks on Nicaragua's oil installations and the CIA-assisted mining of its ports (discussed in more detail on page 212). By that stage the Sandinistas had demonstrated that their political strength was such that it was highly unlikely that the *contra* forces could succeed in overthrowing them. With an eye to the November 1984 US presidential elections, Moscow's calculations must have been that they had little to lose by providing the Sandinistas with just enough military equipment to ensure that the United States could not win without becoming directly involved. After President Reagan's re-election, the USSR's interest in trying to keep the highly assertive US administration tied down in Central America increased, particularly in the light of Washington's linkage of arms control negotiations with the resolution of regional conflicts. In May 1985 Gorbachev took the decision to guarantee Nicaraguan oil supplies, all of which came from the Soviet Union in 1986, 'on terms understood to amount to a free donation' (*The Times*, 3 October 1986, p. 8). The aim of Soviet policy was primarily to establish Nicaragua as a counterweight to Afghanistan in any 'spheres of influence' deal. As relations thawed between Moscow and Washington, and real prospects emerged for the negotiation of agreements, the Soviet Union sought to maximise its bargaining power by stepping up its involvement in Nicaragua. This is what lies behind the fact that both economic and military assistance to the Sandinistas increased dramatically during 1986. In 1987 and 1988, in the light of a new era of superpower cooperation and the withdrawal of Soviet troops from Afghanistan (beginning on 15 May 1988), there were clear indications that the Kremlin could be willing to reconsider its commitment to Nicaragua, a development which will be discussed below.

Moscow and the Sandinista revolution

Political and military policies

The triumph of the Nicaraguan FSLN (Sandinista National Liberation Front) against the dictator Somoza on 19 July 1979 came as a great surprise in Moscow. Richard Feinberg, who visited the Soviet Union in 1981, states that neither experts at the Institute of Latin America nor government officials had predicted such an outcome to the civil war (Feinberg: 1983, p. 376). Abraham Lowenthal, who travelled in the same group as Feinberg, also reports that the editor of *Latinskaia Amerika*, Sergei Mikoian, told him that 'few could see the possibility of a Sandinista triumph even in 1979' (Lowenthal: 1981, p. 10).

The Soviet Union played no active role in the guerrilla war waged by the FSLN and gave no direct material aid. Mikoian told Lowenthal that he had attended a solidarity conference for the Sandinistas in Panama early in 1979 to 'show them that Soviet neglect of them was not absolute' (Lowenthal: 1981, p. 10). Nicaragua's Moscow-affiliated Communist Party (known as the Nicaraguan Socialist Party), which had long been hostile to the armed struggle, maintained for much of the civil war that the Sandinista strategy was too daring, and tried to back US efforts to find an alternative to Somoza. Although the PSN 'fell in line with the Front's military strategy' after the FSLN had unified early in 1979, even in the last few months of the war its role was confined to propaganda support (Ramírez: 1980, p. 92 and Black: 1981, p. 145). Of course, Cuba's military support for the Sandinistas was more significant, although it was by no means decisive, nor did it compare favourably with the quantities of materiel sent by other Latin American countries, notably Panama and Venezuela. Cuba gave some weapons (mostly rifles), training and financial support. According to the US administration an intelligence unit was set up early in 1979 in Costa Rica to monitor the war in Nicaragua, and Castro also sent a few military advisers in the closing stages of the conflict. Cuba's primary contribution was a political one. It was through Cuban mediation that the unification of the FSLN, which was undoubtedly crucial to the success of the war, was achieved. The enthusiastic reception given by the Cuban press to the announcement of the Sandinista victory and Cuba's subsequent involvement in the sending of personnel to help with the implementation of revolutionary policies, such as the health and literacy programmes, suggest that the low profile maintained by the Cuban government prior to July 1979 was deliberately adopted as a means of removing any pretext for stepped-up US action against the Sandinistas. In distinct contrast the Soviet Union, which had paid only desultory attention to the Sandinista campaign, took care to contain its enthusiasm even after the triumph of the revolution. An article in the 19 July 1979 edition of *Pravda*, entitled 'A step towards victory', which reported Somoza's departure from Nicaragua, was very low-key. There was no acclamation of the FSLN success and the emphasis was heavily on the probability of US intervention.

However, as the Sandinistas began to consolidate their power, and Moscow's interest in promoting the Nicaraguan revolution heightened in the light of its involvement in Afghanistan, Soviet commentaries began to adopt a more positive tone. In October 1980 leading Soviet ideologist Ponomarev described the Nicaraguan revolution as 'a major success' and in his speech to the CPSU Congress of February 1981 Brezhnev stated that the revolutions in Ethiopia, Afghanistan and Nicaragua were the most important 'new victories' since 1976. Academic specialists began to argue that the Sandinistas had been able to avoid many of the mistakes made by Allende in Chile, partly because they were 'the only political force to have emerged from the ruins of *Somocismo*'[1] but also because they had understood that the issue at stake in revolutionary Nicaragua was 'not . . . the broadness of the economic reforms but . . . the reliable securing of all (or the maximum possible) fullness of power' (Mikoian: 1980, pp. 110–11).

The successes of the Sandinista government in securing control of the armed forces, promoting a mixed economy in order to avoid antagonising the middle classes and developing organisations of mass participation were all noted approvingly. While some Soviet Latin Americanists, notably Kiva Maidinik, of the Institute of World Economy and International Relations, are sceptical about the alliance between the FSLN and the bourgeoisie, which they see as inherently unstable, other leading experts, for example Sergei Mikoian and Anatoli Shul'govski (author of a respected history of the Mexican revolution), are convinced that the Nicaraguan model, with its proposed incorporation of the private sector, is feasible and could potentially be applied elsewhere in the Third World.

Despite the enthusiasm shown in academic circles for the Sandinista revolution, at an official level Moscow has proved no keener to grant Nicaragua the 'socialist' status which would command a major Soviet

---

[1] Professor Karen Khachaturov, vice-chairman of the Afro-Asian Solidarity Committee with special responsibility for Latin America, cited in Richard Gott and Jonathan Steele, 'Russia turns down the Cuba card', the *Guardian*, 28 April 1983, p. 15.

commitment than it was with Chile. With Castro's 1960–2 successful manipulation of Khrushchev's assertions of 'revolutionary internationalism' in mind, Soviet officials have been careful to avoid giving the Sandinistas any scope for similar manoeuvres. In addition, any Sandinista attempts to emulate Castro's tactics are inherently weakened by the fact that the United States has avoided presenting them with a 'Bay of Pigs'-type rallying point for international and domestic solidarity.

Sandinista statements of adherence to Marxism-Leninism pose a dilemma in that it is difficult for Soviet ideologists to accord the FSLN a status equivalent to the officially recognised Communist parties in Central America. This problem is theoretically resolved by classifying groupings such as the FSLN (and Grenada's New Jewel Movement) as 'vanguard parties' which are capable of leading a developing nation towards socialism, but which are made up of *petit bourgeois* rather than working-class elements and which 'are substantially inferior to Communist parties in the level of the theoretical maturity of their cadres, in the degree of their revolutionary influence on the working people, and in their ideological, political and organisational experience' (Irkhin: 1982, p. 58).

In articles published in November 1980 (in *Kommunist*) and in the *World Marxist Review* in January 1981, Ponomarev wrote that states of 'socialist orientation' were emerging in Asia, Africa and Central America, but no explicit reference was made to Nicaragua (Rothenberg: 1983, p. 7). In general, references to Nicaragua as a state of socialist orientation have been confined to articles in the academic journal *Latinskaia Amerika* and have scarcely appeared in official statements.[2] In any case, even 'socialist orientation' is regarded by Soviet ideologists as a reversible process, and the additional caution shown with respect to Nicaragua suggests that it in fact ranks somewhere below countries such as Angola, Ethiopia, Mozambique and South Yemen.

The Soviet Union has consistently sent out signals designed to reassure the United States above all, but also the West Europeans and the Latin Americans, that its relations with Nicaragua do not have aggressive implications. Although Moscow and Managua exchanged messages indicating readiness to restore diplomatic relations at the

---

[2] The exception was an article on 'The USSR and the developing countries' in *Pravda*, 13 June 1983, which referred to 'countries with a socialist orientation, in particular, Angola, Afghanistan, Nicaragua and also certain Arab states' (Rothenberg: 1983, p. 10, footnote 35).

end of July 1979, it was not until 18 October that normal links were restored. Even then, the Soviet representative at the ceremony in Managua (Yurii Volskii, ambassador to Mexico) was careful to stress that 'Soviet–Nicaraguan relations are not directed against any third country and will not affect any one else' (Managua home service, 19 October 1979, in SWB, SU/6251/A1/9, 22 October 1979). When asked in August 1982 how the USSR would respond in the event of direct aggression against Nicaragua, Yurii Fokin, Secretary-General of the Soviet Foreign Ministry, replied, 'We will support Nicaragua politically in every way', a remark which was broadcast by Radio Havana (Rothenberg: 1983, p. 11). In private, one Soviet official admitted that, 'If the Americans invaded Nicaragua, what would we do? What could we do? Nothing' (Steele: 1983, p. 220).

The Soviet Union has little to gain itself from defending Nicaragua. Even if the Sandinistas had shown themselves willing to provide the USSR with bases, which they have not, it is hard to see what strategic advantage the Soviet Union would enjoy in Nicaragua which it does not already possess in Cuba. This has been implicitly recognised by US officials assessing their own security interests in the Caribbean. One US diplomat, a veteran of the Vietnam pacification programme, put it thus: 'In the event of a war in Europe where we'd have to reinforce NATO, we'd already have to watch Cuba to guard the shipping lanes from the gulf ports. It's more trouble if we have to watch Nicaragua too. That's it. . . . Compared to Cuba, Nicaragua could never amount to anything' (Nairn: 1984, p. 27. His interview, Tegucigalpa, September 1983).

Correspondingly, the political impact of the Nicaraguan revolution was only a relatively minor tremor in comparison with the earth-shattering force with which Castro's victory over Batista and defiance of the United States resounded throughout Latin America. Nicaragua's revolutionary power of example as a model of development is also considerably less than Cuba's in the 1960s, almost exclusively confined to its economically insignificant Central American neighbours. Thus the Sandinista seizure of power held out the prospect only of limited strategic and political gains for the Soviet Union.

Despite the fact that, after an early spate of bellicose threats against Cuba, Reagan's administration has concentrated its attention on Nicaragua and El Salvador, the Soviet emphasis has been very much on 'hands off Cuba' rather than 'hands off Nicaragua'. In an *International Affairs* article of January 1982 there is an explicit condemnation of Washington's attempts to 'subvert Socialist Cuba, as well as other progressive Latin American states, such as Nicaragua and Grenada', but the declaration of Soviet support refers only to Cuba: 'the Soviet Union has supported, and will continue to support the Cuban people in their struggle to protect their sovereignty. All progressive and peace-loving forces are coming out in defence of Cuba and its independence' (Khachaturov: 1982, p. 61).

In the joint communiqué issued after Daniel Ortega's meeting with Andropov on 25 March 1983, he was obliged to concur with the Soviet leader's 'conviction that Nicaragua will be able to uphold its freedom and independence' by emphasising that 'the revolutionary government of Nicaragua has all the necessary resources to defend the motherland' (*Pravda*, 26 March 1983, p. 1). The USSR has also sought to downplay apparent acts of provocation by the United States, such as the harassment of the Soviet vessel *Ulianov*. The Soviet Union delayed for almost a fortnight before finally delivering a note of protest about this incident early in the second week of August 1983. This was in order not to jeopardise a peace initiative by Castro, who in the last week of July wote to all the Contadora presidents expressing Cuba's support for their proposals and its willingness to participate in negotiations. Neither was there any discernible change in policy after the US October invasion of Grenada. On the day of the invasion, TASS issued a statement deploring US activities in Nicaragua as 'a crime against the Nicaraguan people' and 'a direct threat to the security and sovereignty of all Latin American states' (the *New York Times*, 16 October 1983, p. A17). Although the reference was not made explicitly, the statement was clearly intended to deter the United States from taking similar action in Nicaragua. However, Soviet support for the Sandinistas was still expressed only in terms of 'resolute condemnation' of US actions and 'unswerving solidarity' with the Nicaraguan people (the *New York Times*, 16 October 1983, p. A17). Continuing Soviet caution is reflected in the fact that the situation in Nicaragua did not merit a single mention in the speeches at the 27th CPSU Congress in 1986. Nor is Managua included in the itinerary of Gorbachev's projected visit to Latin America (postponed in 1987). Moscow has consistently emphasised its support for the Contadora group initiative (launched by Panama, Mexico, Colombia and Venezuela in January 1983) to bring about a negotiated settlement of the crisis. A government statement welcomed the Central American Peace Plan signed on 7 August 1987, saying that Moscow would promote efforts to translate the plan into reality. In late October 1987 Elliot Abrams, US Assistant Secretary of State for Central America and

Yurii Popov, head of the Latin American department of the Soviet Foreign Ministry met in London for secret talks about Central America, aimed at avoiding misunderstandings of each other's aims in the region. The USSR has also been trying to persuade Western European nations to back the peace process. In a January 1988 visit to Madrid Eduard Shevardnadze said that Moscow wanted to 'create a channel of consultations' with Spain on Central America 'in order to intensify our joint assistance to the process of a peaceful settlement' (the *Guardian*, 22 January 1988, p. 7). The Soviet Union has not signed a Treaty of Friendship and Cooperation with Nicaragua, and it is clear that the Soviet military commitment in the Caribbean is, and is likely to remain, limited to the defence of Cuba.

According to President Reagan, at the December 1987 Washington summit meeting Gorbachev made a unilateral offer to stop supplying arms to the Sandinistas in support of the Central American Peace Plan signed by the Presidents of Costa Rica, El Salvador, Honduras, Guatemala and Nicaragua in August 1987 (variously known as the Guatemala Accord, the Esquipulas Agreement and the Arias Plan). The Soviet clarification issued on 17 December did not withdraw the offer to halt military deliveries to Nicaragua, but stated that it was conditional on Washington's ceasing its aid to the *contras* (*The Financial Times*, 18 December 1987, p. 3). In March 1988, however, Yurii Pavlov, head of the Soviet Foreign Ministry's Latin America department, said that the White House had presented a distorted version of this offer, and that the true Soviet position was that it was prepared to stop all heavy arms deliveries to Nicaragua if the United States would cease supplies of heavy arms to the *contras* and to its other allies in Central America (the *Miami Herald*, 1 March 1988, in *Information Services Latin America* (California), 36:3 (March 1988), p. 180). This reflects Soviet concern about recent deliveries of US modern combat aircraft to Honduras. In a letter to Costa Rican President Arias in early April 1988 Gorbachev reemphasised that the Soviet Union was 'willing to assume, on a basis of reciprocity with the USA, a commitment to respect and strictly fulfil the agreements on matters of security, the control and limitation of weapons . . . within the framework of the Contadora process' (Radio Reloj, San José, 10 April 1988, in *Summary of World Broadcasts*, SU/0123 A1/8, 12 April 1988). These statements, along with the 1987 slowdown in economic support (discussed below), clearly demonstrate the extent to which Moscow's interest in sustaining the Sandinista revolution is constrained by the relative significance of Central America as an issue between the two superpowers.

It is in this context that the USSR's readiness, since late 1981 (when US backing for the counter-revolutionary forces began in earnest), to supply the Sandinistas with sufficient military equipment to keep the *contras* at bay must be understood. Three points should be made concerning the build-up of the Sandinista armed forces (alleged by the Reagan administration to be offensive in intention) and the increase in military supplies from the Soviet bloc. One important fact which is often overlooked is that the Nicaraguans exhausted virtually every possible means of obtaining arms outside the Soviet bloc before Western intransigence forced the issue. In August 1979 Tomás Borge said that an arms deal with the socialist countries 'would be a last resort' (Robert Matthews: 1985, p. 25). By September 1979 the Carter administration had made it clear that the Sandinistas would receive no military supplies from the United States (although the formal announcement of suspension of military aid was not made until June 1980), and pressure from Washington saw to it that when the then Defence Minister Bernardino Larios went on an arms buying mission in the same month to Belgium, West Germany, Spain, Mexico and Brazil, he returned empty-handed (R. Matthews: 1985, p. 28). When, in December 1981, recently elected President Mitterand tried to challenge the Washington dictum against arms supplies to Nicaragua with a sale of $15.8 million worth of equipment (in comparison, France had recently concluded deals worth $2.5 billion with Saudi Arabia and $1 billion with Egypt), the reaction both from the Reagan administration and France's other Western allies proved too harsh for the French government to withstand. In March 1982 President Mitterand privately informed Reagan that the delivery of the helicopters 'would face indefinite delays' and the French have refrained from signing any further arms deals with Managua (R. Matthews: 1985, p. 28). By late 1981 the FSLN, urgently in need of a well-equipped army to combat the increasingly active *contra* forces, was faced with little choice but to obtain military equipment from the only source which was both able and willing to meet its requirements.

Secondly, Sandinista requests for increases in both quantitative and qualitative terms of Eastern bloc supplies can be shown to be in direct response to specific threats to the security of the revolution. Arms shipments from the socialist countries were insignificant in 1979–80. They were estimated by US intelligince sources at $12–13 million worth, and included Soviet ZPU light anti-aircraft guns, SA-7 surface-to-air missiles, RPG anti-tank grenades and East German trucks (Edelman: 1985, p. 49). Apparently, 'After signing a purchase agreement for the trucks, the Sandinistas learned from the Cubans that the model they had ordered performed poorly and that spare parts were hard to obtain. The Cubans suggested cancelling the agreement, but the GDR refused, with party chief Erich Honecker reportedly insisting that "a deal is a deal"' (Edelman: 1985, pp. 49–50). In 1981 the Soviet Union supplied twenty-five T-54 and T-55 tanks (a model which was discontinued in 1963) and two helicopters, 'flown in the ambulance role in support of civilian agencies and one of which was shot down by *Somocista* guerrillas in January 1983' (English: 1984, p. 333).

At the end of November 1981 Defence Minister Humberto Ortega spent one week in Moscow seeking increased supplies in the face of the escalating war against the *contra* groups, which were by then receiving US funds. Nevertheless, it appears that the USSR was not overly forthcoming. US intelligence estimates quoted by the *Los Angeles Times* on 13 January 1984 put Soviet and East European military aid to Nicaragua in 1982 at $56 million, including about 20 more T-54 tanks, 12 BTR-60 armoured personnel carriers, 6 105mm howitzers and around 48 ZIS2 37mm anti-aircraft guns (English: 1984, p. 330). In comparison, the United States supplied $115 million of military aid to other Central American countries during that year. As an additional, most telling comparison, it should be noted that the US administration reportedly subsidised CIA covert operations in Nicaragua to the tune of somewhere between $20–55 million in fiscal year 1982.

The Soviet Union has also given help with training of military personnel. About seventy Nicaraguan pilots and mechanics completed training in Bulgaria in December 1982. In the early summer of 1983, the USSR sent additional military advisers to Nicaragua, bringing the total to one hundred, according to the CIA. Numbers may well have increased since then: according to the White House, 250 Russians in Nicaragua in 1986 were acting as military advisers (the *Guardian*, 9 June 1986, p. 8). Even so, this is by no means a substantial presence.

The worsening military situation in 1983–4 prompted the Sandinistas to request increased support, and US administration sources estimate socialist military aid to Nicaragua at double the 1982 figure, i.e., over $100 million, in 1983. The 1983 level was maintained or slightly augmented during 1984 and 1985, when shipments were valued at $115 million. For comparison, total official US aid to the *contras* from 1981 to 1987 comes to about $237 million (LASA Commission: 1988, p. 21). 1986, the peak year for Soviet aid to Nicaragua, both economic and military, saw a major increase in supplies, with over

23,000 tonnes being delivered, worth about $600 million, according to the Pentagon (*Latin America Weekly Report*, 9 April 1987, pp. 6–7). Equipment sent includes, again according to the Pentagon, over a dozen troop transport helicopters and unknown numbers of An30 reconnaissance aircraft and S14 ground-to-air missiles (*The Times*, 5 November 1986, p. 9 and 20 November 1986, p. 13). This development may have reflected a growing Soviet hope that US policy in Nicaragua could be defeated. In 1985 the Sandinista army had waged two successful campaigns against *contra* forces which were cut off from US Congressional military funds. President Reagan had to fight hard to get his 1986 $100 million aid package through Congress (it was defeated in March but passed in June), and by the time the assistance began to be disbursed in late autumn, the Iran/*contra* scandal was breaking in Washington. Whatever the precise Soviet calculations as to prospects for the Nicaraguan armed opposition, at a time when the US State Department was insisting that Afghanistan and 'regional conflicts' should be on the agenda at the October 1986 Reykjavik summit, it was worth Moscow's while to add weight to its negotiating position by boosting its support for the Sandinistas. Similar considerations (Mr Shultz and Mr Shevardnadze were meeting regularly throughout 1987 to discuss the conflicts in Cambodia, Angola and Central America) lay behind the sustained high level of military shipments during 1987 (21,700 tonnes, according to the Pentagon) and into 1988 (the *Miami Herald*, 26 March 1988, in *Information Services Latin America*, 36:3 (March 1988), p. 181).

The third point is that the USSR has confined its supplies to defensive weapons and, moreover, has allowed the United States to define what it will accept as 'defensive' equipment (just as it has done in Cuba since the Missile Crisis). Five members of the Nicaraguan air-force were in the Soviet Union in mid-1983 to be trained in the use of MIG-21 fighter aircraft. The US administration has, however, succeeded in preventing the supply of these '1950's vintage' aircraft by announcing that their acquisition by the FSLN would justify a US military response. In late 1984, Nicaragua managed to obtain between half a dozen Soviet Mi-24 'Hind' helicopter-gunships, and a further six 'Hinds' arrived in October 1986, according to the Pentagon (Edelman: 1985, p. 51 and *The Times*, 29 October 1986, p. 4). This still leaves the Nicaraguan forces ill-equipped to attack its neighbours: 'El Salvador had 15 combat helicopters in 1984, with nine more on order; Guatemala had 50 helicopters, although not all were operational; Honduras had 15, 10 of them on loan from the United States' (Edelman: 1985, p. 51). Although by late

1983 it was recognised amongst US policy-makers that the *contras* were unable to overthrow the Sandinistas, the main reason for this was political: they had failed to provoke the popular uprising which had been anticipated. Their military effectiveness depended almost entirely upon the level of aid that the US Congress would permit. The Sandinistas have been given just enough, but no more, to ensure the survival of their revolution.

The conclusion must be that, while the Soviet Union approved of the general direction of the Nicaraguan revolution, this in itself was not a sufficient reason to grant the Sandinistas a status which would entitle them to unlimited Soviet protection. This is despite the fact that the Nicaraguans, anxious to indicate to Moscow that they are potentially reliable allies, sought to make their allegiance clear by affiliating to all the major international Communist front organisations and by endorsing Soviet foreign policy on contentious issues such as Afghanistan and Kampuchea. However, the desire to preserve a substantive commitment to non-alignment (a condition for maintaining the political backing of Latin American and Western European nations) has meant that, unlike Grenada, the Sandinistas have not voted with the USSR in the annual UN call for the unconditional withdrawal of Soviet troops from Afghanistan, preferring to abstain, as they did on the motion condemning the Soviet shooting down of the Korean airliner in September 1983. In any case, the Soviet Union has made it clear that, while they are prepared to give political support, to keep the Sandinistas supplied with weapons, and even to grant Nicaragua observer status at Comecon in 1983, they are far from decided to make any public military commitment which might make them a hostage if the Americans decide to escalate the war in Nicaragua.

Economic policy

The Soviet Union's reluctance to be identified with Nicaragua on a political or military level was echoed by the slowness with which economic relations were developed with the Sandinista government. As in the case of military supplies, the increase in Soviet economic aid and trade has been directly related to the policies of the Reagan administration. Initially the Sandinistas themselves were quite happy to let the Soviet Union keep its distance. In the light of a fierce controversy in the United States over whether or not aid should be sent to Nicaragua, Castro was impressing upon the Nicaraguans the need for workable relations with the Americans, not only because of political realities but also for compelling economic reasons. Indeed, many Nicaraguan leaders themselves recognised the deficiencies of Cuba as a model for development. As Xavier Gorostiaga, one of the country's leading economists, put it, 'the politics of isolation' which Cuba had adopted as the price of withstanding US pressures 'offers the world one particular experience that should not be repeated . . . Cut off from its traditional markets and even from neighbouring countries in the region, Cuba has been forced to survive in a Cold War environment, in which socialist countries provided the bulk of the aid needed to survive' (the *Guardian*, 22 August 1983, p. 11).

Particularly in the early stages, Sandinista leaders, who were still relying on privately owned agriculture for the bulk of export revenues, were reluctant to take any action which might provide an unnecessary pretext for US hostility. The Nicaraguan revolution had attracted a lot of support within Latin America and from more progressive European governments, and the Nicaraguans were successful in their attempts to diversify away from the United States without tying themselves to the Eastern bloc.

Emergency aid donated by Moscow in the aftermath of the revolution was of negligible value and far overshadowed by contributions from Western sources. According to the *Latin America Weekly Report*, between July 1979 and November 1980 Comecon aid in loans and donations totalled around $50 million, of which $30 million was a loan from East Germany. (The Soviet contribution apparently consisted of donations of 1.5 million pencils, 1.5 million exercise books, 1,000 transistor radios, 30,000 pairs of boots and ten cars.) By comparison West Germany lent $30 million and countries such as Mexico and Libya each were negotiating commitments far larger than those of the entire Comecon (*LAWR*, WR-81-15, 10 April 1981, p. 1). No significant contacts were made between the Nicaraguan and Soviet governments until March 1980, when a delegation of Sandinista leaders travelled to Moscow,[3] following the suspension of US aid on 23 January 1980 and the cancellation of a $15 million credit offer on 2 March. They returned with a reciprocal most-favoured-nation trading agreement, a protocol on the establishment of trade representations, an agreement on planning cooperation and various other accords providing for Soviet assistance in fishing, water power resources, mining and geological surveys, along with a consular convention and an agreement on air

[3] The delegation included Junta member Moises Hassán, Minister of the Interior Tomás Borge, Minister of Economic Planning Henry Ruiz and Defence Minister Humberto Ortega.

communications. An agreement was signed to foster the development of ties between the CPSU and the FSLN, and the joint communiqué issued at the end of the visit emphasised Soviet–Nicaraguan agreement on a wide range of significant foreign-policy positions.

When the incoming Reagan administration adopted a manifestly tougher approach early in 1981, the Sandinistas started appealing for greater assistance from the Soviet Union. At the February 1981 CPSU Congress one member of the Nicaraguan delegation, Carlos Núñez Telles, speaking in tones reminiscent of Chilean Communists a decade previously, emphasised the need for help from the socialist countries 'even though they are thousands of kilometres away' (Steele: 1983, p. 20). The only tangible response to this appeal came in April 1981, when the US refusal to deliver a Public Law 480 wheat shipment to Nicaragua enabled the USSR to win an easy propaganda victory, and demonstrate its disdain for Washington's grain embargo, by donating 20,000 tonnes of grain and other supplies. Nevertheless, it appears that no official credits were offered until September 1981, when a visit to Moscow by Interior Minister Tomás Borge yielded the opening of a $50 million credit line for the purchase of Soviet machinery and equipment. The only publicly announced result of Miguel d'Escoto's December 1981 visit to Moscow was the signing of a programme for scientific and cultural exchanges.

Around mid-1982 the Sandinistas stepped up the urgency of their search for Soviet support. This can be traced directly to the destabilisation policies adopted by the Reagan administration. These activities, and their consequences within Nicaragua, vindicated the position of those members of the FSLN who argued for integration with the socialist bloc as the best defence against Washington. Daniel Ortega's May 1982 visit to Moscow followed the declaration of a state of emergency in Nicaragua and tougher economic measures indicating a move away from a mixed economy towards a more centralised model with emphasis on the public sector. Ortega (then 'Coordinator', elected President in November 1984) negotiated a $100 million Soviet credit for deliveries of industrial machinery and equipment and a further $50 million for a feasibility study of a hydro-electric power station. He also secured a promise of Soviet assistance in mining, agriculture, communications and the expansion of facilities for ship repair at the Pacific port of San Juan del Sur. (In May 1983 it was reported that this assistance would in fact take a slightly different form, more advantageous to Moscow than to Managua. The USSR was to build a 7,000 ton dry-dock and a 60 foot-long floating pier to adapt

Table 8. *Eastern bloc credits to Nicaragua 1979–1982*

	Granted	Disbursed ($m)
USSR	68.0	1.4
East Germany	82.0	36.2
Czechoslovakia	30.0	0
Bulgaria	18.5	3.6
Hungary	5.0	0
Total	203.5	41.2

Source: LAWR, WR-82-44, 12 November 1982, p. 1.

the port for tuna fishing. For the use of this facility the Soviet Union was to pay the Nicaraguan government an annual rent of $200,000.) In June 1982 the USSR sent $31 million in emergency aid to help repair damage caused by widespread flooding. A succession of visits by Nicaraguan leaders to Moscow in 1982–3, including one by Tomás Borge in September 1982, which was not publicised by Moscow although it was apparently at the invitation of Andropov, and by Daniel Ortega in March 1983, produced relatively little in the way of concrete economic assistance.[4] The results of negotiations following Daniel Ortega's visit were agreements on Soviet cooperation in the development of Nicaragua's mining industry and mineral prospecting, and Soviet assistance in the building of a hospital, two training centres, a power station and an experimental cotton farm (*SWB* SU/7344/A1/14, 27 May 1983).

Figures for March 1982 reveal that the Nicaraguans were in no particular hurry to avail themselves of Eastern bloc credit facilities (see table 8). Total Eastern bloc credits to Nicaragua from 1979 to 1983 add up to $466.7 million, of which the Soviet share was well under half. (By comparison, US economic aid to El Salvador nearly doubled from $105 million to $186 million between fiscal years 1981 and 1982.) This accounts for one-fifth of Nicaragua's total borrowing from 1979 to 1983, a further 25.5 per cent of which came from multilateral organisations, 32.2 per cent from Latin America and 11.2 per cent from

[4] The other visits were as follows: In November 1982 Daniel Ortega attended Brezhnev's funeral and the following month Jaime Wheelock went to celebrations to mark the 65th Anniversary of the USSR. In February 1983 Henry Ruiz, Minister of Planning, held talks with Soviet economic planners. The following July Bayardo Arce, head of the Sandinista political commission, travelled to Moscow to discuss implementation of the CPSU-FSLN agreement, and in July Jaime Wheelock went to negotiate an agricultural agreement.

Western Europe, according to the Nicaraguan Central Bank (Berrios: 1984, p. 10).

In 1984 and 1985 the US government succeeded in pressurising multilateral organisations to the extent that aid from these sources, which in 1979 represented 78 per cent of Nicaragua's total borrowing, was stopped altogether. Aid from Western countries also decreased from 51 per cent of total borrowing in 1983 to 40 per cent in 1984, thus obliging the FSLN to turn to the Eastern bloc. The decline in Western aid, the percentage of which dropped by over half again in 1985, can be attributed to disillusionment with the Sandinistas amongst sections of the Socialist International in Europe, which prompted the French government and the EEC to allow existing programmes to lapse. West Germany also cut off bilateral aid in 1985. Eastern bloc sources accounted for over 80 per cent of Nicaraguan borrowing in 1985 and 84 per cent in 1986 (John Weeks, seminar on War and the economy in Nicaragua, St Antony's College, Oxford, 20 May 1986 and *The Times*, 23 July 1986, p. 13).

Agreements announced in 1984–5 include one signed in January 1984 for the construction of a $20 million yarn mill to enable Nicaragua to substitute imported yarn, a May 1985 agreement to set up a joint commission on economic, trade, scientific and technical cooperation, the supply in late 1985 of a ground-based satellite communications station to enable Nicaragua to join the Intersputnik system, an April 1986 agreement on agricultural cooperation and a series of other projects (mostly long-term) to develop Nicaraguan fishing, mining and energy resources. Plans were also made in late 1985 for a large irrigation project, fourteen textile factories to make Nicaragua self-sufficient in clothing and a dairy project (the latter involving the Soviet Union in cooperation with Czechoslovakia and Cuba) (*LAWR*, 8 November 1985, pp. 10–11).

Figures for sources of Nicaragua's bilateral economic aid from 1979 to April 1985 were as in table 9. In 1985 alone Soviet aid was estimated at $247 million (over a quarter of Nicaraguan import needs), and towards the end of 1986 an agreement was signed for 1987 also worth about $250 million. US economic aid to El Salvador in 1987 was double that, at $502 million.

In January 1988 the Soviet Union and Nicaragua agreed an economic plan involving $294 million worth of Soviet aid per annum through to 1990. Given that this figure includes supplies of 300,000 tonnes of crude oil each year (worth about $100 million), it represents a reduction in previous levels of economic support (*The Miami Herald*, 17

Table 9. *Sources of aid to Nicaragua 1979–1985 (millions of dollars)*

Mexico	500
USSR	300–400*
East Germany	200
Bulgaria	200*
Libya	100–200*
Cuba	150*
Spain	60
Brazil	50
France	45

* Estimate
Source: diplomatic missions and Nicaraguan press, cited in *The Financial Times*, 10 April 1985, p. 5.

January 1988, in *Information Services Latin America*, 36:1 (January 1988), p. 148).

The USSR's reluctance to make an economic commitment can be explained by the fact that, as was the case with Chile in 1970, there is very little compatibility between the Nicaraguan and the Soviet economies. Before the revolution Soviet–Nicaraguan trade was at a negligible level. In the peak year 1976 Comecon received under 1 per cent of Nicaraguan exports (all to Poland) and supplied about one quarter per cent of Nicaragua's imports (again, mostly from Poland). According to Soviet figures, the volume of Nicaraguan–Soviet commercial exchange rose between 1979 and 1987 as shown in table 10. Even so, Soviet exports in 1983 accounted for about one twentieth of Nicaraguan imports. Other Comecon countries, particularly Cuba and East Germany, were more significant suppliers and, in March 1983, Bulgaria signed a $165 million trade and economic assistance agreement with Nicaragua. However, Nicaraguan imports from Comecon as given below (table 11) can be compared with 1983 figures of $157 million from the United States, $124 million from the Central American Common Market and $189 million from other Latin American countries. Moscow's exports to Nicaragua have increased quite dramatically since 1983, partly reflecting the fact that in 1985 the Soviet Union assumed the burden of providing virtually all of Nicaragua's oil (see below) and partly the fact that much of the so-called economic 'aid' is in fact credit for the purchase of Soviet machinery and equipment.

The USSR has, however, proved highly reluctant to import Nicaraguan goods at subsidised prices. Even in good years Nicaragua has

Table 10. *Soviet trade with Nicaragua 1980–1987* (millions of rubles)

	1980	1981	1982	1983	1984	1985	1986	1987
Exports								
Machinery, equipment and transport	0	0	0	37.117	57.555	61.530	157.950	n/a
Textile industry equipment	0	0	0	0	0	4.000	1.268	
Road-building equipment	0	0	3.778	5.133	2.854	1.067	3.605	
Light motor vehicles	0	0.238	0.775	1.879	2.700	2.690	3.11	
Spare parts for light motor vehicles	0	0	0	0	0	2.163	2.960	
Printing equipment	0.098	0.124	0.082	0.286	0.449	0.350	0.427	
Tractors	0	0	4.35	1.782	6.697	2.605	7.442	
Heavy goods vehicles	0	0	9.424	4.026	9.885	15.614	16.683	
Aerial communication equipment	0	0	12.665	7.917	19.346	10.971	95.778	
Metalwork machinery	0	0	0.651	0.857	0.691	0.188	0	
Metal extraction equipment	0	0	0	0.722	0.119	0.095	0	
Transport equipment	0	0	0.014	2.318	0.805	1.794	1.412	
Tractor spare parts and equipment	0	0	0.690	0.514	0.410	1.887	1.671	
Lorry spare parts and equipment	0	0	0.900	1.306	1.921	4.226	9.432	
Specialised motor vehicles	0	0	0	1.853	4.826	1.822	3.141	
Agricultural machinery	0	0	0.041	0.447	0.386	1.018	0.360	
Oil and oil products	0	0	0	0.930	49.148	105.893	68.510	
Rolled metals	0	0	0	1.037	2.818	8.317	10.686	
Chemical products	0	0	0	0	0	2.758	4.251	
Polythene	0	0	0	0	0	1.415	0.891	
Medicaments	0	0	0	0	0	0.172	0.064	
Cotton cloth	0	0	0	0	0	3.373	4.093	
Fertilizer	0	4.281	0	0	3.109	8.211	6.338	
Paper	0	0	0	0.774	2.294	0	1.713	
Tinned fish	0	0	0	0	0	0.440	1.195	
Lard	0	0	0	0	3.369	3.304	2.346	
Rice	0	0	0	0	5.822	0.191	0	
Butter	0	0	0	0	5.266	5.094	4.109	
Others	0	0	0	0	1.911	0	0	
Total	0.1	4.7	36.6*	42.4	138.0	212.9	277.1	166.1

Table 10 (*cont.*)

	1980	1981	1982	1983	1984	1985	1986	1987
Imports								
Natural coffee	2.560	5.647	4.805	3.747	0	0	0	n.a.
Raw sugar	2.976	0	0.958	2.395	0	0	7.626	
Cotton	0	0	0	3.011	0	0	0	
Philately	0	0	0	0	0.292	0.014	0	
Fuel, minerals and metals	0	0	0	0	0.209	0.219	0.105	
Total	5.5	5.7	5.9	9.5	0.5	0.2	7.7	13.2

* This is the total given, although these figures add up to 33.37 million rubles. Indeed, most of these totals are inaccurate but are as given.
Source: Vneshniaia torgovlia SSSR, 1980–6; 1987 figures from *Foreign Trade* (Moscow), January 1988.

Table 11. *Nicaragua's imports from Comecon ($m)*

1979	1980	1981	1982	1983
0	2	33	89	134

Source: Nicaraguan government sources, cited in Berrios: 1984, p. 3.

little to offer the Soviet Union, for its exports consist primarily of sugar, coffee and cotton, which are already supplied by Cuba or other, more powerful, developing nations with which Moscow is anxious to develop trading relations. For example, from 1981 to 1984 the Soviet Union imported nearly 400 million rubles' worth of sugar from Brazil. Soviet purchases of Nicaraguan goods remained static for the first three years after the revolution, rose to only 9.5 million rubles in 1983, and in the following two years declined to an almost negligible level, despite the fact that on 1 May 1985 the Reagan administration announced a total embargo on all trade with Nicaragua, affecting some $45 million worth of Nicaraguan exports and $158 million worth of imports (1984 figures). In January 1986 it was announced that the Soviet Union and Cuba would buy 30 per cent of the year's Nicaraguan sugar exports at the preferential price of 17 cents per pound (three times the prevailing market price) (*The Financial Times*, 8 January 1986, p. 24). Even so, the deal is worth only $10 million, which accounts for approximately 2.5 per cent of Nicaragua's export revenue. A similar deal was signed at the end of 1986 involving the purchase of coffee, but as the figures for 1987 imports show, the quantities were not significant. Neither has the shortfall been made up by other Comecon countries so far: Nicaraguan sales to the group (including Cuba) accounted for 3 per cent of total exports in 1980, 6 per cent in 1981, 5 per cent in 1982, 13 per cent in 1983 and 6 per cent in 1984 (Edelman: 1985, p. 49). Most of Nicaragua's cotton still goes to Japan, and its coffee to Western Europe. Sugar exports were diverted to Algeria, Libya and Iran following 1983 cuts in the US quota (*The Financial Times*, 2 May 1984, p. 5).

Like Cuba, Nicaragua is almost totally dependent on imported oil. Under the San José agreement of 1980 it received its supplies, until 1984, at below market prices from Mexico and Venezuela, as do a total of ten Caribbean nations of varying political tendencies. Venezuela halted the flow in August 1982, claiming that it was because of Nicaragua's inability to meet payment deadlines; however, since no other Central American country was paying on time, this decision was widely perceived as a political one. Mexico picked up the slack until late 1983, when Nicaragua's payment problems once more became an issue. In the light of Mexico's own economic crisis, it was reported in Mexico that the de la Madrid government was under IMF pressure not to sell oil to Nicaragua (Edelman: 1985, p. 47). In autumn 1983 counter-revolutionary forces sabotaged the only three oil-unloading ports in Nicaragua. In September, rebels destroyed 400,000 gallons of fuel at the Atlantic port of Benjamín Zeledón and wrecked facilities at Puerto Sandino. The following month oil storage tanks at the main port of Corinto, on the Pacific, were machine-gunned from speed boats, resulting in the loss of more than 3.2 million gallons of petrol and other liquid fuels. As a result of these attacks, Exxon temporarily stopped leasing the tankers which had been used to deliver the Mexican oil, and because of this disruption the first Soviet tanker to supply Nicaragua arrived at Corinto in January 1984 (*Petroleum Economist*, LI:5 (May 1984), p. 190). In the same month, counter-revolutionaries announced that they had mined Puerto Sandino and Corinto with, it was subsequently revealed, the active involvement of the CIA. By the end of 1984 the Soviet Union was providing about half of Nicaragua's oil requirements, the remainder of which had been resumed by Mexico after Nicaragua had formally recognised its debt and promised to repay it. On 16 April 1985, however, de la Madrid caused near-panic in Managua by informing visiting FSLN minister Henry Ruiz that in future Nicaragua would have to pay 80 per cent cash for oil deliveries (an impossibility for a country which has no hard currency reserves) (the *Guardian*, 3 September 1985, p. 19). This was what prompted Daniel Ortega's ill-timed visit to Moscow in early May, which worsened the mood in Washington to the extent that a Congress which had vetoed a $14 million aid package for the *contras* subsequently approved an administration request for $27 million, and President Reagan judged it timely to announce the embargo on trade to Nicaragua. Ironically, in protest against this, the Mexican government decided to resume oil supplies to Managua and, on 29 May, the two countries signed a trade agreement worth $26 million for 1985. $7 million worth covered a countertrade deal by which Nicaragua would pay for oil with exports of frozen meat and shellfish, but the remainder of the crude supplied would be added on to Managua's existing $500 million oil debt with Mexico (*The Financial Times*, 31 May 1985, p. 6). However, 80–90 per cent of Nicaragua's 1985 oil imports and all of its 1986 fuel supplies were met by the Eastern bloc.

In summary, although there has been a substantial increase in Soviet development aid to Nicaragua since mid-1984, the USSR has not shown itself willing to provide either significant subsidised support for Nicaraguan exports or the hard currency that the Nicaraguan economy, with a balance of payments deficit of upwards of $400 million each year since 1979, so desperately needs. In addition to the lack of economic complementarity between the Soviet Union and Nicaragua, it would have been easy for Soviet leaders to foresee that the Nicaraguan economy would rapidly reach a point where its major short-term need would be for the hard-currency loans which the Kremlin is so reluctant to provide. The Sandinistas came to power after a lengthy period of civil war which proved highly destructive to both the manufacturing and agricultural sectors. In order to implement their reforms and sustain the revolutionary momentum, Managua was forced to import massive quantities of basic goods in 1980–1. The results of these policies began to emerge in 1982 in the inevitable form of a severe balance of payments crisis, a critical shortage of foreign exchange and the need to curb imports to borrow heavily on the international markets. The economic situation was exacerbated around mid-1982, since when attacks by the US-inspired counter-revolutionary forces have obliged the government to divert a considerable percentage – an estimated 40–50 per cent in 1986 and 1987 – of its resources to defence spending. By early 1983, Nicaragua had joined most Latin American countries in failing to service its external debt, which reached the level of $3 billion in September 1983 (*Latin America Regional Report: Central America and the Caribbean*, RM-83-08, 23 September 1983, p. 6). Ortega was reported to be seeking $200 million cash from Moscow during his May 1985 visit (*The Times*, 30 April 1985,

p. 6); instead he obtained an equivalent sum in credits, $130 million of which were to cover oil imports.

Indeed, Ortega said, following his 1985 visit to Moscow, that although the Soviet bloc states had pledged economic help, 'We are not expecting abundance and a solution to all our problems from this' (*The Times*, 11 May 1985, p. 5). At the June 1985 Comecon summit in Warsaw Nicaragua was lobbying for more aid. Henry Ruiz (former Minister of Planning, now Minister for Foreign Cooperation and a known advocate of Soviet-style development) made it clear that the Sandinista government needed much more assistance from the Soviet bloc (*The Times*, 28 June 1985, p. 5).

This echoes the experience of other developing nations who have attended Comecon as observers. The record shows that no status in Comecon short of full membership (which entitles the incoming nation to benefit from specific Comecon measures designed to raise the levels of economic development of its less-developed member states) necessarily leads to a substantial increase in involvement with the Eastern bloc economies. Ethiopia and the People's Democratic Republic of Yemen, both countries with which the Soviet Union has low economic complementarity, have had observer status at Comecon for some years without seeing their trade volumes with the Soviet Union reach significant levels. Soviet–Ethiopian trade turnover in 1987 was R142 million; Soviet–PDRY trade in the same year totalled R85.6 million.

Perhaps the most pertinent example is the case of Mozambique. In 1981 the Frelimo government tried to gain full Comecon membership; it failed to do so, apparently because Soviet leaders were apprehensive both about the potential costs to other members and the likelihood that it would set an unwelcome precedent (Smith, Alan: 1982, p. 114), and received so little assistance from the socialist bloc that it was obliged, in March 1984, to sign an agreement with South Africa. Within South America, Guyana has attended Comecon sessions as an observer for several years but, in 1978, had its application for 'formal association' rejected (Leiken: 1982, p. 70).

In the case of Nicaragua, the Sandinistas, for their part, are still anxious to maintain their economic links with the Western capitalist economies. In mid-June 1985 the Nicaraguan government signed rescheduling agreements with 130 private banks in New York, in an attempt to pave the way for further loans. Despite drastic hard currency shortages, Managua has since maintained debt service payments as an indication of its commitment to remaining within the international economy. The Sandinistas have had some success in circumventing the US embargo (obtaining spare parts from US subsidiaries in Canada and Mexico), helped by the decision of the twenty-four countries of the Latin American Economic System (SELA) to support their attempts. Even in the peak year of Soviet bloc assistance, 1986, around 60 per cent of Nicaragua's trade was with non-socialist nations. Soviet–Nicaraguan trade turnover was substantially lower in 1987 than in the previous year (see table 10). Moreover in August 1987 the Soviet Union signed a trade agreement to buy coffee and sugar from Honduras and officials announced that, if fully implemented, the accord could raise turnover to $20 million per annum.

Events in 1987 left the Sandinista leaders in no doubt as to the dangers inherent in reliance upon the Soviet Union. In late May the Nicaraguan government publicised its growing concern about sources of oil shipments for the year. External Cooperation Minister Henry Ruiz announced that of the 765,000 tonnes of oil Nicaragua would need in 1987, the Soviet Union was expected to supply only 300,000 tonnes, the last shipment of which arrived at the end of that month. Other Comecon countries were due to send a further 320,000 tonnes, which still left the country (and, most importantly, the armed forces, whose need for fuel to fight the *contras* largely accounted for the increase in oil imports from 600,000 tonnes in 1985) some way short of its estimated requirements. In early June vice-president Sergio Ramírez set off on a tour of the Eastern bloc, but to no avail, for less than two weeks after the signing of the Esquipulas Agreement on 7 August, he was obliged to state that 'a country that does not have its oil resources assured for the rest of the year cannot have the security needed to engage in a process of this magnitude' (the *Guardian*, 20 August 1987, p. 5). Nicaragua's attempts to obtain oil from Mexico or Venezuela, Iraq, Iran, Yugoslavia, Greece and Algeria had all proved fruitless, and Ramírez announced that the Sandinistas would run out of oil before the end of the year unless an immediate donation of $1.6 million worth of crude were forthcoming. A week later Soviet Foreign Ministry spokesman Gerradi Gerasimov responded that, 'if other countries cut back, it does not automatically mean the USSR should increase its supplies', but stated that Moscow was prepared to negotiate on the issue. An agreement to send a further 100,000 tonnes was announced in early September, thus averting a crisis, although a shortfall of some 55,000 tonnes remained. The Soviet Union could not have made plainer its reluctance to remain the sole supplier of such a crucial commodity.

Several factors lie behind Gorbachev's decision to make public the USSR's less than total commitment to the Sandinistas. The policy was probably intended as a signal to Washington that Moscow would be prepared to negotiate a solution to the conflict in Nicaragua. It may also have been a means of applying pressure on the Sandinistas to be flexible in the negotiations which resulted in the signing of the Guatemala Accord and to be prompt and thorough in their compliance subsequently. In addition, it expressed the Soviet leaders' irritation with Sandinista economic mismanagement and alleged wastefulness of Soviet aid, an accusation which Minister of External Cooperation Henry Ruiz has accepted as 'legitimate'. Even though disrupted supplies in 1987 obliged the Sandinistas to increase petrol prices several times over and to tighten rationing, petrol is still cheap in Nicaragua and therefore not always used economically. Retrenchment was also a way of reminding the Nicaraguans that they should not fall into the trap of making policy on the assumption that Moscow will always bail them out.

Whatever the outcome of Managua's relationship with Moscow, all the indications are that any Soviet commitment has been made cautiously, reluctantly, and largely in response to US policies towards revolutionary Nicaragua, which opened a window of opportunity for the USSR to counter US pressure on Afghanistan. It appears that Moscow has studied the 'lessons of Cuba' rather more closely than Washington.

8   Conclusion

The preceding chapters have attempted to redress the balance in the analysis of Soviet–Latin American relations by considering them not in isolation, but with reference to both parties' relations with other powers, primarily of course the United States of America. This context is essential for an understanding of the Soviet role in Latin America, given that the area is one of low priority for the USSR and its interest in establishing a presence there is motivated primarily by the dynamics of superpower rivalry. Because the region is highly sensitive for the United States, the Soviet Union knows that its Latin American policy has to be considered in terms of whether its desire is to appease, challenge or provoke Washington. This is the most imposing constraint on any attempt by Moscow to expand its influence in the sub-continent.

Additional political factors have often been adduced to explain the low level of the Soviet presence in Latin America, most notably the concept of 'geographical fatalism', the traditional anti-Communism of Latin American elites and the instability of Latin American politics. While these considerations can largely explain the almost minimal Soviet involvement in the region prior to the Cuban revolution, they have become far less significant over the past quarter century, owing to the opening up of Soviet foreign relations after the death of Stalin, the consolidation of the Castro regime and the tendency of most Latin American countries from the early 1970s onwards to develop broad multi-lateral relations and more consistent foreign policies.

Over the past twenty-five years the Soviet Union has moved from ostracism to acceptance in Latin America. It by no means follows, however, that Moscow enjoys significant political influence in the region. The relationship with Cuba is exceptional and in itself suggests the need for a reassessment of established preconceptions about the degree of leverage which a greater power can realistically expect to exert on a lesser power. Moscow shows no signs of entering into the

217

same kind of total commitment to Nicaragua that Castro managed to secure in the early 1960s. The remaining Latin American countries maintain relations with the Soviet Union primarily to counteract US influence and to assert their independence as sovereign states. Such ties serve a dual role as an escape valve from US pressure and a probe of Washington's tolerance. Governments of varying orientations (all imbued with a strong sense of nationalism) have preferred to keep political ties with the USSR to a minimum and confine their relations to the commercial sphere. This is particularly true of two major regional powers with which the Soviet Union would be especially keen to enjoy political influence: Argentina and Brazil. Moscow's closest political ties in Latin America (with the exceptions of Cuba and Nicaragua) are with Mexico, which has, by virtue of its geographical position, particular incentives to assert its independence of the United States. Much has been written on the increasing Soviet 'penetration' of Central America: however, the indications are that Moscow is far more interested, especially in the long term, in cultivating its political ties with the major powers of the region – Mexico, Venezuela, Brazil and Argentina – particularly in the latter two cases, in which economic considerations are also significant factors. In 1982 A. Glinkin and P. Yakovlev wrote that 'The US ruling elite calculates that however important in strategic or political relations the individual small countries of the region are the outcome of the opposition between the forces of progress and reaction on the soil of Latin America is being decided in key countries – Brazil, Mexico, Argentina' (Glinkin and Yakovlev: 1982, p. 79). Given that the Soviet Union's attitude towards Latin America is primarily informed by its global competition with the United States, Moscow officials are likely to shape their policy around US perceptions of the key issues in the region.

An initiative directed at the major Latin American powers is consonant with a revision of Soviet policy towards the Third World which was indicated in the new CPSU Programme adopted at the 27th Party Congress in February 1986, in which it was stated that 'The practice of the USSR's relations with newly liberated countries has shown that real grounds for cooperation . . . exist with young states that are travelling a capitalist road' (*Pravda*, 7 March 1986, in *SWB*, SU/8206/C/41, 14 March 1986).

There is little to suggest that such an initiative in Latin America will be any more successful than has been the case in the past. As indicated above, the political climate is not propitious, and the previous chapters have presented evidence for the existence of fundamental economic constraints which operate to ensure that the Soviet presence in Latin America, while markedly expanded since 1959, is still limited and likely to remain so. These have been identified as (i) the daunting physical barriers to effective communications, which would in any case tend to discourage Soviet links with the sub-continent, and (ii) the lack of economic complementarity between the two regions. Prospects for the development of a long-term, mutually beneficial trading relationship between the Soviet Union and Latin America are not encouraging. Soviet analysts themselves believe that '. . . the USSR and Latin American countries have not yet established comprehensive and stable trade relations . . . The existing trade links are still at the initial stage, and it will take time before mutually beneficial patterns of trade are established, consumers find out more about new products, and wider contacts are set up between business communities' (Zinoviev: 1981, p. 100).

Beyond Argentina and Brazil, it is hard to find a Latin American country where there is a real possibility for the development of a stable trading relationship. Apparent exceptions are found, on closer examination of the data, to conform to the general rule. For example, Colombia has proved relatively receptive to the import of Soviet equipment, having bought trolley-buses and Soviet cars in the past. Contracts have also been signed on the supply of Soviet hydraulic power engineering equipment for the Urrá-1 and Urrá-2 hydro-electric power stations, but these developments have been postponed until after 1990. The limitations of the relationship are graphically demonstrated by the fact that the protocol for 1984–90 set a target for the annual export of only 17–20 million rubles' worth of Soviet equipment. Trade with Peru increased steadily in the early 1980s, turnover rising from 20.9 million rubles in 1983 to 67.6 million rubles in 1984 and 119.8 million rubles in 1985. It fell back again in 1986 to 63.7 million rubles, rising the following year to 87.3 million rubles. However, the bulk of these exchanges consisted of Soviet imports from Peru which, under an agreement signed in November 1983, were being transferred to the USSR in part-repayment of debts Peru incurred with its 1970s purchases of Soviet aircraft and weaponry. The Soviet Union selects from an agreed list of Peruvian exports and has accepted a ceiling of 25 per cent on its purchases of commodities (such as metals, fishmeal and coffee) which Peru can more readily sell for hard currency. Most of its other imports are textiles, currently subject to harsh restrictions in the US market. Early in 1987 Peru's only significant computer manufacturer, Novotec, signed a contract worth $450-500 million to supply

100,000 IBM-compatible personal computers. At first payments were to be in hard currency to help cover initial manufacturing costs, but subsequent deliveries were to be part of counter-trade against the debt. A further rescheduling arrangement was made in January 1988 to cover the next three years. It is worth $600 million, a figure which includes $156 million in debt service, and the Soviet Union has agreed to reduce the interest rate on Peru's $1 billion debt to 3.5 per cent from 7 per cent (*The Financial Times*, 22 January 1988, p. 4). It is hardly surprising that Moscow should prefer deals such as this to a renewed paper debt which the Peruvians are unlikely to be able to make good in the short or even the medium term. Moreover, there is a small amount of political capital to be made out of accepting textiles which US protectionism has barred and by adapting a sympathetic and constructive approach to debt renegotiation. However, Soviet officials rejected an initial proposal by Peruvian textile manufacturers for a package worth $96 million a year, once again indicating that their approach to trading with Latin America is purely commercial (the *Washington Post*, 26 August 1984, p. H2).

Bolivia would appear to be a more promising market, given the scope for exchanging tin (which the Soviet Union lacks) for mining equipment (which is of competitive quality). In April 1978 the state company Comibol signed a contract for the delivery of various types of equipment for the processing of low-content tin ores and in July 1982 a fuming factory at La Palca near Potosí was put into operation. This has never functioned satisfactorily, however, and over the past few years Soviet–Bolivian trade has dwindled away to a very low level.

One possible exception to the overall pessimism may be Uruguay, which has increased its imports of Soviet equipment over the past couple of years to the point where trade is nearly balanced. The first session of a Soviet–Uruguayan Mixed Commission was held in September 1984 and President Sanguinetti, who visited Moscow in March 1988, has expressed interest in expanding economic links with Moscow. As of 1987, however, we are talking about a trade turnover of only 21.8 million rubles (a significant drop from the 1985 figure of 65.9 million rubles).

Thus there is not a single instance of lasting and mutually satisfactory economic convergence between the Soviet Union and a Latin American country (even Cuba would be a dubious exception). Structural incompatibility means that Moscow finds it extremely difficult to activate any means of payment for its agricultural purchases in Latin America other than the hard currency which it is so anxious to conserve for imports from the industrialised West. The majority of Latin American nations (themselves desperately short of foreign exchange and historically integrated economically with the developed capitalist world) clearly prefer to trade with the West, or with other developing countries. While they may be prepared to cultivate limited commercial links with the Soviet Union either because certain one-off deals are economically advantageous or because such trade acts as a counterweight to economic relations with the United States, they have not so far proved willing to undertake the considerable degree of economic adjustment which would, in most cases, be necessary to allow for the absorption of a significant level of Soviet exports.

The integration of Cuba into Comecon is often cited as 'proof' that any lack of economic complementarity will not be a significant factor in Soviet decision-making if the prospective political gains are sufficiently enticing. However, this book has shown that there was in fact a material basis (albeit restricted) for the Soviet–Cuban commitment (oil for sugar) which helped to maintain the momentum of relations between the two countries at a time when the political situation was far from clear. In any case, the Soviet–Cuban relationship (essentially a lucky accident as far as the USSR was concerned) came about through a unique combination of circumstances which had more to do with the manoeuvrings of Eisenhower and Castro than with initiatives from Moscow. In the light of their experience in Cuba, Soviet leaders have been far more cautious in their response to more recent 'revolutionary' governments in Latin America, and have as yet proved reluctant to pay the high opportunity costs of ensuring the economic survival of such regimes. In 1987 Gorbachev said explicitly that 'we are not in favour of ultra-radical approaches to development problems such as the rupture of the historically established economic links between the United States and Latin America' (*International Herald Tribune*, 26 May 1987, p. 1). In a Third World area of low priority, the importance of economic factors in determining Soviet policy may be more important than has hitherto been recognised.

Appendix

Soviet trade with Latin America and the Caribbean[1] 1950–87 (millions of rubles)

	1950	1960	1961	1962	1963	1964	1965
Argentina:							
Imports	0.1	19.5	17.9	8.8	16.6	17.9	68.4
Exports	0	12.6	9.5	7.2	0.8	4.0	18.3
Brazil:							
Imports	1.4	8.4	21.6	32.2	39.1	33.4	29.5
Exports	0	14.2	16.5	27.1	26.5	21.6	24.9
Colombia:							
Imports	0	0	0	0	0	0	0.4
Exports	0	0	0	0	0	0	0.3
Jamaica:							
Imports	0	0	0	0	0.1	2.6	0
Exports	0	0	0	0	0	0	0
Mexico:							
Imports	0	3.0	0.3	6.6	7.4	1.9	0.3
Exports	0	0.7	0.1	0.1	0.1	0.3	0.7
Peru:							
Imports	0	0	2.2	5.2	0.2	0	0
Exports	0	0	0	0	0	0	0
Uruguay:							
Imports	0	1.2	3.7	13.8	4.7	0.9	2.7
Exports	0	1.2	0.5	0.2	0.2	0.2	0.4
Latin America and the Caribbean:							
Imports	1.5	32.1	45.7	66.6	68.1	56.7	101.3
Exports	0	28.7	26.6	34.6	27.6	26.1	44.6

	1966	1967	1968	1969	1970	1971	1972
Argentina:							
Imports	96.6	20.8	25.8	23.0	28.2	30.4	22.9
Exports	6.7	4.3	2.9	6.1	1.7	1.9	1.8
Bolivia:							
Imports	0	0	0	0	3.1	9.0	2.5
Exports	0	0	0	0	0	0	0.8
Brazil:							
Imports	27.6	31.2	25.1	43.9	20.8	41.7	65.8
Exports	24.9	10.8	12.4	10.9	2.4	2.0	7.1
Colombia:							
Imports	2.1	0.7	3.1	3.8	9.4	4.3	1.2
Exports	1.0	1.4	1.9	2.3	1.5	1.1	2.7
Costa Rica:							
Imports	0	0	0	4.7	6.2	2.2	2.8
Exports	0	0	0	0	0	0	0
Dominican Republic:							
Imports	0	0	0	0	0	0	2.8
Exports	0	0	0	0	0	0	0
Ecuador:							
Imports	0	0	0	12.5	0.7	3.3	2.3
Exports	0	0	0	0.2	0.1	0	0.1
El Salvador:							
Imports	0	0	0	0	0	0	2.8
Exports	0	0	0	0	0	0	0
Jamaica:							
Imports	0	0	0	0	0.7	2.3	1.0
Exports	0	0	0	0	0	0	0
Mexico:							
Imports	9.3	8.3	7.6	5.0	0.3	9.2	7.8
Exports	0.6	0.7	2.4	0.8	0.7	0.3	0.6
Peru:							
Imports	0	0	0	0	0.2	0.2	1.8
Exports	0	0	0	1.3	0.1	0	0.2
Trinidad:							
Imports	0	0	0	0	0	0	8.4
Exports	0	0	0	0	0	0	0
Uruguay:							
Imports	8.3	3.3	1.4	0.9	1.0	1.2	2.2
Exports	0.5	0.4	0.6	0.8	0.8	0.9	1.2
Venezuela:							
Imports	0	0	0	0	0	0	4.1
Exports	0	0	0	0	0	0	0.1
Latin America and the Caribbean:							
Imports	143.8	65.4	74.2	93.9	70.9	104.7	135.7
Exports	33.8	17.7	20.3	22.6	7.8	13.2	26.5

	1973	1974	1975	1976	1977	1978	1979
Argentina:							
Imports	72.3	131.5	293.7	222.2	192.9	308.8	288.7
Exports	4.5	6.0	10.7	8.5	13.4	22.4	24.8
Bolivia:							
Imports	12.2	11.4	9.6	12.3	27.7	34.3	32.4
Exports	4.0	4.1	3.0	4.2	3.6	5.3	5.2
Brazil:							
Imports	116.5	112.0	302.8	369.4	209.6	130.2	160.0
Exports	9.3	9.0	93.3	76.1	104.4	34.9	19.9
Colombia:							
Imports	9.3	4.3	7.1	3.3	7.4	0.1	3.0
Exports	0.8	1.0	1.9	1.7	1.8	5.5	8.2
Costa Rica:							
Imports	5.1	1.6	0	2.2	3.6	5.6	0
Exports	0.2	0.6	0.5	0.6	0.2	0.1	0.3
Dominican Republic:							
Imports	15.6	0	0	0	0	0	0
Exports	0	0	0	0	0	0	0
Ecuador:							
Imports	0.7	4.4	12.9	7.4	9.8	3.3	0
Exports	0.2	0.5	0.6	0.4	0.5	0.6	0
El Salvador:							
Imports	3.7	0	0	0	0	0	0
Exports	0	0	0.1	0	1.1	0	0
Guatemala:							
Imports	4.3	0	0	0	0	0	0
Exports	0	0	0	0	0	0	0
Guyana:							
Imports	6.9	4.5	24.5	0	1.6	3.5	0
Exports	0	0.2	0	0	0	0.6	0
Jamaica:							
Imports	3.9	9.5	11.2	0	0	0	0
Exports	0	0	0	0	0	0	0
Mexico:							
Imports	0.1	1.3	1.7	11.1	1.7	11.0	4.1
Exports	0.5	1.1	4.4	6.0	1.2	2.4	0.7
Panama:							
Imports	0	0	0	0	0	0	0
Exports	0	0	2.6	3.8	5.7	5.2	10.3
Peru:							
Imports	15.4	4.7	90.2	18.1	20.4	15.7	9.9
Exports	4.3	4.6	28.3	13.9	26.4	16.8	2.8
Surinam:							
Imports	0	0	0	0	0	15.7	0
Exports	0	0	0	0	0	0	0
Trinidad:							
Imports	0	0	0	0	1.8	0	0
Exports	0	0	0	0	0	0	0
Uruguay:							
Imports	5.3	24.7	14.0	4.1	8.6	12.4	11.4
Exports	0.8	0.8	1.0	1.3	1.2	0.9	1.6
Venezuela:							
Imports	0.6	0	0	0	0	0	0
Exports	0.6	0.2	0.2	0.3	2.7	0.7	0
Latin America and the Caribbean:							
Imports	284.4	309.9	767.7	653.3	485.1	540.6	509.8
Exports	41.2	28.1	146.2	116.8	162.1	98.4	73.5

	1980	1981	1982	1983	1984	1985	1986	1987
Argentina:								
Imports	1162.1	2372.3	1265.4	1299.6	1104.3	1229.9	171.9	374.2
Exports	30.4	30.6	27.5	25.9	25.6	62.4	50.7	30.6
Bolivia:								
Imports	20.0	11.7	19.1	13.1	2.6	0.7	0	0
Exports	5.5	9.0	2.8	0.7	1.0	0.2	0	0
Brazil:								
Imports	252.9	533.9	415.5	590.6	372.5	380.0	200.0	189.6
Exports	22.1	16.3	179.9	106.8	95.3	70.3	24.6	42.8
Colombia:								
Imports	12.0	12.1	13.4	13.3	14.5	21.2	0	2.1
Exports	9.1	3.3	6.8	3.3	3.7	5.2	4.9	3.2
Costa Rica:								
Imports	8.4	0	0	0	0	0	0	0
Exports	0	0	0	0	0	0	0	0
Ecuador:								
Imports	0	3.4	6.1	0	0	0	0	0
Exports	0	2.7	1.7	0	0	0	0	0
Mexico:								
Imports	1.9	18.7	21.0	8.7	14.4	16.1	7.2	21.0
Exports	11.9	4.0	7.8	2.9	1.7	4.2	4.0	5.6
Panama:								
Imports	0	0	0	0	0.1	0	0	0
Exports	15.1	26.1	8.2	8.8	9.3	10.4	7.4	11.9
Peru:								
Imports	10.2	22.2	10.7	16.2	42.6	108.5	57.6	47.2
Exports	3.1	12.5	14.5	4.7	25.0	11.3	6.1	40.1
Uruguay:								
Imports	21.4	49.9	52.2	52.6	46.8	32.4	20.4	21.2
Exports	2.4	1.8	1.0	1.6	22.7	33.5	3.8	0.6
Latin America and the Caribbean:								
Imports	1480.5	3029.9	1809.3	1994.1	1597.8	1788.8	465.0	668.5
Exports	99.6	111.0	286.8	154.2	184.3	197.5	328.3	300.9

[1] No figures are given for Cuba because such statistics tend to be misleading and throw little light on the relationship between Moscow and Havana. Figures for Chile and Nicaragua can be found on pages 129 and 210 respectively. The totals for Latin America are inclusive of these figures.

Bibliography

(1) PRIMARY SOURCES: NEWSPAPERS AND PERIODICALS

Soviet sources

1. In Russian
(Published in Moscow unless stated otherwise)
Pravda
Izvestiia
Latinskaia Amerika (also published as *América Latina*)
Mirovaia ekonomika i mezhdunarodnye otnosheniia
Vneshniaia torgovlia SSSR

2. In English
Current Digest of the Soviet Press (American Association for the Advancement of
    Slavic Studies, USA)
Foreign Trade
International Affairs
New Times
Summary of World Broadcasts: The USSR (British Broadcasting Corporation
    Monitoring Service)
World Marxist Review (Prague)

3. In Spanish
América Latina
Panorama Lationamericana

Latin American sources

1. In Spanish
Barricada (Managua)
Granma (Havana)
La Prensa (Buenos Aires)

2. In English
Economic Information on Argentina (Buenos Aires)

British and US sources

The *Guardian*
The Times
The Financial Times
Latin America Commodities Report (London)
Latin America Economic Report (1974–9)
Latin America Political Report (1974–9)
Latin America Regional Reports (Southern Cone, Brazil, Central America and the Caribbean, Mexico, Andean)
Latin America Weekly Report (1979 onwards)
Market Report (International Wheat Council)
The *New York Times*

(2) SECONDARY SOURCES

Abouchar, Alan (1981), 'The case for the US grain embargo', *The World Today*, Royal Institute of International Affairs (RIIA), 37:7, 277–81
Academy of Sciences of the USSR (1973), *Sovetskii Soyuz i Kuba, 15 let bratskogo sotrudnichestva* (Moscow)
Adelman, Alan and Reid Reading (eds.) (1984) *Confrontation in the Caribbean Basin: international perspectives on security, sovereignty and survival* (Latin American Monograph and Document Series, no. 8, Centre for Latin American Studies, University of Pittsburgh)
Adomeit, Hannes and Robert Boardman (1979), *Foreign policy making in Communist countries* (Saxon House, Farnborough, Hants.)
Agentstvo Pechati Novosti (1978), *USSR-Cuba, friends forever* (Moscow)
Aguilar, Luis (1968), *Marxism in Latin America* (Alfred A. Knopf, New York)
(1978), 'Fragmentation of the Marxist Left', *Problems of Communism*, 19:4 (July–Aug.), 1–11
Alba, Victor (1954), *Historia del comunismo en América Latina* (Ediciones Occidentales, Mexico)
(1959), *Historia del Frente Popular* (Libro Mex, Mexico)
(1961), 'The Chinese in Latin America', *China Quarterly*, no. 5, 53–61
(1964), *Historia del movimiento obrero en América Latina* (Libreros Mexicanos Unidos, Mexico)
Alexander, R. J. (1957), *Communism in Latin America* (Rutger's University Press, New Brunswick, New Jersey)
Allen, Robert Loring (1959), *Soviet influence in Latin America: the role of economic relations* (University of Virginia, Washington)
Altamirano, Carlos (1977), *Dialéctica de una derrota* (Siglo Veintiuno Editores, Mexico)
Angell, Alan (1972), *Politics and the labour movement in Chile* (Oxford University Press for the Royal Institute of International Affairs, London)
Attwood, William (1967), *The reds and the blacks: a personal adventure* (Hutchinson, London)

Avarina, V. and M. Danilevich (1963), *Ekonomicheskie problemy stran Latinskoi Ameriki* (Izdatel'stvo Akademii Nauk SSSR, Moscow)

Avetisián, Artur (1983), 'Colaboración en el campo de la energética', *América Latina* (Moscow), no. 4 (April), 56–63

Bailey, Norman A. (1967), *Latin America in world politics* (Walker and Company, New York)

Banco Nacional de Comercio Exterior de México (1964), *Misión a Europa* (Mexico)

Bark, D. (ed.) (1986), *The red orchestra: instruments of Soviet policy in Latin America and the Caribbean* (Hoover Institution Press, Stanford)

Barston, R. P. (1983), 'Soviet foreign policy in the Brezhnev years', *The World Today*, RIIA, 39:3 (March), 81–9

Bartley, Russell H. (1978), *Imperial Russia and the struggle for Latin American independence 1808–1828* (Latin American monographs no. 43, Institute of Latin American Studies, University of Texas at Austin)

Beijing Review (1980), 'Where is Nicaragua heading?', no. 1 (7 Jan.), 12–13

Bekarevich, A. D. (ed.) (1980), *Sovetsko-Kubinskie otnosheniia, 1917–1977* (Academy of Sciences of the USSR, Institute of Latin America, Moscow)

Berrios, Rubén (1984), *Economic relations between Nicaragua and the socialist countries* (Working Papers, no. 166, The Wilson Centre, Washington)

Best, Edward (1987), *Regional security in Central America and United States policy* (Gower, Aldershot)

Bialer, Seweryn (1981), *The domestic context of Soviet foreign policy* (Studies of the Research Institute of International Change, Columbia University, New York)

Bierck, Harold A. (ed.) (1967), *Latin American civilisation: readings and essays* (Allyn and Bacon Inc., Boston)

Bitar, Sergio (1979), *Transición, socialismo y democracia: la experiencia Chilena* (Siglo Veintiuno Editores, Mexico)

Black, George (1981), *Triumph of the people* (Zed Press, London)

(1983), 'Garrison Guatemala', *NACLA Report on the Americas*, 17:1 (Jan.–Feb.), 2–35

(coordinating editor) (1985) and Robert Armstrong, Marc Edelman and Robert Matthews, 'Sandinista foreign policy: strategies for survival', *NACLA Report on the Americas*, 19:3 (May–June), 13–56

Blasier, Cole (1981), 'The Soviet Latinamericanists', *Latin American Research Review*, 16:1, 107–23

(1983), *The giant's rival: the USSR and Latin America* (Pitt Latin American Series, University of Pittsburgh Press, Pittsburgh, Pa.)

and Carmelo Mesa-Lago (eds.) (1979), *Cuba in the world* (University of Pittsburgh Press, Pa.)

and Aldo Vacs (1983), 'América Latina frente a la Unión Soviética', *Foro Internacional* (Colegio de México), 24:2 (Oct.–Dec.), 199–211

Bond, Robert D. (1981), *Venezuela, the Caribbean Basin and the crisis in Central America* (Wilson Centre Working Papers, no. 94)

Bonsal, Philip W. (1971), *Cuba, Castro and the United States* (University of Pittsburgh Press, Pa.)

Boorstein, D. (1968), *The economic transformation of Cuba: a first hand account* (Modern Reader Paperbacks, New York and London)

Borge, Tomás (1981), *Los primeros pasos: la revolución popular Sandinista* (Siglo-Veintiuno, Mexico)

Boughton, George J. (1974), 'Soviet–Cuban relations 1956–1960', *Journal of Inter-American Studies*, 16:4 (Nov.), 436–53

Bourne, Peter (1987), *Castro* (Macmillan, London)

Brown, Archie and Jack Gray (eds.) (1977), *Political culture and political change in Communist states* (Macmillan, London)

Brown, Archie and Michael Kaser (eds.) (1982), *Soviet policy for the 1980s* (St Antony's/Macmillan, Oxford)

Brundenius, Claes (1984), *Revolutionary Cuba: the challenge of economic growth with equity* (Westview Special Studies on Latin America and the Caribbean, Colorado)

Burmistrov, Vladimir (1982), 'The first Soviet-Cuban long term trade agreement (1976–80): its results', *Foreign Trade* (Moscow), no. 1 (Jan.), 7–11

Butler, Nick (1983), 'The US grain weapon: could it boomerang?', *The World Today*, RIIA, 39:2 (Feb.), 52–9

Caballero, Manuel Antonio (1986), *Latin America in the world revolution: the Communist International 1919–1943* (Cambridge University Press, Cambridge and New York)

Campa, Valentín (1978), *Mi testimonio: experiencias de un comunista mexicano* (Ediciones de cultura popular, Mexico)

Cantero, Manuel (1977), 'The role and character of external factors', Lessons of Chile, Article 7, *World Marxist Review*, 20:8 (Aug.), 37–45

Carr, Barry (1985), 'Mexican Communism 1968–1981: Euro-Communism in the Americas?', *Journal of Latin American Studies*, 17:1 (May), 201–28

Carter, James Richard (1971), *The net cost of Soviet foreign aid* (Praeger Publishers Inc., New York)

Cassen, Robert (ed.) (1985), *Soviet interests in the Third World* (Sage Publications/RIIA, London)

Castro Ruz, Fidel (1969), *History will absolve me* (the Moncada trial defence speech), Santiago de Cuba, 1953 (Cape, edition 22, London)

(1971), *Chile 1971: habla Fidel Castro* (Editorial Universitária, Chile)

(1972a), *Fidel in Chile, a symbolic meeting between two historical processes* (International Publishers, New York)

(1972b), *Fidel Castro speaks*, edited by Martin Kenner and James Petras (Pelican Latin American Library, Penguin Books, Harmondsworth)

(1981), *Speeches: Cuba's internationalist foreign policy 1975–1980* (Pathfinder Press, New York)

(1985), *Fidel y la religión, conversaciones con Frei Betto* (Oficina de publicaciones del consejo de estado, La Habana)

Centro de Investigación y Docencia Económicas, AC (1983), *Estados Unidos: perspectiva Latinoamericana* (Cuadernos Semestrales, no. 12, Mexico)

Cerdas Cruz, Rodolfo (1983), *Sandino, el APRA y la Internacional Comunista:*

Antecedentes Históricos de la Nicaragua de hoy (Comisión Nacional de Ideología y Doctrina del Partido Aprista Peruana, Lima)

(1986a), *La hoz y el machete* (Editorial universidad estatal a distancia, San José)

(1986b), 'Nicaragua: One step forward, two steps back', in Di Palma and Whitehead: 1986, 175–94

Cheston, T. S. and B. Loeffe (eds.) (1974), 'Aspects of Soviet policy toward Latin America' (MSS Information Corporation, New York)

Chigir', N. N. (1975), *SSSR-Kuba v Edinom Stroyu k Obshchei Tseli* (Biblioteka Mezhdunarodnika, Moscow)

Claudín, Fernando (1975), *The Communist movement: from Comintern to Cominform* (Penguin Books, Harmondsworth)

Clissold, Stephen (ed.) (1970), *Soviet relations with Latin America, 1918–1968: a documentary survey* (Oxford University Press/RIIA, London)

Corvalán, Luis (1964), *Nuestra vía revolucionaria* (Santiago)

(1969), *El poder popular, única alternativa patriótica y revolucionaria. Informe al XIV Congreso Nacional del Partido Comunista de Chile* (Santiago)

Crahan, Margaret E. (n.d. *c.* 1984), *The church and revolution: Cuba and Nicaragua* (La Trobe University Institute of Latin American Studies)

Crawford, William R. (1963), *A century of Latin American thought* (Harvard University Press, Cambridge, Massachusetts)

Dabat, Alejandro and Luis Lorenzano (1984), *Argentina: the Malvinas and the end of military rule* (Verso, London)

Dahl, Victor (1976), 'Soviet bloc response to the downfall of Allende', *Inter-American Economic Affairs*, 30:2 (Autumn), 33–47

Dalton, Roque (1986), *Un libro rojo para Lenin* (Editorial Nueva Nicaragua, Managua)

Davis, Nathaniel (1985), *The last two years of Salvador Allende* (Tauris and Co. Ltd, London)

Dawisha, Adeed and Karen Dawisha (eds.) (1982), *The Soviet Union in the Middle East: policies and perspectives* (Heinemann/RIIA, London)

Dawisha, Karen (1980), 'The limits of the bureaucratic politics model: observations on the Soviet case', *Studies in Comparative Communism*, 13:4 (Winter), 300–46

and Philip Hanson (eds.) (1981), *Soviet–European Dilemmas* (Heinemann/RIIA, London)

Debray, Regis (1971), *Conversations with Allende: socialism in Chile*, translated from the French and Spanish MS by Peter Beglan; with introduction, notes and appendix tr. from the French and Spanish by Ben Brewster, Marguerita Sánchez and Peter Gowan (NLB, London)

(1977 and 1978), *A critique of arms* (Penguin Books, Harmondsworth, vols. 1 and 2)

Devlin, Kevin (1968), 'The permanent revolution of Fidel Castro', *Problems of Communism*, 17:1 (Jan.–Feb.), 1–11

Dinerstein, Herbert (1962), *The making of a missile crisis* (Balt. & Co., Baltimore)

(1967), 'Soviet policy in Latin America', *American Political Science Review*, 61:1, 80–90

(1971), 'Soviet and Cuban conceptions of revolution', *Studies in Comparative Communism*, 4:1 (Jan.), 3–22

Di Palma, G. and L. Whitehead (1986), *The Central American impasse* (Croom Helm, London and Sydney)

Dmitriyev, V. (1982), 'The crisis of imperialists' colonial policy in Latin America', *International Affairs* (Moscow), no. 10 (Oct.), 33–41

Domínguez, Jorge (1980), *The success of Cuban foreign policy* (Occasional Papers, no. 27, New York University)

(1982), *Cuba: internal and international affairs* (Sage Publications, Harvard University Centre for International Affairs)

(1984), 'Cuba's relations with Caribbean and Central American countries', in Adelman and Reading: 1984, 165–202

Donaldson, R. H. (ed.) (1981), *The Soviet Union in the Third World: successes and failures* (Westview Press, Colorado) esp. Sigmund, Paul E., 'The USSR, Cuba and the revolution in Chile', 26–50

Draper, Theodore (1961), 'Castro's Cuba: a revolution betrayed?', *Encounter*, 16:3 (March), 6–23

(1962), *Castro's revolution: myths and realities* (Thames and Hudson, London)

Dulles, John W. F. (1983), *Brazilian Communism, 1935–1945: Repression during world upheaval* (University of Texas Press, Austin)

Duncan, W. Raymond (1971), 'Soviet policy in Latin America since Khrushchev', *Orbis*, 15:2 (Summer), 643–69

(1978), 'Caribbean Leftism', *Problems of Communism*, 27:3 (May–June), 33–57

(1984), 'Soviet interests in Latin America: new opportunities and old constraints', *Journal of Inter-American Studies*, 26:2 (May), 163–98

(1985), *The Soviet Union and Cuba: interests and influence* (Praeger, New York)

Dunkerley, James (1982), *The long war: dictatorship and revolution in El Salvador* (Junction Books, London)

Edelman, Marc (1985), 'Lifelines: Nicaragua and the socialist countries', *NACLA Report on the Americas*, 19:3 (May–June), 33–56

(1987), 'The other superpower: the Soviet Union and Latin America 1917–1987', *NACLA Report on the Americas*, 21:1, 10–40

Edmonds, Robin (1983), *Soviet foreign policy: the Brezhnev years* (Oxford University Press, Oxford)

Edquist, Charles (1983), 'Mechanisation of sugarcane harvesting in Cuba', *Cuban Studies* (Pittsburgh), 13:2 (Summer), 41–64

English, Adrian J. (1984), *Armed forces of Latin America: their histories, development, present strength and military potential* (Jane's Publishing Co., London)

Entrevista a Konstantin Katushev, embajador de la URSS en Cuba, América Latina (Moscow), no. 5 (May) 1985, 75–7

Fagan, Richard R. (1975), 'The United States and Chile: roots and branches', *Foreign Affairs*, 53:2, 297–313

Fairhall, David (1971), *Russia looks to the sea: a study of the expansion of Soviet maritime power* (André Deutsch, London)

Falk, Pamela S. (1985), *Cuban foreign policy: Caribbean tempest* (Lexington Books, Lexington, Mass.)

Farber, Samuel (1983), 'The Cuban Communists in the early stages of the Cuban revolution: revolutionaries or reformists?', *Latin American Research Review*, 18:1, 59–83

Fauriol, G. A. (1984), *Foreign policy behaviour of Caribbean states: Guyana, Haiti and Jamaica* (University Press of America, Lanham and London)

Feinberg, Richard (ed.) (1982), *Central America: international dimensions of the crisis* (Holmes and Meier, New York)

(1983), 'Centroamérica: el punto de vista de Moscú', in *Centro de Investigación y Docencia Económicas*, 375–80

Ferrer, Aldo (1980), 'The Argentine Economy 1976–9', *Journal of Inter-American Studies*, 22:2 (May), 131–62

Ferris, Elizabeth G. and Jennie K. Lincoln (eds.) (1981), *Latin American foreign policies: global and regional dimensions* (Westview Special Studies on Latin America and the Caribbean, Westview Press, Boulder, Colorado)

Fiorini, Mario (1957), 'El comunismo en el Perú', *Estudios sobre el comunismo* (Santiago), no. 16 (April–June), 67–71

Flores Galindo, Alberto (1980), *La agonía de Mariátegui, la polémica con la Komintern* (Centro de Estudios y Promoción del Desarrollo, Lima)

(1982), *El pensamiento comunista, 1917–1945* (Mosca Azul Editores, Lima)

Fortín, Carlos (1975), 'Principled pragmatism in the face of external pressure: the foreign policy of the Allende government', in Ronald G. Hilton and H. Jon Rosenbaum (eds.), *Latin America: the search for a new international role* (Sage Centre for International Relations, Beverley Hills, California), 217–45

'Four more years' (a symposium on Central America and the second Reagan term), *NACLA Report on the Americas*, 19:1 (Jan./Feb. 1985), 15–55

Franco, Carlos (1981), *Del Marxismo eurocéntrico al Marxismo Latinoamericano* (Centro de Estudios para el Desarrollo y la Participación, Lima)

Franco, Jean (1967), *The modern culture of Latin America: society and the artist* (Pall Mall Press, London)

Frondizi, Arturo (1963), *La política exterior Argentina*, (2nd edition, Transición, Buenos Aires)

Fuchs, Jaime (1965), *Argentina: su desarrollo capitalista* (Editorial Cartago, Buenos Aires)

Furci, Carmelo (1982), 'The Chilean Communist party (PCCh) and its third underground period, 1973–1980', *Bulletin of Latin American Research*, 2:1 (May), 81–96

García Treviño, Rodrigo (1959), *La ingerencia rusa en México* (Editorial América, Mexico)

Garner, William R. (1968), 'The Sino–Soviet ideological struggle in Latin America', *Journal of Inter-American Studies*, 10:2 (April), 244–55

Ghoshal, Animesh (1983), 'Lessons of the 1980 grain embargo', *The World Economy*, 6:2, 183–94

Gil, Federico, Ricardo Lagos and H. Landsberger (eds.) (1979), *Chile at the turning point: lessons of the socialist years, 1970–3* (Institute for the Study of Human Issues, Philadelphia)

Gillespie, Richard (1982), *Soldiers of Perón – Argentina's Montoneros* (Oxford University Press, Oxford)

Gilmore, Richard (1982), *A poor harvest – the clash of policies and interests in the grain trade* (Longman, New York)

Ginsburgs, George (1975), 'The Soviet view of Chinese influence in Africa and Latin America', in Alvin Z. Rubinstein, *Soviet and Chinese influence in the Third World*, (Praeger, New York), 197–220

Girardi, Giulio (1986), *Sandinismo, Marxismo, Cristianismo: la confluencia* (Centro Ecuménico Antonio Valdivieso, Managua)

Gladkov, N. (1975), 'Trade and economic relations between the Soviet Union and the developing Latin American countries', *Foreign Trade* (Moscow), no. 12 (Dec.), 11–20

Glinkin, Anatoli (1985), 'URSS-Brasil: 40 años de relaciones diplomáticas', *América Latina* (Moscow), no. 5 (May), 83–5

and P. Yakovlev (1982), 'Latinskaia Amerika v global'noi strategii imperializma', *Mirovaia ekonomika i mezhdunarodnye otnosheniia*, Oct., 65–82

Goldenberg, Boris (1963), 'The Cuban revolution: an analysis', *Problems of Communism*, 12:5 (Sept.–Oct.), 1–8

Goldhamer, Herbert (1972), *The foreign powers in Latin America* (Princeton University Press, New Jersey)

González, E. (1968), 'Castro's revolution, Cuban Communist appeals, and the Soviet response', *World Politics*, 21:1 (Oct.), 39–68

(1972), 'Comparison of Soviet and Cuban approaches to Latin America', *Studies in Comparative Communism*, 5:1 (Spring), 21–35

(1976), 'Castro and Cuba's new orthodoxy', *Problems of Communism*, 25:1 (Jan.–Feb.), 1–19

Gott, Richard (1973), *Rural guerrillas in Latin America*, (the Pelican Latin American Library, Penguin Books, Harmondsworth)

Gouré, Leon and M. Rothenberg (1975), *Soviet penetration of Latin America* (Centre for Advanced International Studies, University of Miami)

(1980), 'Latin America', in K. London (ed.), *The Soviet Union in world politics* (Westview Press, Colorado), 233–62

Gouré, Leon and J. Suchlicki (1971), 'The Allende regime: actions and reactions', *Problems of Communism*, 20:3 (May–June), 49–61

Gouré, Leon and Julian Weinkle (1972), 'Cuba's new dependency', *Problems of Communism*, 21:2 (Mar.–Apr.), 68–79

Grabendorff, Wolf, Heinrich-W. Krumwiede and Jörg Todt (eds.) (1984), *Political change in Central America: internal and external dimensions* (Westview Special Studies on Latin America and the Caribbean, Westview Press, Boulder and London)

Graham, John A. (1980), 'The Non-Aligned Movement after the Havana summit', *Journal of International Affairs*, 34 (Spring/Summer), 153–60

Grayson, George (1972), 'El viaje de Castro a Chile, Perú y Ecuador', *Problemas Internacionales*, 19:3 (May–June), 1–15

(1980), *The politics of Mexican oil* (University of Pittsburgh)

Grenada: history, revolution, US intervention (1984), Latin America: Studies by Soviet Scholars, no. 4 ('Social Sciences Today' Editorial Board, USSR Academy of Sciences, Moscow)

Gruzinov, V. P. (1979), *The USSR's management of foreign trade*, edited by E. A. Hewett, translated by M. Vale (Macmillan, London)

Guan-Fu, Gu (1983), 'Soviet aid to the Third World, an analysis of its strategy', *Soviet Studies*, 35:1 (Jan.), 71–89

Guardia, Alexis (1979), 'Structural transformations in Chile's economy and in its system of external economic relations', in Sideri: 1979, 45–101

Guevara, Ernesto (Che) (1967), *Che Guevera speaks, selected speeches and writings* (Merit Publishers, New York)

(1968), *Complete Bolivian diaries and other captured documents*, edited and with an introduction by Daniel James (Allen and Unwin, London).

Haig, Alexander (1984), *Caveat: realism, Reagan and foreign policy* (Weidenfeld and Nicolson, London)

Halperin, Ernst (1963), 'Castroism – challenge to the Latin American Communists', *Problems of Communism*, 12:5 (Sept.–Oct.), 9–18

(1965), *Nationalism and Communism in Chile* (The MIT Press, Cambridge, Massachusetts)

Halperin, Maurice (1972), *The rise and decline of Fidel Castro* (University of California Press, Berkeley, Los Angeles and London)

Hanson, Philip (1970), 'The Soviet Union and world shipping', *Soviet Studies*, 22:1 (July), 44–60

(1981), *Trade and technology in Soviet–Western Relations* (Macmillan Press, London)

Haya de la Torre, Victor Raúl (1961), *Nuestra América y el Mundo* (Ediciones Pueblo, Lima)

Herman, Donald L. (ed.) (1973), *The Communist tide in Latin America: a selected treatment* (University of Texas Press, Austin)

Hobsbawm, E. J. (1970), 'Guerrillas in Latin America', *The Socialist Register* (The Merlin Press, London), 51–61

(1973), *Revolutionaries: contemporary essays* (Weidenfeld and Nicolson, London)

Hodges, Donald C. (1974), *The Latin American revolution, politics and strategy from Apro-Marxism to Guevarism* (William Morrow & Co., Inc., New York)

(1977), *The legacy of Che Guevara: a documentary survey* (Thames and Hudson, London)

(1986), *Intellectual foundations of the Nicaraguan revolution* (Texas University Press, Austin)

Hoffman, Erik P. and Frederic J. Fleron (eds.) (1980), *The conduct of Soviet foreign policy* (2nd edition, Butterworths, London)

Holland, Stuart and Donald Anderson (1984), *Kissinger's kingdom? A counter-report on Central America* (Spokesman, Nottingham, U.K.)

Holsti, K. J. with Miguel Monterichard, Ibrahim Msabaha, Thomas W. Robinson, Timothy Shaw and Jacques Zylberberg (1982), *Why nations realign: foreign policy restructuring in the postwar world* (Allen and Unwin,

London), esp. Robinson, Thomas W., 'Restructuring Chinese foreign policy, 1959–1976: three episodes', 134–71 and Zylberberg, Jacques and Miguel Monterichard, 'An abortive attempt to change foreign policy: Chile, 1970–3', 172–97

Horelick, Arnold L. (1964), 'The Cuban missile crisis: an analysis of Soviet calculations and behaviour', World Politics, 16:3 (April), 363–89

Horowitz, I. L. (ed.) (1969), Latin American radicalism: a documentary report on Left and nationalist movements (Jonathan Cape, London)

(1984), Cuban Communism (Transaction Books, New Brunswick)

Hough, Jerry (1981), 'The evolving Soviet debate on Latin America', Latin American Research Review, 16:1 (Spring), 124–43

(1986), The struggle for the Third World: Soviet debates and American options (The Brookings Institution, Washington)

Huberman, Leo and Paul Sweezy (1961), Cuba: anatomy of a revolution (2nd edition, Monthly Review Press, New York)

Hurrell, Andrew (1985), 'Brazil, the United States and the debt', The World Today, RIIA, 41:3, 62–4

(1986), 'The quest for autonomy: the evolution of Brazil's role in the international system 1964–1985' (University of Oxford, D.Phil manuscript)

Ingenieros, José (1950), Enseñanzas económicas de la revolución rusa (Los Tiempos Nuevos, Buenos Aires)

Irkhin, Yu. V. (1982), 'Avangardnye revoliutsionnye partii trudiashchikhsia v osvobodivshikhsia stranakh', Voprosy Istorii, no. 4 (April), 55–67

Ishchenko, Irina (1983), 'Soviet-Brazilian negotiations on trade, economic, scientific and technological cooperation', Foreign Trade (Moscow), no. 1 (January), 49–50

Jackson, D. Bruce (1966), 'Whose men in Havana?', Problems of Communism, 15:3 (May–June), 1–10

(1969), Castro, the Kremlin and Communism in Latin America (John Hopkins University Press, Baltimore)

Jahn, Egbert (ed.) (1978), Soviet foreign policy: its social and economic conditions (Allison and Busby, London)

James, Daniel (1970), Che Guevara: a biography (Allen and Unwin, London)

Jaster, Robert S. (1969), 'Foreign and economic development: the shifting Soviet view', International Affairs (London), 45:3 (July), 452–64

Johnson, Cecil (1970), Communist China and Latin America, 1959–1967 (Columbia University Press, New York and London)

(1972), 'China and Latin America: new ties and tactics', Problems of Communism, 21: 4 (July–Aug.), 53–66

Johnson, Dale L. (ed.) (1973), The Chilean road to socialism (Anchor Books, Doubleday and Co., Inc., New York)

Joxe, Alain (1967), El conflicto Chino-Soviético en América Latina (Editorial Arca, Montevideo)

Kanet, R. E. (ed.) (1974), The Soviet Union and the developing nations (Johns Hopkins University Press, Baltimore)

Karol, K. S. (1971), *Guerrillas in power* (Jonathan Cape Ltd, London)

Katz, Mark N. (1983), 'The Soviet–Cuban connection', *International Security*, 8:1 (Summer), 88–112

Kaufman, Edy (1976), *The superpowers and their spheres of influence* (Croom Helm, London)

Keal, Paul (1983), *Unspoken rules and superpower dominance* (Macmillan, London)

Khachaturov, K. (1982), 'Washington's Latin American policy', *International Affairs* (Moscow), no. 1, 52–61

(1985), 'South America: past experience and prospects for the future', *International Affairs* (Moscow), no. 4 (April), 33–41

Khrushchev, N. (1970), *Khrushchev remembers*, translated and edited by Strobe Talbot, introduction, commentary and notes by Edward Crankshaw (Little, Brown and Co., Boston)

Klinghoffer, Arthur J. (1977), *The Soviet Union and international oil politics*, (Columbia University Press, New York)

Klochkovski, L. (1977), *Neocolonialismo económico* (Academy of Sciences of the USSR, Institute of Latin America, Moscow)

Kolodov, Viktor (1984), 'USSR–Cuba: development of foreign trade', *Foreign Trade* (Moscow), no. 7 (July), 13–16

Koshelev, Pyotr (1982), 'The USSR's economic and technical cooperation with the countries of tropical Africa', *Foreign Trade* (Moscow), no. 10 (Oct.), 8–12

Krestyaninov, V. (1981), 'Washington's Caribbean plan', *International Affairs* (Moscow), Dec., 82–90

Kubálková, V. and A. A. Cruickshank (1980), *Marxism-Leninism and the theory of international relations* (Routledge and Kegan Paul, London)

Kuznetsova, Galina and Anatoli Manenok (1986), 'Soviet–Argentine trade and economic relations: problems and prospects', *Foreign Trade* (Moscow), no. 3 (March), 23–5

Laferrte, E. (1961), *Vida de un Comunista* (Partido Comunista, Santiago)

Lambert, Francis (1977), 'Cuba: Communist state or personal dictatorship?', in Brown and Gray: 231–52

Latin America Bureau (1982), *The European challenge: Europe's new role in Latin America* (Latin America Bureau [Research and Action Ltd], London)

LASA (Latin American Studies Association) Commission on Compliance with the Central America Peace Accord (1988), *Final report*, University of Pittsburgh

Leiken, R. S. (1982), *Soviet strategy in Latin America* (The Washington Papers, 10:93, Centre for Strategic and International Studies, Georgetown University)

(ed.) (1984), *Central America: anatomy of conflict* (Pergamon Press, New York)

Leogrande, William M. (1980), 'Evolution of the Non-Aligned Movement', *Problems of Communism*, 29:1, 35–52

Leonov, N. (1981), 'El drama Salvadoreño', *América Latina* (Moscow), no. 9 (Sept.), 4–26

Levèsque, Jacques (1976), *L'URSS et la révolution Cubaine* (University of Montreal Press)

Levine, Barry B. (ed.) (1983), *The new Cuban presence in the Caribbean* (Westview Special Studies on Latin America and the Caribbean, Boulder, Colorado)

Levine, Daniel H. (ed.) (1980), *Churches and politics in Latin America* (Sage Publications, California)

Lindell, Erik (1982), 'US–Soviet grain embargoes: regulating the MNCs', *Food Policy*, 7:3 (Aug.), 240–6

Liss, Sheldon B. (1984), *Marxist thought in Latin America* (University of California Press, Berkeley and Los Angeles)

Lloyd's Bank Ltd (1973 and 1974), Overseas Department – Export Promotion, *Economic report, Cuba 1972* and *1973* (London)

Lockwood, Lee (1969), *Castro's Cuba, Cuba's Fidel* (Vintage Books, New York)

López, José Andrés (1983), 'Relaciones comerciales Argentina–URSS; balance y perspectivas', *América Latina* (Moscow), no. 8 (Aug.), 55–64

Losman, Donald (1979), *International economic sanctions: the cases of Cuba, Israel and Rhodesia* (University of New Mexico Press, Albuquerque)

Lowenthal, Abraham (1977), 'Cuba's African adventure', *International Security*, 2:1 (Summer), 3–10

(1981), 'A Latin Americanist encounters the USSR: informal notes' (unpublished)

Löwy, Michael (ed.) (1982), *El Marxismo en América Latina de 1909 a nuestras dias: Antología* (Era, Mexico)

MacDonald, Hugh (1975), *Aeroflot, Soviet air transport since 1923* (Putnam, London)

Madariaga, Salvador de (1962), *Latin America between the eagle and the bear* (Hollis and Carter, London)

Maier, Joseph and Richard W. Weatherhead (ed.) (1964), *Politics of change in Latin America* (Frederick A. Praeger, New York)

Malcolm, Neil (1984), *Soviet political scientists and American politics* (Macmillan Press, London)

The Malvinas (Falklands) crisis: the causes and consequences (1984), Latin America: Studies by Soviet Scholars, no. 3 ('Social Sciences Today' Editorial Board, USSR Academy of Sciences, Moscow)

Mariátegui, José Carlos (1959), *Defensa del Marxismo. Polémica revolucionaria* (Empresa Editora Amauta, Lima)

Marin, Gladys (1977), 'The working class and its policy of alliance', *World Marxist Review*, 20:7 (July), 53–63

Martz, John D. and David J. Myers (1977), *Venezuela: the democratic experience* (Praeger, New York)

Matthews, Herbert L. (1969), *Castro: a political biography* (Allen Lane, Penguin Books Ltd, London)

(1975), *Revolution in Cuba* (Charles Scribner's Sons, New York)

Matthews, Robert (1985), 'The limits of friendship: Nicaragua and the West', *NACLA Report on the Americas*, 19:3 (May–June), 22–32

Medhurst, Kenneth (1972), *Allende's Chile* (Hart-Davis, MacGibbon Ltd, London)

Medvedev, Roy (1982), *Khrushchev* (Basil Blackwell, Oxford)

Mercurio, El (1974), *Breve historia de la Unidad Popular* (Santiago)

Merin, Boris M. (1977), 'La etapa actual en la Latinoamericanística Soviética', *Latin American Research Review*, 22:12, 171–5

Mesa-Lago, Carmelo (1970), *Ideological Radicalisation and Economic Policy in Cuba*, Studies in Comparative International Development, 5:10 (1969–70), (Rutger's University, New Brunswick, New Jersey)

  (1971), 'Ideological, political and economic factors in the Cuban controversy on material versus moral incentives' (unpublished, deposited in Latin American Centre Library, St Antony's College, Oxford)

  (1973), 'Castro's domestic course', *Problems of Communism*, 22:5 (Sept.–Oct.), 27–38

  (1978), *Cuba in the 1970s* (University of New Mexico Press, Albuquerque)

  (1981), *The economy of socialist Cuba: a two decade appraisal* (University of New Mexico Press, Albuquerque)

  and J. S. Belkin (1982), *Cuba in Africa* (Latin American Monograph and Document Series, 3, University of Pittsburgh Press)

Mikoian, Sergei (1974), 'Chile: algunas lecciones', *América Latina*, no. 2, 75–84

  (1980), 'Las particularidades de la revolución en Nicaragua', *América Latina*, 3 (March), 101–15

Milenky, Edward S. (1978), *Argentina's foreign policies* (Westview Press, Boulder, Colorado)

Mining Journal (1979), *Mining annual review*, 1979, (London)

Ministries of Foreign Affairs of Mexico and the USSR (1981), *Sovetsko-Meksikanskie otnosheniia 1968–1980* (Moscow)

Moore, Carlos (1986), *El Caribe y la política exterior de la revolución Cubana, 1959–1984* (Documentos de Trabajo, no. 19, Centro de Investigaciones del Caribe y América Latina, Universidad Interamericana de Puerto Rico)

Moran, Theodore (1979), 'The international political economy of Cuban nickel development', in Blasier and Mesa-Lago: 1979, 257–72

Morgan, Dan (1979), *Merchants of grain* (Weidenfeld and Nicolson, London)

Morse, Richard (1967), 'Towards a theory of Spanish American government', in Bierck: 1967, 221–35

Moskoff, William (1973), assisted by G. William Benz, 'The USSR and developing countries: politics and export prices, 1955–69', *Soviet Studies*, 24:3 (Jan.), 349–63

Moulián, Tomás (1982), *Evolución histórica de la Izquierda Chilena: influencia del Marxismo* (FLASCO, Santiago)

Munck, Ronaldo (1984), *Revolutionary trends in Latin America* (Monograph series, no. 17, McGill University, Centre for Developing-area Studies, Montreal)

Muñiz Ortega, Carlos (1968), *La URSS y América Latina (50 años de relaciones diplomáticas y económicas)*, (Francisco Moncloa Editores, Lima)

Muñóz, Heraldo (1984), *Inserción internacional de los partidos de la Izquierda*

Chilena (Material para Discusión, no. 10, Centro de Estudios del Desarrollo, Santiago de Chile)

Nairn, Allan (1984), 'Endgame: a special report on US military strategy in Central America', *NACLA Report on the Americas*, 18:3 (May/June), 19–55

Neruda, Pablo (1974), *Confieso que he vivido: memorias* (Seix Barral, Barcelona, 7th edition, 1983)

Nogee, J. L. and R. H. Donaldson (1981), *Soviet foreign policy since World War II* (Pergamon, New York and Oxford)

Nogee, J. L. and J. W. Sloan (1979), 'Allende's Chile and the Soviet Union: a policy lesson for Latin American nations seeking autonomy', *Journal of Inter-American Studies*, 21:3 (Aug.), 339–68

Nolan, David (1984), *The ideology of the Sandinistas and the Nicaraguan Revolution* (University of Miami, Florida)

O'Brien, Philip (1986), '"The debt cannot be paid": Castro and the Latin American debt', *Bulletin of Latin American Research*, 5:1, 41–64

Olivari, Ricardo E. (1963), *El comercio exterior Argentino: reorientación necesaria* (Edinorte Editores, Buenos Aires)

de Olivera, E. (1962), *Revolucão e contra-revolucão no Brasil* (Rio de Janeiro)

Ortega Saavedra, Humberto (1980), *50 años de lucha Sandinista* (Editorial de Ciencias Sociales, La Habana)

O'Shaughnessy, Hugh (1984), *Grenada, revolution, invasion and aftermath* (Sphere Books with the *Observer*, London)

Oswald, J. G. (1966), 'Contemporary Soviet Research on Latin America', *Latin American Research Review*, 1:2 (Spring), 77–96

(ed.) (1970), *The Soviet image of contemporary Latin America: a documentary history, 1960–68* (University of Austin, Texas)

and Anthony J. Strover (eds.) (1970), *The Soviet Union and Latin America* (Institute for the Study of the USSR, London)

Pan, Luis (1964), *Justo y Marx* (Ediciones Monserrat, Buenos Aires)

Pérez-López, Jorge F. (1988), 'Cuban–Soviet sugar trade: price and subsidy issues', *Bulletin of Latin American Research*, 7:1, 123–47

Philip, George (1982), *Oil and politics in Latin America* (Cambridge University Press)

Poitras, Guy (1981), 'Mexico's foreign policy in an age of inter-dependence', in Ferris and Lincoln: 1981, 103–14

Política exterior de la Cuba socialista: Documentos (1982) (No publisher given, Moscow)

Ponomarev, B. (1971), 'Aktualnye problemi teorii mirovogo revoliutsionnogo protsessa', *Kommunist*, no. 15 (October), 37–71

Poppino, Rollie E. (1964), *International Communism in Latin America: a history of the movement, 1917–63* (The Free Press of Glencoe, Collier Macmillan Ltd, USA)

Poterov, V. and Y. Godunsky (1972), 'US ideological expansion in Latin America', *International Affairs* (Moscow), no. 7 (July), 35–40

President's National Bipartisan Commission on Central America (1984), *Report* (Macmillan, New York)

Prieto Rozos, Alberto (1985), *El movimiento de liberación contemporáneo en América Latina* (Editorial de ciencias sociales, La Habana)

Ramet, Pedro and Fernando López-Alves (1984), 'Moscow and the revolutionary Left in Latin America', *Orbis*, Summer, 341–63

Ramírez, Alvaro (1980), 'Nicaragua: from armed struggle to construction', *World Marxist Review*, 23:1 (Jan.), 90–3

Rapoport, Mario (1986), 'Argentina and the Soviet Union: history of political and commercial relations (1917–1955)', *Hispanic American Historical Review*, 66:2, 239–85

Ratliff, William E. (1976), *Castroism and Communism in Latin America, 1959–76: the varieties of Marxist-Leninist Experience* (Hoover Institute Studies, 56, Washington)

Ravines, Eudocio (1951), *The Yenan way* (Charles Scribner's Sons, New York) (1957), *La gran estafa* (2nd edition, Editorial del Pacífico, Santiago)

Recabarren, Luis E. (1965), *Obras escogidas*, vol. 1 (Editorial Recabarren, Santiago de Chile)

'La revolución es irreversible – plática con Carlos Carrión Cruz y el padre Fernando Cardenal, miembros de la Asamblea Sandinista del FSLN' (1983), *América Latina* (Moscow), no. 1 (Jan.), 44–57

Rice, Desmond and Arthur Gavshon (1984), *The sinking of the Belgrano* (Secker and Warburg, London)

Richards, Edward B. (1965), 'Marxism and Marxist movements in Latin America in recent Soviet historical writing', *Hispanic American Historical Review*, 45:4 (Nov.), 577–90

Riding, Alan (1986), *Distant neighbours: A portrait of the Mexicans* (Vintage Books, New York)

Robbins, Carla Anne (1984), 'The "Cuban threat" in Central America' in Grabendorff et al: 1984, 216–27
    (1985), *The Cuban threat* (Institute for the Study of Human Issues, Philadelphia)

Rodó, José Enrique (1900), *Ariel*, edited by Gordon Brotherston (Cambridge University Press, 1967)

Rodríguez, Pedro (1977), 'Defending the people's power', *World Marxist Review*, 20:6 (June), 47–55

Rodríguez Llompart, Hector (1985), 'Present-day Cuban–Soviet economic cooperation', *Foreign Trade* (Moscow), no. 1 (January), 21–4

Rothenberg, Morris (1983), 'Latin America in Soviet eyes', *Problems of Communism*, 32:5 (Sept.–Oct.), 1–18
    (1984), 'The Soviets and Central America', in Leiken: 1984, 131–59

Roy, M. N. (1964), *Memoirs* (Indian Renaissance Institute, Bombay)

Ruilova, Leonardo (1978), *China Popular en América Latina* (Instituto Latino-americano de Investigaciones Sociales, Quito)

Rumer, Boris (1981), 'The "second" agriculture in the USSR', *Soviet Studies*, 33:4 (Oct.), 560–72

Ryabov, Yakov (1984), 'USSR–Cuba: fruitful cooperation', *Foreign Trade* (Moscow), no. 1 (Jan.), 4–9

Samuel, Raphael and Gareth Stedman Jones (eds.) (1982), *Culture, ideology and politics: essays for Eric Hobsbawm* (Routledge and Kegan Paul, London)

Schneider, Ronald M. (1976), *Brazil, foreign policy of a future world power* (Westview Press, Boulder, Colorado)

Secretaria General de Gobierno, República de Chile (n.d.), *Libro blanco del cambio de gobierno en Chile, 11 de septiembre 1973* (Editorial Lord Cochrane, Santiago).

Segal, Gerald (ed.) (1983), *The Soviet Union in East Asia: predicaments of power* (Heinemann/RIIA, London)

Selcher, Wayne A. (1978), *Brazil's multilateral relations: between First and Third Worlds* (Westview Press, Boulder, Colorado)

(1981), *Brazil in the international system: the rise of a middle power* (Westview, Boulder, Colorado)

Shcherbakov, V. (1983), 'A year after the Malvinas crisis', *International Affairs* (Moscow), no. 7 (July), 109–13

Shearman, Peter (1985), 'The Soviet Union and Grenada under the New Jewel Movement', *International Affairs* (London), Autumn, 661–73

(1987), *The Soviet Union and Cuba* (Routledge and Kegan Paul for RIIA, London)

Shevchenko, Arkady N. (1985), *Breaking with Moscow* (Jonathan Cape, London)

Sideri, S. (ed.) (1979), *Chile 1970–3: economic development and its international setting (self-criticism of the Unidad Popular government's policies)* (Martinus Nijhoff, The Hague)

Sigmund, Paul E. (1977), *The overthrow of Allende and the politics of Chile, 1964–1976* (University of Pittsburgh Press)

Sizonenko, A. I. (1971), *Ocherki istorii sovetsko-latin-amerikanskikh otnoshenie* (Izdatel'stvo 'Nauka', Moscow)

(1972), *La URSS y Latino-América ayer y hoy*, translated by Venancio Uribes (Progress Publishers, Moscow)

(1974), 'Sovetski-Meksikanskim otnosheniiam – 50 let', *Latinskaia Amerika*, no. 4, 6–23

Skidmore, Thomas and Peter Smith (1984), *Modern Latin America* (Oxford University Press, New York and Oxford)

Smirnova, N. Yu. (1982), 'Nicaragua: la revolución en marcha', *América Latina*, no. 7 (July), 4–12

Smith, Alan H. (1982), 'The influence of trade on Soviet relations', in Dawisha and Dawisha: 1982, 103–23

Smith, Wayne S. (1972), 'Soviet policy and ideological formulations for Latin America', *Orbis*, 15:4 (Winter), 1122–47

(1982), 'Dateline Havana; myopic diplomacy', *Foreign Policy*, no. 48 (Fall), 157–74

Steele, Jonathan (1983), *World power: Soviet foreign policy under Brezhnev and Andropov* (Michael Joseph, London)

Stepan, Alfred (1978), *The state and society* (Princeton University Press, Princeton, New Jersey)

Suárez, Andrés (1963), 'Castro between Moscow and Peking', *Problems of Communism*, 12:5 (Sept.–Oct.), 18–26

(1967), *Cuba, Castro and Communism 1959–1966*, Translated by J. Carmichael and E. Halperin (Studies in International Communism, no. 12, Centre for International Studies, Mass. Institute of Technology, Cambridge, Mass.)

Szulc, Tad (1986), *Fidel: a critical portrait* (Hutchinson, London)

Theberge, James D. (ed.) (1972), *Soviet seapower in the Caribbean: political and strategic implications* (Praeger Special Studies in International, Political and Public Affairs, New York)

(1974), *The Soviet presence in Latin America* (New Strategy Information Centre, Inc., New York)

Theriot, Laurence H. (1982), 'Cuba faces the economic realities of the 1980s', in Horowitz: 1984, 68–90

Thomas, Hugh (1977), *The Cuban revolution* (Harper and Row, New York)

Tikhonov, O. (1982), 'Revolutionary Cuba making strides', *International Affairs* (Moscow), no. 2 (Feb.), 25–9

Torres Ramírez, Blanca (1971), *Las relaciones Cubano-Soviéticas 1959–1968* (El Colegio de México)

Turrent, Isabel (1983), 'The Soviet Union and Chile's Popular Unity 1970–3' (unpublished M.Litt thesis, University of Oxford)

(1986), 'La Unión Soviética en América Latina: el caso de Brasil', *Foro Internacional* (Colegio de México), 27:1 (July–Sept.), 75–101

Ulam, Adam B. (1983), *Dangerous relations, The Soviet Union in world politics 1970–82* (Oxford University Press, Oxford)

Ulyanovsky, R. (1971), 'The Third World – problems of socialist orientation', *International Affairs* (Moscow), no. 9 (Sept.), 26–35

UNCTAD (1982), *Cuba: Recent economic developments and future prospects* (Report to the Government of Cuba)

Vacs, Aldo (1984), *Discreet partners: Argentina and the USSR* (University of Pittsburgh Press, Pittsburgh)

Valenta, Jiri (1981), 'The USSR, Cuba and the crisis in Central America', *Orbis*, 25:3 (Fall, 1981), 715–46

(1983), 'Soviet policy in Central America', *Survey*, 27:118–19 (Autumn–Winter), 287–303

and Herbert J. Ellison (eds.) (1986), *Grenada and Soviet–Cuban policy* (Westview Press, Boulder)

Valenta, Jiri and William C. Potter (eds.) (1984), *Soviet decision-making for national security* (Centre for International and Strategic Affairs, University of California, Los Angeles, Allen and Unwin, London)

Valenta, Jiri and Virginia Valenta (1984), 'Leninism in Grenada', *Problems of Communism*, 33:4 (July–Aug.), 1–23

Valkenier, Elizabeth Kridl (1979), 'The USSR, the Third World and the global economy', *Problems of Communism*, 28:4 (July–Aug.), 17–33

Vallejo, César (1970), *An anthology of his poetry*, introduction and notes by James Higgins (Pergamon Press, Oxford)

Vanden, Harry (1979), 'Mariátegui, Marxismo, Comunismo and other biblio-
graphic notes', *Latin American Research Review*, 14:3, 61–86

Vanderlaan, Mary B. (1986), *Revolution and foreign policy in Nicaragua* (Westview Press, Boulder)

Vanin, V. (1986), 'Soviet–Brazilian relations keep developing', *International
Affairs* (Moscow), no. 2 (Feb.), 37–40

Varas, Augusto (1981), *América Latina y la Unión Soviética: Relaciones interesta-
tales y vínculos políticos* (Facultad Latinoamericana de Ciencias Sociales,
Santiago de Chile)

(1982), *La Unión Soviética en la política exterior de América Latina: los casos de
Chile, Argentina, Brasil y Perú* (Facultad Latinoamericana de Ciencias
Sociales, Santiago de Chile)

(1984), 'Ideology and politics in Latin American–USSR relations', *Problems of
Communism*, 33:1 (Jan.–Feb.), 35–47

(ed.) (1986), *Soviet–Latin American relations in the 1980s* (Westview Press,
Boulder)

Vasena, Adalbert Krieger and Javier Pazos (1973), *Latin America: A broader
world role* (Ernest Benn Ltd, London)

Veliz, Claudio (1963), 'Obstacles to reform in Latin America', *The World Today*,
(Jan.), 18–30

Viktorova, I. and N. Yakovlev (1980), 'Modern trends in Brazil's foreign
policy', *International Affairs* (Moscow), no. 1 (Jan.), 57–64

Vol'skii, V. V. (1967), *SSSR i Latinskaia Amerika 1917–1967* (Academy of
Sciences of the USSR, Institute of Latin America, Moscow)

Walker, Thomas W. (ed.) (1982), *Nicaragua in Revolution* (Praeger, New York),
esp. Vanden, Harry E., 'The ideology of insurrection', 41–62

Walters, Barbara (1977), 'An interview with Fidel Castro', *Foreign Policy*, no. 28
(Fall), 22–51

Weinstein, Martin (ed.) (1979), *Revolutionary Cuba in the world arena* (Institute
for the Study of Human Issues, Inc., Philadelphia)

Wesson, Robert (ed.) (1981), *Communism in Central America and the Caribbean*
(Hoover Press, Stanford)

Wetter, Gustav A. (1966), *Soviet ideology today: dialectical and historical
materialism*, translated by Peter Heath (Heinemann, London)

Wheelock, Jaime (1983), 'El pueblo revolucionario de Nicaragua es invencible',
América Latina (Moscow), no. 10 (Oct.), 14–17

Whitehead, Laurence (1973), 'Why Allende fell', *The World Today*, RIIA, 29:11
(Nov.), 461–74

Williams, E. J. (1982), 'Mexico's Central American policy: Apologies, motivations and principles', *Bulletin of Latin American Research*, 2:1 (Oct.),
21–42

Zea, Leopoldo (1963), *The Latin American mind*, translated by James H. Abbott
and Lowell Dunham (University of Oklahoma Press)

Zhuravlev, Yu. P. (1976), 'Latinskaia Amerika – SEV: tendentsii vzaimoot-
noshenii', *Latinskaia Amerika* (Moscow), no. 4, 13–30

Zhuravleva, Olga (1983), 'The food aspect of economic cooperation between the socialist states and Latin American countries', *Foreign Trade* (Moscow), no. 1 (Jan.), 44–8

Zimmerman, William (1969), *Soviet perspectives on international relations 1956–67* (Princeton University Press, New Jersey)

Zinoviev, Nikolai (1981), 'Soviet economic links with Latin America', *International Affairs* (Moscow), no. 1 (Jan.), 100–7

(1983), 'Dinámica de las relaciones económicas', *América Latina*, no. 3 (Mar.), 4–15

Zorina, I. (1971), 'Kharakter i perspektivi revoliutsionnogo protsessa v Chili', *Mirovaia ekonomika i mezhdunarodnye Otnosheniia*, no. 12 (December), 54–63

Index